ARTHUR FREEMAN

Madness to Magic

First published by Healcyon 2023

Copyright © 2023 by Arthur Freeman

All rights reserved. No part of this publication may be reproduced, stored or transmitted in any form or by any means, electronic, mechanical, photocopying, recording, scanning, or otherwise without written permission from the publisher. It is illegal to copy this book, post it to a website, or distribute it by any other means without permission.

Arthur Freeman asserts the moral right to be identified as the author of this work.

Designations used by companies to distinguish their products are often claimed as trademarks. All brand names and product names used in this book and on its cover are trade names, service marks, trademarks and registered trademarks of their respective owners. The publishers and the book are not associated with any product or vendor mentioned in this book. None of the companies referenced within the book have endorsed the book.

First edition

ISBN: 979-8-218-23128-6

Editing by Diana Hernandez
Illustration by Stuart Freeman
Proofreading by Blair Parke
Advisor: Hui-Chun Li-Lan
Cover art by Farrukh Bala

This book was professionally typeset on Reedsy. Find out more at reedsy.com

Foreword

What can I share for this memoir that complements, and hopefully enhances it? I have struggled for several weeks with the perspective to embody before putting fingers to keyboard on this Earthly month of Taurus of 2023. In my dream state last night, words came to me that I am afraid to admit publicly: how vulnerable it is to write what is truly on our minds and hearts. In this, I applaud Arthur for his courage to recount and reflect on the roller coaster life of his 20s from 2014-2018. At the same time, however, I fear for him.

Fear, though, has always been a motivating factor for me to look deeper into the stories that engender it.

I first read Arthur's book in the Libra month of October 2021, two years after I first met him at a small healing arts practitioners' gathering in Durham, North Carolina. As a licensed acupuncturist who has always welcomed collaborative efforts with massage therapists, I worried that the publishing of his book about his past would prevent him from practicing and teaching massage therapy by our relevant overseeing authorities. Why so? Because there is an expectation that a practitioner in the healing arts is meant to be more "together and composed" than the people they work with, especially in a field where relaxation is the key. The underlying principle from which this worry stems is both a social reality to be aware of, as well as an institutional hypocrisy that resists nuanced reflection on the relationship between experience and practice – What harsh expectations we have of each other as well as of ourselves. When I shared my fears about his memoir being published, my heart softened as I heard the fear in his voice as well as his soul's determination in sharing his past with readers in hopes of being able to help others. I knew then that I would stand beside him in support.

In the summer of 2020, Arthur was the first tenant of a treatment room in the wellness clinic I steward, Armonia Health LLC, and – at the outset – I very much appreciated his gentle demeanor as well as his acute attunement to space. That spring and summer of 2020 was saturated with fear, as were the next few years of the Covid-19 pandemic and societal upheaval. Reflecting back, 2020 was experienced by many as the start of a new epoch; there was no way to continue on the same road. Little did I know that 2020 marked the start of an intense spiritual transformation that Arthur has helped me to navigate.

Arthur's Bipolar diagnosis was made known to me in the fall of 2020. He did not want me to share his diagnosis with other practitioners at Armonia Health as he did not feel it was necessary for them to know about his mental health diagnosis. I respected his wishes; the level of privacy that I keep for people comes from nearly twenty years of being a Chinese medicine practitioner and that caveat transfers over for everyone I know, regardless of the relationship.

This was in contradiction with how I felt and know in my soul as to how a truly harmonious community and society can be: our world would be a better place if we honestly accept, understand, care for, and support a person with all their gifts and challenges. All it takes is for us all to be more open minded and kind. In this sense, my idealism is naïve, but idealism is a limiting word to describe the truth. Life experiences continue to teach me that idealism is possible, it just does not look the way my ego self sees it, and that realization of the reality of our times continues to humble me.

I felt then that I could hold Arthur in the middle of the circle of support that I had created at Armonia Health, a respite of calmness and peace for the community amidst the cacophony and emotional chaos of the world. It was not time to share with others what I knew then – that his bipolar label does not have to derail the larger perspective of what his soul has in mind. This memoir is part of his soul's work.

Knowing Arthur's challenges then, I remember feeling that we as a society need to stop insisting that those that need the most support be labeled as marginalized. This insistence manifests in the ways we speak to, treat, and act toward such persons – locking them away in various forms so that those leading 'normal' and 'productive' lives are not tainted by seeing, interacting with, or feeling their intense pain even as it triggers emotions many suppress or project onto others.

If you imagine your community or "pod" –the word that arose during the COVID-19 pandemic of families and friends trying to keep each other safe and cocooned – as several closed concentric circles; then being marginalized constructs those most vulnerable as the misfits who would be on the outskirts of these circles. How is being marginalized ever going to be healing for us all as a whole? The word under debate here, <u>marginalized</u>, is an observation of the current truth, but let us move towards changing that presentation. This book aligns with this movement if you choose to read it with an open heart and mind. On the other side of this coin, let us catch ourselves from living in the shallowness of what we see, like skin color and mental health labels.

I have learned time and time again that my idealism of a harmonious community clashes with how hard it is for humans to be kind to each other – an aspect of reality that is deeply saddening for me. Our mind is so complex, when our souls are not.

In the late summer of 2020, when the COVID-19 pandemic turned our lives 360 degrees, at one of the first conversations we had sharing why we are healing arts practitioners and him being a renter practitioner at Armonia Health, Arthur told me candidly that he would like to help others connect with their soul. I marveled then, as I have many times since, how direct and frankly he spoke the words in his heart. I marvel because I struggle to express through words what I feel and know in my soul and also see how difficult it is for each person's creative Light, their soul's gift, to both shine in the world and have it be seen. I could feel his sincere level of deep care for helping others.

I had felt this quality of caring since I met him in 2019 but did not have words for my felt-sense then, but my innate Pisces sense has never failed to deeply enrich my life. My logical mind saw that our interest in the wide scope of East Asian healing arts and philosophy was complementary and we might make a good team in order to help others. This has been the foundation of our facilitation and teaching about the Chinese Five Elements.

In the spring of 2021, while weeding my vegetable garden and asking for inspiration for Tones for your Bones, an experiential workshop started by my multi-instrumentalist husband Alex Weiss and I for sharing my understanding of the Chinese Five Elements using music, Qi gong, and meditations, Arthur came to mind for teaching the *Qi Gong* portion. It was no coincidence that this inspiration came during the spring, a season represented by the Wood Element, which happens to be Arthur's Chinese *Bazi* astrology Day Master, a core aspect of his being.

Tones for your Bones was offered online in 2021 and we continue to share the video recordings from that fruitfully intense time. It felt imperative to creatively offer connection and ways for coping during the pandemic. Since then, Arthur and I have co-facilitated several in-person nature-based retreats during the equinoxes and solstices as well as co-created a unique type of combo session using acupuncture, bodywork, Qi healing, and soul listening that we have named 'Elemental sessions'.

We have noticed there is much we can teach each other in the healing arts. I share with him Chinese medicine diagnosis theory on aspects of the psyche as well lifestyle habits that support a calmer mind. "Emotional Issues are in our tissues", coined by Willhelm Reich, a contemporary of Sigmund Freud and Carl Jung, is a foundation of modern bodywork in the west – an aspect that has been observed and documented in Asia for over 2000 years. Arthur has taken what I have observed about him and enhanced his understanding through specific *Qi Gong* practices, as well as further habituating lifestyle habits he was already cultivating.

I have been attending his monthly embodied western astrology and dream circles online since 2020 and have used it for my own self-awareness and now also for my patients. He has mentored me on how to use Chinese *Bazi* astrology to guide me in my business decisions, a practice very commonly used in Asia and various indigenous cultures to this day. This holistic approach allows for a more embodied relationship with success and failure, as well as cultivates interpersonal harmony and equilibrium with a wide variety of forces – 'natural' but also 'transcendental.' We both share an innate alignment with *Qi Gong* and meditative cultivation, an uncommon trait in modern American society.

Amidst this mutual learning and collaboration, we both have supported each other to move through our lives, its challenges, and the mind's emotional turmoil as a journey that can be managed with care. I greatly appreciate Arthur's sharp mind and kind heart as well as his commitment to overcoming personal mental/emotional obstacles. This commitment to oneself is one that many struggle with, as I have observed in my professional practice. I greatly appreciate his support for me and Armonia Health and have witnessed the evolution of his passion towards teaching.

So now that I have painted the background of how I have come to know Arthur, I would like to shine the spotlight on one of my favorite subjects, one that I have kept hidden from sharing with many – the concept of magic, part of the title for this book. For all its hype, disdain, taboo, and fear-engendering feelings, as well as being a "sin fin," meaning "without end" in Spanish, source of creative inspiration, this quote best explains my matter-of-fact belief about magic:

"Magic for one culture is the reality for another", Wikipedia says, as I googled the word magic while sitting on the toilet one morning a few years ago.

This personal story reflects my belief.

My best friend in middle and high school in Honduras went to a church with the name Berea and Cristiano, I did not know at the time that this small one room church with no religious art nor effigies of saints nor a bleeding Jesus on the Cross per the norm of the predominant Catholic religion of Latin America was affiliated with the Southern Baptist Church of the USA. My best friend's mother was Swiss but grew up in Honduras, she is a rosy-cheeked light skinned statuesque woman amidst shorter brown and olive-skinned persons, and was very vocal about helping others who were not of Christian faith reach heaven. I did not know at the time that this was called conversion and is a tenant of the Baptist faith, but I had an innate response that only now, in my 40s, I have the inclination as well as the accuracy of words and perspective to voice more publicly.

One afternoon, her mother is driving me to her home to spend the afternoon doing homework, playing the piano, and hanging out with my best friends' sisters, pet parrot, and bunnies. She nonchalantly turns her head towards me in the back seat as she is turning into their driveway, "Your parents should come to our church and make Christ their Savior." I quickly retorted in Spanish, my third language after Taiwanese and Mandarin Chinese, "Pero son chinos/But they are Chinese." I could tell that she did not understand me nor my explanation, and at the time I did not know how to convey and explain my feelings and reasoning. I thought that what I said at the time was sufficient to stop her desire to convert my parents.

The context of our two sentence interaction is as vast as the Pacific Ocean that separates Asia from America. It was one thing that at the time I believed in one God and Christian tenants, being a teenage sponge, thirsty to learn and having a budding interest in philosophy, having grown up and attended schools that taught the American curriculum and the civic patriotism of Latin America and Spain. It is another matter that my parents, who grew up in Taiwan as Buddhist, Daoist, and Confucian, should be forced to change their beliefs. On a deeper level, it felt like an assault that infringed on another person's spiritual beliefs, and I resented her for being so upfront and inconsiderate about it. As I have done most of my life, I kept my thoughts and feelings of anger outside the home to myself.

Is this story a good example of one culture's magic being another's reality?

Maybe it is just a nice way of framing it. In this day and age of the discourse in the USA on racism, the Me Too movement, microaggressions, white fragility, religious condemnation, emotional upheaval, irrational reasonings, and the marginalized being more vocal, one could take my story above and write an entire doctoral thesis. Does this not point towards madness?

This memoir just might make you contemplate your own madness. Can you be humble enough to do so? As you read this book, notice if you question the definition of these two words, madness versus magic, switching them like a see-saw going up and down. Dr. Nida, an internationally known Tibetan medicine teacher, in an introductory teaching on the nature of the mind, calls this Bi-Polar.

As Arthur and I discussed one afternoon several years ago, before I knew he was writing this book, that mental illness is a label used and placed on those who cannot conform and act according to society's norms of what is considered normal. The human mind is capable of creatively overcoming obstacles, and this book is its manifestation. From nearly twenty years of observing, listening, following, and helping patients as a Chinese medicine practitioner, I have noticed that the healing process is non-linear and involves aspects of creativity, openness, and a supportive environment, albeit magic.

Expect in this memoir intimate stories that open doors of questioning, knowledge, and insight into what is reality and what is magic as Arthur maneuvers the medical mental health system, the teachings from other cultures as well as non-conventional approaches to managing mental health. More directly, it is meant to question your own perception of madness and magic in your life. What is your definition? Are they both sides of the same coin? Can using these concepts help you live a more authentic life?

As you read and imagine your way through Arthur's writing, make note of your visceral response. Notice how you feel when amidst confusion, loss, and grief, there is still lucidity and love. "Do not judge a book by its cover," in this case, do not judge a person by their past nor by the stories we create around their labels. As you make note of your body's response while reading, can you notice that your mind is not separate from the body? That, dear reader, might just be this memoir's take-home message.

If you read this book more than once, make note of the changes in your feelings and thoughts compared to the first read; wouldn't this be an example of the precarious reality of the mind, of the nature of impermanence? Uh oh, beware reader, as this book might just make you notice the nature of your own mind! The mind is a mysterious and intense realm of exploration. I encourage you to find wise teachers and mentors, choose discerningly who you allow yourself to be influenced by, and take responsibility for your own minds' actions.

Religion and spiritual faiths are full of magic, it can be quite comical if one starts to analyze all the myths and stories from around the world. You'll have to admit, don't we all love that mysterious spark of magic? Don't we all love the force of LOVE in a story? Don't we all resonate with the struggle between Dark and Light, Good and Evil; the search for love; the grief from mistakes and the roads we missed taking; the reflections of looking back at life in the hope of helping ourselves reach grace and redemption or if one is not so lofty and ambitious, perhaps one merely reaches some aspect of understanding about our past to heal our wounds.

Our shit is not so pretty to look at, it stinks, it is confusing, it is intense. This is part of the nature of the mind. The other side of the mind, what Buddhism calls the heart mind, is spacious like the sky...Again, do you notice a bi-polar quality? It can't be helped, this Dr. Jerkyll Mr Hyde syndrome. The mind can be managed, though, and you'll travel through Arthur's writing how that is so, even if it is out of survival mode and the grief of personal relationships. Through his narrative, we hope you remember the resiliency of your heart and its healing capacity.

In writing this foreword, amidst taking a break to practice Qi Gong – a Chinese movement art form introduced to me by my father when I was a teenager in Honduras and which has always helped me feel relaxed and connected to my body – I peruse a bookshelf and find my attention magnetized to a book by His Holiness the Dalai Lama and Howard C. Cutler, MD. From years of practice, setting an intention of asking "What can I learn from this present moment?" I allow my heart rather than my mind to teach me. I open the book the way one would throw a dice or pick an oracle card to a section titled A Supple Mind.

"Perfect words of inspiration and conciseness for Arthur's foreword!" is my delighted internal response.

> "The ability to shift perspective, the capacity to view one's problems 'from different angles,' is nurtured by a supple quality of mind...A supple mind can help us reconcile the external changes going on all around us. It can help us integrate all of our internal conflicts, inconsistencies, and ambivalence. Without cultivating a pliant mind, our outlook becomes brittle and our relationship to the world becomes characterized by fear....It is through our efforts to achieve a flexible mind that we can nurture the

resiliency of the human spirit."[1]

When you take a step back from being drawn into the mind of another to reflect on your community, your family dynamics, and your personal relationships, do you see parallels? Can you find the commonality of being human? Through the honest knowing of another's mind, it allows one's own to be more supple and flexible. By feeling the vulnerability of another, it allows one's heart to soften and feel more love and compassion. This has been so for me reading Arthur's memoir and knowing him. My sincere wish is that this be so for you, dear reader.

At the end of the day, does the distinction between madness and magic matter? Are these words a play for a mind that is forever restless and searching? Maybe what matters behind our innate desire to be seen, understood, and accepted is kindness, compassion, and the endless quest toward what it means and looks like to love unconditionally, starting with ourselves.

"You are not your thoughts" is a quote attributed to Buddhist teachings. I leave that for you to ponder what that means for you.

I close this foreword with my favorite quote from my early teenage years so that you may begin your journey with Arthur. At my current age of 44, I continue to feel the same and live by this quote:

> *"Don't walk in front of me; I may not follow.*
> *Don't walk behind me; I may not lead.*
> *Just walk beside me and be my friend".*

This quote is attributed to Albert Camus, French philosopher, author, and journalist who won the Nobel Prize in Literature at the age of 44 in 1957.

It seems no coincidence to me that 44 are both our ages as I googled to make sure I remembered the quote correctly. I am tickled with Leo child-like delight at this synchronicity! These days, magic is part of my everyday life.

---

[1] Lama, Dalai (2009). *The Art of Happiness*. Penguin Publishing Group.

I hope you are inspired to find yours as you witness Arthur's journey.

In alignment,

Li-Lan Hsiang Weiss *Licensed Acupuncturist and steward of Armonia Health LLC* Chinese Buddhist name: Xiang Hui-Chun/Serving the Community

Preface

"Did you ever consider that your very existence is the door that Death chose?

What lies ahead of that passage is Life and it is difficult. It's supposed to be difficult and wear you down, all the while tempting you with four opportunities to thwart death's quest for life.

This is the dichotomy of good and evil, God and the Devil. God is the road forward and the Devil is the four doors.

So, what reward does Life offer that made Death choose that door?

It is simple, grasshopper. Life is a vector of physical entropy. The embrace of physical difficulty transforms Life's temporal structure until it can exist beyond its physical gravity and no longer be tempted by doors. To eschew difficulty is to forego that transformation leaving Life's energy to precipitate completely into chaos."

-Terry Freeman "Dad"

I never made a habit of speaking bluntly or directly, although I'd like to start you off on that note, brave reader. This book is filled with esoteric ramblings, divine insights, spiritual vagueness, and plenty of madness. I wish to convey a sense of magic—the wonder and freedom inherent in Life. Let me be forthright so that you can decide whether these are waters worth diving into.

Madness to Magic is for those that have dabbled with the former or know someone who has. Madness, in its extreme form, is mental illness, but it is also something that can be observed in the common streets of life as any deviation from a shared sense of reality. This shared reality we are taught to believe is complete and all that there exists is called "consensual reality." In my view, everyone has an individual sense of reality and their own madness, which only becomes mental illness when their reality becomes incongruent with functioning in daily situations and relationships. Madness can be a tempting fountain to drink from, promising the alluring fantasy of life being whatever one thinks it is, a disconnect from the transcendent reality beyond what is consensual, a distortion of the Truth (or however you refer to a Higher Absolute.) Everyday people drink from this fountain from time to time: when Life is too cruel; when one can't bear to see what is happening before them; when the distance between one's heart is too great to bear; and most of all when one loses someone or something that is most precious to them.

Magic is what happened when my own sense of reality became a personal journey of connection to the Sacred, the Divine, the luminous nature of EnLightenment. Magic reveals itself to me when I learn to listen to the whispers of my soul in a language only few can understand and begin to take steps into the unknown to see that which is waiting to be discovered. Magic occurs the more I shift from the view of life as a painful process to be endured to an adventure worth embracing.

The format I have chosen to share my narrative is journal entries that are told in real time. More than anything I feel called to generate some empathy for the lived experience of mental illness, and the present tense captures that best. I also use capital letters to emphasize certain words, to bring forth and highlight a deeper perspective that these words may contain. The Magic that comes from reflection is available here, and I hope that you use the lens of my book to revisit certain words and realities that were perhaps mapped out thoroughly.

Before we explore the exciting landscape of Magic, I must first start in the places that are difficult to witness. It is the Dark that gives birth to the Light, and this book will hopefully grant you the inside look of what it means to suffer fully and completely with madness. May it give you new eyes to see: yourself, your loved ones, and those that struggle with battles you may even glimpse.

I

Madness

1

Waking Up

Yin and Yang. Everything has two sides. There are only two kinds of people in this world.
Truth is loss of Self. To succeed is to Die.
Nothing ever changes until it does
Everything was the same until it was not.
Balance is to Live, to rock back and forth. On every scale, on every level. Every single thing is just something in a different form. The one true form, the god particle, the divine. There is a silver lining in everything, but that's not the light—it's God.
I see everything, literally everything. We eat things that are dead. Everything is a cycle. All the shapes are becoming clear in an infinite pattern. Everything has everything else contained in it. We are all one.
Spiritual needs have finally been met.
Now I understand the lines that divide us. The judgements and truths, the light and the dark. The least enlightened are those who do the most extraordinary things.
The most enlightened are those that are content.
And I am the Ghost.
The light. And the Dark.
Just like I had said all along.
-March, 2014

People think Hell is a place you only go after you die.
Those of us here now are tortured with a different truth.

I wake up in Heaven. I figure it's Heaven because an angel greets me; she's dressed in all white. The agony of Hell doesn't seem to be here, but everything is fuzzy, and I keep going in and out. They have drugs that are strong as hell in heaven, which would really be of better use numbing the tortured souls in Hell. I wake up and I'm watching *Family Guy* with my dad. *Family Guy* is always able to make me laugh, there's just something about absurd chaotic humor: POW! Gets me every time.

I hide my plush yeti under my sheets and knees when the red people come in. These people aren't angels per say; they do vital routine things for my physical body.

Lucidity snaps me back when an angel, a sitter they call her, is asked to change shifts. She puts her hand up to the replacement sitter and looks at me until she gets my attention. I'm floating around in a few different planes of existence, but when she stares at me like that, I come to Center for a nice clear moment.

She looks at me and she says, "Listen to me. When you get out of here, don't ever let anyone tell you what to do." Well since she's an angel, I engrave that in my heart with permanent ink. Later people would debate and say, "Wasn't her saying that ... telling you what to do?" However, that's just some philosophical technicality. I know a clear spiritual message when I hear one.

I'm probably getting ahead of myself, or behind myself. I figure a linear telling of the story would be nice, but if I tell all the events as they come to me, maybe they'll paint a picture in your mind that you can only see once it's done. I have a friend now who paints like that. She'll be painting and have no idea what she's making, but once it's done, it's like she had the whole picture the entire time.

A lot of things in life are like that.

Flowing with what's going is something of a gift of mine. Gift is a strong word though, because I lost track a long time ago of the subtle line between a gift and a curse. It is all a matter of perspective.

My name is Arthur Freeman, and I love Life. *Magic to Madness* is a journey through what it means to be alive, to wake up, and to feel it in every cell of your body. A journey through the United States' mental health system. An exploration of altered states of consciousness, achieved through various methods. A romantic sojourn through the crests and valleys of the heart, and what it means to truly love. A fragment of an inkling of a hint of what it means to be human, at least for those of us that Dream. Above all, this is my story. If we haven't met, I trust the invisible part of yourself that gently fills your sails. May your Soul guide you to read this book—or put it down—as best suits what it wants to See.

Enjoy the ride.

2

Falling to the Depths

I'm not Crazy, I just Love you
March 2014
I'm here in the hospital, or heaven, because for me, it sure as hell is heaven and I have no idea who I am. I'm at least awake enough to play a *Magic the Gathering* game with my girlfriend—I play a Red/Green Gruul Smash deck. I rock back, forth, and side to side on my feet as she takes her time with her turns, even though time is all happening at once, and I'd already won before she got in her car that morning. Excuse me, our car, a Red 1998 Mitsubishi Eclipse convertible that we call "The Sex Machine"; its roof leaks, and we cover it every night with a black shower curtain. Funny story about that car, it plays a key role in how all the events unfolded and gives some nice context.

Let me go back to the third day of a Qi Gong workshop in Asheville, North Carolina, when I'm driving The Sex Machine up a large hill to the hotel. She's been having problems starting lately-alternator problems we figure—but she makes it up the hill and I leave her parked on the grass.

I quickly found who I'll refer to as "Water Girl," for privacy, inside the workshop. Water Girl's able to calm down my Fire, which due to the intense amounts of Qi Gong and various Rebirthing breath exercises, has shattered through a lot of my Metallic boundaries and limits in my mind. During a break, I am outside walking around with Water Girl, feeling as Free as my last name. I take my shoes off and leave them on the grass. They are a nice pair of black Nikes, but hey, they are black like the clothes I was wearing the first day of the workshop and signify a burned-out flame or metallic energy. I feel the earth underneath my feet, and it's like I'm feeling it for the first time—all moist and soft. Next I figure, "Hey what the hell do I need ANY of this for?" and take out my wallet. Water Girl touches my hand with her soothing magic and guides it back into my pocket. I immediately agree. "Yeah, you're right, that's a bit much."

I called my ex-wife on a different break. Haven't spoken to her in years, but her number is still as clear in my heart as it was when she smiled and gave it to me the last day before Spring break of my high school senior year. She's having some health problems and is in a bit of a funk. I throw all the Qi I can muster at her. "Don't you remember? You're a Fire Girl! Don't you remember our passion? We met in creative writing class! Remember that! You have the heart of a poet and the voice of a magician, please don't forget your Fire."

The best part of that day was we all held hands in a prayer circle, a chain of about 150 people or so (hell maybe 200) and the workshop host kept going on about some problems in Ukraine or something. Thing is I can't stop laughing for the life of me; the whole thing is a Big Joke. And I'm not talking about the prayer or the workshop! I keep laughing—must've laughed for forty minutes straight—and the guy next to me starts cracking up. Finally Water Girl starts laughing too; I mean Water resists getting evaporated by Fire but it's so much freer to be steam!

At the end of the day, I hug her and I say, "I love you' (this was maybe the 340th time I said it to her by the way, when you open your heart, nothing but Love comes out), but this time she melts—her whole body literally relaxed into my arms—and she says, "I know." If only I knew then it wasn't about repetition but timing! Damn. Everything feels completely perfect. Harmonious. No one's in illusion about anything.

Outside, The Sex Machine won't start and I don't miss a beat. I get out smiling—no shoes and all—and begin hitching a ride. I'm completely confident I'll get one. Sure enough a beautiful Wood-type Crone takes me back to my hotel.

Earth Girl [that's what I'll call my girlfriend who I had met through Fate two and a half years prior] isn't doing too well. She spent the day in the room because she's not a morning person and didn't come with me so she could have the car. I don't remember much of that night, but it must've been better than the night before (where I didn't sleep a wink and was up all night scribbling the secrets of the universe that I eventually gave to Water Girl). They were chicken scratches that made perfect sense to me, but to my surprise she took them into her hands as if they were the most valuable treasure in the world.

Well, the fact that The Sex Machine isn't working doesn't thrill Earth Girl too much. On the workshop's fourth and final day, we check out of the hotel and take a cab over to the workshop's hotel. Turns out The Sex Machine got towed! Annoying, I mean who tows a car that's parked in a parking lot (nevermind that it was on the grass overflow lot)? She goes over to the front desk to see what's up with the car, and I go see Water Girl. I take Water Girl's name tag off because I told her I had a magic trick ready for her. I say, "Tadaa! Now who are you!?" The ripping-off part startled her through and I read that as the bad kind of startled. I get really self-conscious about that, worrying that it is a mistake and all, and go over to beg the man for a blank name tag so I could undo my trick. I give it back to her and she laughs at how seriously I'm taking these symbolic gestures.

Earth Girl comes over at the first break to inform me, all organized and laid out on paper, of our options for dealing with our car situation. I mean she has to return to Raleigh in two days for an interview with her prospective new job designing happiness—err video games—so it isn't exactly a pressure-free situation. I introduce Earth and Water to each other, and Water Girl remarks on what a wonderful partner I have. "Make her your everything," she texts me later. I didn't know what to do with that, like a lot of good advice I've gotten over the years.

Anyway, I point to the option that says, "Take a cab to the towing place and see what's up" by method of what they call "intuition" (or as I prefer it, "Fate"). We go over there and wouldn't you know it! The place is empty (of people) and I'm all fired up, thinking of the nerve of people to both tow my car from a place I had a right to park in AND then not be there when we come to pick it up! Following Fate, I go over and climb a fence, to which Earth Girl warns me of the posted sign "BEWARE OF DOG." As soon as she says it, a little tabby cat scurries across my vision at the bottom of the hill. I roar with laughter back at her, "HAH! It's just a cat! THERE IS NO DOG!" having found another secret of the universe. Fears are much bigger in the Mind than in Reality.

I get down to where The Sex Machine is. I start rattling the gate—that's locked—like I'm sort of a caveman, when Earth Girl calmly finds that she can unscrew a bolt on the lever that holds the gate together and the gate slides apart wide open.

I get in the car and—VRROOM, it starts on the FIRST try! I'm high on the Qi-feeling magic surge through to the alternator, and we tear out of Asheville like it's on fire, like we've done something wrong but really we're in our own car and on our own Way. About halfway down the mountain it starts snowing, and time starts to slow down. I can see every fat snowflake as it drifts down to kiss the ground; the pure beauty thaws the ice inside me a bit more.

I drive pretty much non-stop back to Raleigh. I feel like I need to come down from the mountain "high" energetically as well as literally. We land at a Whole Foods because I'm ready for radical changes in my diet, but I feel compelled to stop by my friend Reck's house on the way back. He is in a bit of a rut, and I knew that he deserved every bit of happiness that I'd found. I enter to find him playing Leona on *League of Legends*. I watch as he becomes immortal. He continues living through dangerous situations with slivers of health when my words finally break through his exterior to get some laughs out of him.

"You're like the Sun! See! You can't die with solar power!"

We get home. As Earth Girl makes dinner, she gets stuck at a crossroads—make an appetizer or just have the main meal? It feels like a *Real Serious* decision, one that reflects her entire life over the past year where she didn't know how to hit the start button; a year off work where I encouraged her to discover what she really wants to do moving forward while I took care of the bills. Without hesitating, I say, "Let's have both! Just do it!" She lights up like a Star. "Yes! That's what was missing! Just do it!" She makes a delicious meal with beets. The flavors of everything are so intense that it takes me a very long time to eat. Even the plain glass of water I can only sip. Slowly. Each time I do, I repeat like a mantra:

"Water always brings me back."

~~Reintegration~~ Disintegration

The next day, I wake up feeling that Earth Girl and I have the power to save the entire world! She shows me some video about a guy who's talking about his bipolar episodes. He says he felt like Jesus, and I empathize with him 100% while completely missing the message that Earth Girl is telling me: I'm a little manic right now and need to address these violent mood swings.

> *Mania is characterized by a feeling of high energy, pressure, anxiety, and intensity. Someone who is experiencing mania may seem "amped up" and become more likely to engage in risky behaviors.*[2]

I call up my Latvian brother, Staeg, and unload the full force of my Flame on him. I say Flame because I call him "FIRE BROTHER" and do all I can to pass on a torch from my Inferno. The raw emotion reaches him! In my rant, I create the phrase UKIUKI. U know it, U know [you] know it! I get him to repeat that phrase, and it has all the markings of the chant for the Religion of ALIVE!

"That's enough for today." That guy who wrote *Zen and the Art of Motorcycle* died this year (2017), and he laid out his madness in quite a logical format and paused often enough. He inspires me to aim for a higher ideal.

---

[2] Grunze, H. (2015). Bipolar disorder. In Neurobiology of brain disorders (pp. 655-673). Academic Press.

FALLING TO THE DEPTHS

I'm also hesitating to continue, because the next part isn't all sunshine and rainbows. I mean I foreshadowed it clearly enough that we're going to Hell. At least let's jump in feet first—

I go to work at the massage spa and get smiles and rainbows out of most people. My first client has a nice crescent moon tattoo that keeps me focused and present—especially since she asked for deep tissue specific work. I talk with one of my coworkers who is feeling a bit stuck on my break, and she is swayed to call her husband, who is stationed over in the Middle East. She has a meaningful conversation with him. All sunshine and rainbows. Then my next client arrives for her first massage appointment ever.

Now, I know the protocol, but here (like in the mountains) my Metal energy [discipline, boundaries, rules] is nowhere to be seen, and I have a tenuous relationship at best with paperwork in my life. I check on her a few times because my sense of time is on fast forward compared to her Earthy, slow rhythms. Third time I ask for the paperwork, and she still hasn't even really started on it. Impulsively, I say, "We don't need to do the health history paperwork. Just sign the consent form and come back to the room." I listen to her attentively and tell her to get on the table facedown under the sheets.

When I return to the room to start the massage, I find her fully clothed on top of the sheets, but I don't skip a beat. I figure I'll go with it rather than explain how to properly receive healing. As if there were a "right" way. I start improvising the massage and do a lot of shaking movements. I also do some heavy breathing and exhale, like she's accumulated a lot of darkness in her and I have to breathe it all out. After who knows how many minutes, she tells me that she's feeling pretty sick in her stomach. I figure she's anxious as hell and that I'm getting stuck emotions moving, but the Metal boundary I still respect is her saying "No." We stop the massage, and I take her back to the front to check out. While I'm changing the sheets, a front desk girl comes in. Apparently my client is weirded out as hell and has complained for a refund. I apologize profusely; my co-worker asks me if I'm on any drugs.

I pause.

"Is happiness a drug?" I say straight to her soul, through her eyes. Something shifts in her expression and she replies, "No." I think in that moment she realized that behind my normally calm and quiet demeanor, there was always a lot of suffering–and a lot of that suffering had been lifted (or was in the process of being lifted). Or maybe she responded to truth and clarity, as most people do in some form or another. She tells me that I should go home anyway, even though I implore her that I want to see my next client, a regular of mine. "I know how to handle my regular. She's someone I know! Let me help her with my newfound awareness! I'll follow the guidelines and share my breakthrough with her." Yet it's too risky in her eyes.

I leave. No matter how much my Fire burns, it is not expressed as anger at my workplace. I call my stepdad, and his slow cadence in tone alerts me to the fact that he is emotionally back in his younger years. His voice is slow and relaxed, and he understands the things I am going through. It is refreshing to hear him actually connect with me from the heart, rather than the usual montage of all the taxes I have to file or registrations I have to renew. Paperwork. Later I learn that this is from the heart too because it is his expression of worry and love.

Back at the NuNest (the name of our duplex apartment), my energy bursts through the door like a strong gust of wind or a raging inferno; I feel like only Water Girl can calm me down. I don't know how to surrender my arrogance and armor to let Earth Girl truly take care of me. Or maybe I simply don't want to be on earth right now. I resist her attempts to instruct me on how to handle my emotions. Well, not even my emotions—I have been neglecting Earth matters like eating, sleeping, and drinking fluids. You know? Those things that the body requires to function…

The worst part is she thinks I'm faking these emotional reactions. Like I'm acting out or something. My body's shaking uncontrollably with Qi and probably fear, and this pushes me over the edge—I gotta get out of here.

Of course this makes her even more nervous—I'm clearly a loose cannon, and I'm trying to fire myself off into the night. I drive off anyway, ending up at McDonald's somehow, where I realize that zombies are real and I've found them at 0 dark-thirty. I am in a full panic attack, feeling like I'm about to die. I plead with the cashier to "call an ambulance!" She literally isn't fazed. She has a face like the world could catch Fire in front of her eyes, and she'd be there chewing bubblegum like it was some old action flick she'd seen a hundred times. She doesn't say a word in response. I call my stepdad again, and he tells me to get something to eat. Perhaps it's his male energy, or something to do with his stars, but when he talks to me, I slow down and listen. I get a McMuffin and some OJ. Then before I know it, I'm out driving again.

Driving isn't the right word, since I'm not really conscious of where I am, where I am going, or even that I'm driving. I notice a few red lights here and there, stop at them, but for the most part, I'm on some spiritual auto-pilot. It is safer than drunk driving (aka literally "Jesus take the wheel!" but I am still unconscious all the same). I have my bamboo sword with me. Holding it in my left hand, it keeps moving as if to tell me which way to turn.

I switch on the radio by pressing buttons and twisting knobs at an erratic pace. As if by magic, some classical music comes through the speakers. The music is heavenly enough that I realize it's Earth Girl! She's dreaming up the reality I'm in! I feel her love through the music—sent to calm me down and get me through.

I shift out of the dream when the sun rises. The dawn light greets me over a wide green field, with trees laughing in the distance. I walk out of my car, up the hill, and halfway through the field, admiring the beauty of a new day. On the edge of reality, I feel as if I could walk off into that sunrise—keep walking and that life would carry me forward to unimaginable places and people, where everything would be taken care of by invisible forces. Even with that faith in my heart, I turn back anyway, feeling that the time for an Endless Adventure isn't now.

I take a wonderful poop right there in the middle of the field, releasing years of grief and emotional debris with it. Returning to the car, my mind remembers how to use GPS, and I see I'm about twenty to thirty miles east of Raleigh.

I get home, and my newly activated sensitivities feel a distinct absence. Visually, Earth Girl's there on the bed, but I don't feel her presence at all; my mind leaps to the dark conclusion that she's killed herself out of the stress I caused her. I yell out loudly a sharp "AH," which snaps her soul back into her body. I feel her presence again, and she lets out a drowsy, "Mew?"

Makes sense that my mind jumped to that conclusion. Part of why I have been reluctant to go to sleep is that everytime I try, I feel my awareness leaving my body—well yeah, how else does one dream of far-off places!? Still, it's terrifying and intense. Like the reverse of sleep paralysis. I don't want to die. I don't want to fall asleep to the new me I have discovered.

She gets up with a cute, sleepy look on her face and has a few cups of coffee. Before coffee, her mind isn't fully online or sharp. She's got feline soul through and through. As for me, I go into our makeshift massage studio (but is-a-moldy-storage-never-used-second bedroom) and relax on my massage table, talking with God for the first time in five to ten years or so. Did I mention my massage table is named Spirit? God's telling me mostly about how to treat Earth Girl, things I have to be aware of now, lessons to learn, and other metaphysical things. Next thing I know, Earth Girl comes in and is giving me a massage! She must have somehow learned through absorption, or her body knew how from all the ones I'd given her. It feels like heaven washing over my body in waves. My entire body is vibrating with peace and relaxation, but my left arm is going haywire. I find out a few years later that during my motorcycle crash, my energy channels were "blown up" at my wrist, but at this moment, all I know is my left arm is flying around as if plugged into an electrical socket.

This massage turns out to be the best foreplay of my life that leads into mind-blowing sex, as I let myself experience the pleasure that I normally hold back from. I had always been terrified reaching that edge of ecstasy because it felt like the top of my head would explode and I'd die. I let go with her now because stopping a freight train at this point, with any resistance, would be like spitting into a storm-force wind. Surrendering to primal forces has an upside after all!

I collapse, satisfied, and Earth Girl tucks me in, assuring me that when I wake up, I will be in a whole new world. I curl up like a child and am ready to give in to unconsciousness when my mind kicks back in and freaks out that I haven't taken a shower after being out all night. I get up and take one. In a flash of brilliance, I decide to take a cold shower. Cold showers for me have always been purifying, but in this case, it stimulates me again and doesn't help me get to sleep. Instead, I rediscover the amazing technology that we call today a cell phone, and I begin to call the people I love. My mother is one of the first who responds along the lines of, "I'll need time to digest this. I'm getting the image of a torrential waterfall rather than the slow faucet stream I normally receive when talking to you."

I have a prayer bead bracelet that Earth Girl got in Asheville for being helpful. I hold on to one bead per person that I call. [synchronicity: apparently Buddhists actually do this while chanting mantras to liberate beings from Samsara!] A hostess I used to work with answers the phone—we hadn't talked in years. I do a magic trick over the phone and get her to smile a bit, but then I talk too long, and she worries something is quite wrong with me after all. I'd like to think I took a nap at some point and woke up before twilight.

I play a game of Hearthstone, and it all plays out in slow motion. The feelings are so intense I can only handle one round. Who knew games were designed to be so much fun!?

Underneath the twilight sky, I walk around my neighborhood with my wooden sword and the Sex Machine's black shower curtain as a cape. I wander up to the top of the hill that's between two roads: right where Western Blvd meets up with Hillsborough Street behind the Family Car Wash. Watching the sunset, I get the same sense that I could wander off into the distance and let the flow carry me where it may. Instead, I turn back east and practice letting go by falling down the hill and tumbling all the way to the bottom. Outside my house, my neighbor is coming back with his girlfriend and their dog, and my sword falls out of my hand while I'm swinging it around. This grabs their attention; I look him straight in the eyes and say, "You gotta start the revolution. If you want it, then you gotta start it!" That freaks him out, probably because he knows it's truth and is the answer to all the existential struggles he's been facing lately about the world and things being screwed up.

Earth Girl makes a delicious and wholesome meal, and I take a very long time to eat it, the pace that intensity demands. Later she goes to bed, but I stay up, feeling the great unwinding of Qi happening in my body. She beckons me to bed, and then we are fighting. This time it's really explosive, and I throw a bunch of my suitcases in my car, intending to drive off east to who knows where. I tear out of our driveway despite her attempts to reign me in.

I drive for a long time with my bamboo sword as a guide. I have no awareness of where I am or where I am headed. I finally come to rest beside a field again (I've often wondered if it was the same one as before), but this time it's dark. I have a glass of water in my cup holder, and I finally feel relaxed and sleepy enough to doze off into sweet, sweet slumber...

I wake up to the sound of a knock on the glass. A police officer. He politely informs me that my car is reported stolen, and I politely show him my ID and registration that prove—no, it's not stolen; I'm here in my own car. At this point, I'm freezing, or nervous as hell, or both, and I'm shaking uncontrollably.

He asks me to step out of the car, to which I comply. I channel my stepdad's advice, and his mannerisms come into play; I act real cooperative and pleasant with the cops. I start telling them my story, not the whole one here but just the Asheville parts with the hotel and the tow company. He stops me and asks a very pointed and difficult question: "Your story is missing some key details. What's the name of the taxi company you took to the tow place?"

Now, since I'm all cooperative and not very perceptive at this point, this question feels like it has the weight of the entire world on it—I believe if I can't answer, then this cop won't believe me! I start panicking, shaking more, and call Earth Girl. She doesn't pick up, and then I panic scroll through my dialed numbers to match up dates and timelines. Fun fact: when you're on Fire, dates and time seam together, and you lose track of all those dates and orderly things that make up day-to-day life. Of course I haven't saved the taxi's number, so it's not named, and I end up calling a few to see if it goes to a taxi voicemail.

Since I can't answer, the cop uses this pressure as an excuse to find my story very fishy and a motive to search my car. I'm not thinking at the moment except *Sure what do I have to hide?* So I let them search my car, and they have me sit on the cold, early spring asphalt. I'm shaking on the ground and ask for my glass of water, which they deny—they probably think I'm shaking because of drug use.

Karma Breaks on the Shore

FALLING TO THE DEPTHS

Let me meander through some backstory, and what better place than Hawai'i? This was five years earlier in 2009.

I live on Makiki Street, living with my wife and roommate Bob. Bob isn't his real name (something he let slip while he was really high once, so I'm going to call him "Bob"). Bob taught me with his actions the wisdom of "easy come, easy go" one day when he abandoned his yellow 50cc moped on the side of the road halfway to the North Shore of Oahu when it stopped working, and he didn't look back. I didn't apply that lesson so well during my divorce, but that's another story.

Bob also taught me that I shouldn't do anything that I can pay someone else to do for me if I make more per hour. That was his reason for eating McDonald's, since he figured he made about $20 an hour, and that an hour of cooking would be a waste compared to what he could pay to have it made for him. Well that and the fact that he had cancer. It's amazing what I can learn from a dying man on how to live. Well, I had to unlearn the "pay someone else" bit after I found out how fulfilling it is to enjoy the fruits of my own labor. Sometimes I wonder how simple and pleasant life would be to simply farm my own food, eat it, and share with my animals and family...

Bob smoked every day, and he had plenty of medical marijuana to enjoy. I smoked with him only once. I was pretty adverse to drugs, since that one time I got really high. My vision split in two while I was playing poker at Jimmy's. It felt like my feet were bleeding, and my body was really hot in that altered state. I called Fire Girl to tell her that I was probably dying and that I loved her. I tried to tell myself that no one's ever died from smoking weed, and Jimmy reassured me the same, but in the moment I couldn't help but think I was a special snowflake and let paranoia take over.

Anyway, I had this nice, little pipe I had picked up in Cozumel, Mexico. It had a gecko on it and was the colors of the Brazilian flag. I showed it to Bob and we smoked it one time, and there was a little leftover burnt bud in the pipe. I don't know much about drugs and their sizes, but I estimate it was a 1/16oz? 1/32oz? One puff's worth? See where I'm going?

Memories within Dreams

Back in humble, old North Carolina, half a decade later, karma hits me in the face as the cops act like they hit the jackpot when they find that pipe I had forgotten all about. They find it buried in my luggage that was filled with manically stuffed clothes and whatever the hell else I needed to run away from my problems. This is where reality really starts breaking for me again, and I'm not even conscious enough to say common sense things like, "Ok so you give me a warning or a ticket and I can go back to sleep?" No, the next thing I know I'm in handcuffs that I'm rubbing my hands against in an attempt to slip out.

An old habit I picked up from the first time I had handcuffs on, which is a related enough story tangent because it's the first time I had a whiff of the mental health system. I'm sitting there in a teenage catatonic state in 2007 with the "Orange Range" opening from Bleach playing in my head on a loop. Well, only the first lines anyway ... "miyagata yozoro no hoshi tachi no hikari." Something about looking at the night stars ... It's hard to say whether that song kept me sane. In retrospect, what I know about stars now, I would say yes.) Anyway, I have pretty thin wrists, not even the tightest setting on standard handcuffs fit around me so I can wriggle in them quite a bit. Even though I knew I couldn't really take on two armed cops sitting in their office, I daydream of my escape. Right on the edge of slipping through, the intuition of one of the cops seem to trigger, and he takes my handcuffs off to let me get comfortable. I am waiting in the station for hours on end—in a catatonic state, you really don't know what time it is and your biological functions all slow down anyway.

Finally, a woman arrives, apparently licensed to determine my sanity, aka my risk of hurting myself or others. I argue with her vehemently about a person's right to choose whether they want to live or not in front of my nerve-wrecked poor mother. I'm very careful with my arguing thanks to a full teenage life of being a smartass cynic. After having been assaulted verbally as the focal point for my rage for the entire broken system of society, she is ready to pull the trigger and have me taken to a mental hospital. I see the fulcrum point and flip the tables by reminding her that not once did I threaten to take my own life or admit to any suicidal thoughts. My mother almost jumps out of her chair, agreeing wholeheartedly. The woman concedes the point—cold, hard logic has its perks like that–and lets me go. As I walk out the door, my mother implores me to thank the woman who just let me off the hook and decided I wasn't insane. I come to a complete stop in the hallway, turn my head around, and stare right through her overworked soul, and say:

"I'll never thank anyone who takes away the freedom of others."

A few days later, it's Valentine's Day. The whole world is blanketed in a pure white soft snow, and I ride my bike a cold three miles to the house my crush lives in. She takes my Valentine's Day card and gift with a "Why are you here?" look on her face, as her father closes the door on me. *I didn't want to warm up for a while inside, no, thanks for asking*, I thought. When some unnamed government official somewhere deems the roads safe enough to open school again, I'm drifting around numbly through eggshell white concrete hallways. At the end of a school day, I turn the corner of the stairs to find my crush talking with an enamored smile on her face to another boy—a friend of mine, because of course it would be. Weighed down with the despair of one who has tasted Love in far-off lands, the catatonic state sinks in.

On the first level, Mimi is in the common area. Not the crush who crushed me, but a wonderful human being on the periphery of my social life. Her kindness breaks through the wall of pain I'm in, and I smile without her saying a word. I fall in Love with her right then without even knowing it. I tuck this memory—a gem that will never be forgotten—deep into the ocean of my Being. I ask her why she always seems so happy, and she responds, "I like seeing your smile," with the sweetness of a thousand falling petals. Yet this warmth is too much to bear in my current inner wasteland, and I convince myself she's only being nice because of how pathetic a state I am in. My self-worth nears the depths of the ocean... sinking...

I go to that optional follow-up visit (I lied to my mom by saying it was mandatory) at some mental health clinic three days after my first evaluation at the police station. I calmly tell the woman that I have had plans to kill myself for a while and that I am fully determined to do it. The same, cold logic wins in the system—no matter what state a person is in, if they say the magic words, the door to hospitalization opens. She implores me to go voluntarily because it's much easier to get in and out of the system that way, but I stand by my principles and refuse to go willingly into a broken system. Nevermind the fact that I had just knowingly told them words I knew would get me committed, after voluntarily going to the follow-up visit: this was for my aesthetic, as it would be going on some permanent record of my life story somewhere. Oh hey, I'm writing a piece of that now, aren't I? Heh.

They take me on a long police car ride down to Snowden. It's a facility in Fredericksburg, Virginia, despite what the name brings to mind these days. The important part is that Fate is at play and that the car stops along the way at a police scene. Some terrible "accident" occurred, and the authorities are cleaning it up. A lot of bodies and a lot were mutilated. The stench of death wafts into the sheriff's car—not the smell of rot but of some fresh vileness—but it doesn't move my frozen heart one inch. The symbolism reaches my mind, however...

I have the whole scene of my death planned out in my mind—I imagine that mental hospitals are places where they forcibly inject you with sedative drugs. I envision myself jumping out of the window of the third or fourth story, resisting any attempts to be controlled through pharmaceuticals. My body falls in a slow arc, along with the shattered glass and the snow drifts down with my last breaths. Freedom.

Snowden is a one-story facility; my dream is ruined. I bide my time for the three days of involuntary commitment until I can appear before a judge and show them I am clearly sane and in control of my faculties. On the witness stand, I stare out with intense eyes forged in the dark winter nights of my soul. I start my defense with all the anger and disdain that had been successful during the first psych evaluation.

Something that I didn't anticipate occurs: evidence is brought against me. Evidence against my sanity? Yes, it is none other than a series of suicide letters I had written to people that I loved.

Everyone experiences life differently, so, of course, everyone thinks of their own death differently. I've known a lot of people in depression that want to die in the shadows, fading out of existence as if they had never existed. These, perhaps, are compassionate souls overwhelmed with life but keenly aware of how their deaths may impact the ones they love. I had no such kindness, and I wanted to go out with a bang to at least make use of all the potential life force I was ending. Of course I wrote letters in just such a case! Hidden in my backpack, my mom had come across them while searching for schoolwork for me. I don't know what compelled her to bring them to court against me. Some would say Love; others would say Fear. In my eyes back then, her actions were nothing short of a complete betrayal of my entire being. It broke my heart. Again. The first time was ... well, I'm sure there will be another time and place to share that. Enough flashbacks within flashbacks!

My father rises to the occasion in my defense, which also surprises me. He argues that the letters are merely creative writing outlets and a way to express my feelings. He is right of course, and I feel Love from him for the first time in a long time. I feel understood. Like he sees my soul. Understands its pain. His birthday is one day before mine, on June 27th. We are Crabs. We understand each other's depths, pains, and Lunacy at times.

The judge is not moved by such deep crab-felt emotions and cares only for the hard facts weighed on the cold scales of Justice. I am judged guilty. I am judged insane. I am taken away in handcuffs yet again, as my father watches from the other side of the sheriff's car with tears in his eyes. It's the only time I've ever seen him cry. My heart breaks a little more.

Getting out of the system is almost as easy as getting in, once you know that you have to get out. (Being a good actor helps.) My fury at my mother ignites a new desire to live. My father's Love opens a path of change I had not anticipated in the dark night of depression. He invites me to live with him in Tysons Corner. Now with the stirrings of some Fire, I play the part of a compliant patient. One night, the other teenagers beckon me to the common room, and we find the door to the yard outside unlocked. We all stand there, eyeing the potential freedom. Yet being the comfortable caged animals, we are turned away from the opportunity. In my mind's eye, I see only the cold snow and the eventuality of dogs tracking me down in that timeline. The fence to the yard is pretty high up too and, as a solid wooden fence, it has no real way to get footing. I decided to gain my freedom the official way; I set my heart on the promise of change that moving one county away to live with my father offered. I am too young to know that no matter where I go, there I am.

Inferno

The cop's viciousness wakes me up in 2014, as he growls, "If the judge asks us, we're going to take a hammer and SMASH IT TO BITS." I speculate that he's referring to my pipe. I don't know what the hell this guy's issue is, but it really is just a 1/32 oz burnt piece of weed in a sentimental pipe. He's training some rookie at the moment, so the whole process of arresting me is pretty long and drawn out, which is doing wonders for my dissociation as I float in and out of awareness.

Next thing I know, I'm in some other bureaucratic machine with yellow-tan concrete walls. I don't know if you've ever slowed down time before, but doing it at 3 a.m. and seeing into the exhausted souls of all those government workers is NOT a pretty sight. Everyone has red eyes. It's enough to make you believe in Hell on earth. After a few eternities, I am led into some little booth where the kind-hearted rookie advises me to copy down some important phone numbers out of my cell phone before they confiscate it. I think I put Earth Girl's down.

I'm in some other processing room where I catch sight of a worker's book. It's a classic, *1984*. When I mention it to the man, his eyes light up with passion and life, as if someone had finally seen him for the first time in years. I figure people that work in this cold, metallic place live for these kinds of moments; the brief respite from waves of people being jammed through the system. The guy tells me that if I can't get bail, there's a hearing in the morning where the judge will decide my fate.

Now, I'm finally in a semi-open room with the freedom to walk around and use the telephone to fish for some bail money. I completely forgot about (or lost) the piece of paper because I don't call Earth Girl. I call my mother and stepdad instead because that's a number I have down pat. It rings once, twice, and then a few more times before I hang up frustrated. At the moment, I convince myself with complete certainty that it's not going through and it's not going to voicemail either, so the whole situation seems rigged. I call again and the same endless ringing happens, so I walk over to a woman at the desk.

I ask her for the numbers of some bail bondsman because I figure that's my path out of here at this rate. She replies casually that they don't have any numbers, and that I'll just have to wait until my hearing. Of all that transpired tonight, this dilemma breaks me. A jail ... with no way to get out? No phone numbers to try and get a bail bondsman? How the hell do people in most need of it get in touch with bail bondsmen?

I sit down in a room that has glass windows and a doorless entryway. I sit there with my head in my hands, and then everything suddenly makes sense. All the events that had been woven together: Hawai'i, the empty towing place, the explosive fight with Earth Girl. It all comes together to make a complete and perfect tapestry: I'm dreaming. In reality, I'm parked at the side of the road where I finally fell deeply asleep for the first time in a week.

Yes. I'm dreaming, of course. Why didn't I think of it before? The stone bench in front of me calls to me as the solution, as I haven't been able to will myself awake any other way. On my knees, I place both hands on the bench and rear my head back. I let out some blood-curdling scream and slam my head into the bench. My head bounces off it without me feeling an ounce of pain, which of course reinforces my dream theory. I know the scream was blood-curdling because two men appear instantly on both sides of the doorway, and I get up knowing full well to comply with them. I'm taken directly to a very tiny holding cell with a toilet, and shown no concern for my bleeding forehead. The walls are a vomit yellow-white color, and the toilet is a cold, steel gray.

Note to the Reader:

A warning that my tone may change from here on out. I came back from a gathering with friends and family in Brasil, where I shared my story in an abridged form and it had the inspiring effect of bringing everyone together. People let go of their irritations and frustrations with each other and were reminded about "What it's all about." In this context, it was a Christian retreat, so "Love One Another" became the focus once again.

I don't consider myself serious, but I come off that way a lot to people. I was also probably downplaying the pain I experienced in these places because other people have been through much worse. However, it's a matter of intensity, and where was I going with that thought? [Honestly, to stop writing in the middle of a sentence.] My point is, sharing my story in front of a crowd in Brasil allowed me to experience Grace. I felt like the pain of these experiences served a purpose and helped ground people in what really matters. I hope that, in this light, this story moves you to be a bit kinder to strangers, and even kinder to the ones close to you. People are the ones that will change the world, one act of Agape at a time.

———

Safe to say, I am on the edge of a complete breakdown in the middle of this tiny cell. No—truly, I AM mid-breakdown! I realize I am not asleep, but deep in Hell in Dante's Inferno. My acts outside in the purgatory area must have led to me going down a few rings of Hell (not that I was keeping track). Let this be a lesson: struggling and resisting in Hell will only serve to deepen one's experience of pain and spiral down further. As for me, I can only push my desire to escape any and all situations to the limit. I see a vent above the toilet, and I try jumping for it a few times. When that fails, I slam my fists against the window of the cell and look out at the people there—the indifferent zombies of 4 a.m. Hell. I am desperately looking for any trace of humanity. I only need one person to look at me with compassion—or at least even to acknowledge my pain! No one turns an eye. My madness makes them too uncomfortable. It is easier to ignore suffering that we do not understand. I imagine many of you reading this have some part of yourself locked away in this Hell, with no one being able to look at it without flinching: it has been forgotten below the tides of forgetfulness.

Please take some time to look within yourself, for if no one else will, then surely it is up to you to gaze upon your own suffering. I wish there that you find the eyes of love to see with. Think of this as an exercise to explore yourself, and my only guideline is to be gentle. I invite you to sit still, actually sit, and ask yourself if there is any pain that has not been acknowledged that would like to arise now. Breathe with that pain, and release it in whatever way feels natural to you.

FALLING TO THE DEPTHS

What did you see?

Don't worry; I haven't gone anywhere. I'm still in this cell. I take my wallet out and scatter the cards and plastic around—searching for some symbolism—some meaning in this hell. No answers shine back at me. The only solution I find is to take a defiant dump in the cell. Yes you read that correctly, and it was hard for me to type it. That is the truth of this story, of the ugliness that I felt at that time. Put the book down if it is too much, but the truth is often like that. I pull down my pants and shit right on the cell floor. I figure that will break the cycle—at the very least someone will wake up and realize how terrible it is to treat humans this way.

On cue, the cell door opens, and a large Black man shouts in shock and incredulity. It's enough to bring me back halfway to a consensual reality. He brings me cleaning supplies and orders me to clean up my own feces. The scene shifts—I'm being strip-searched. Ordered to bend over, I feel vulnerable and incredibly afraid that I will receive a swift kick in the ass that will launch me upward to a new plane of existence and out of my body. Squatting down, the kick doesn't come, and the scene changes.

I sit at a desk in some sort of judgment area. A man who holds my fate in his hand looks over my record while another Fire person stands behind him. The hellion reads my full name slowly: "Arthur Benjamin Freeman. This is a very presidential name," he proclaims. I take that to heart as some sort of destiny. Not a destiny I am happy about having at all because it seems like an incredibly narrow and long journey to achieve. Not to mention the fact that "destinies" discovered in Hell scream of punishment.

He looks up from my records and says to the Fire person, "You want him in the general population ... are you sure?" The Fire person looks right into my eyes and says, "Yeah ... he's not crazy. He just hates being in jail." I stare back with defiant eyes, yet satisfied knowing full well that he has seen me. This Fire person is another one who operates on pure instinct, an intuition refined in the flames of battle. I respect him, despite my own fiery hatred for my current place in this ring of hell.

In "General Population," with the other freshly arrested men, I keep to myself. All the other souls trapped in this terrible place are living through their own nightmares. I feel a strong connection to Earth Girl through the aether—I feel her will is working to free me from this place. Time in hell passes in decades or eternities ... I feel as if years are going by as she changes society and the entire outside world until it is a place that can handle me. I feel like Nelson Mandela waiting all those actual years for the world to be ready for him to play his part. I do Tai Chi-like movements, as the sentence, "Don't fall asleep in hell" continues to echo in my head. A girl is on the other side of the window pane, in some other processing level of hell. She looks remarkably like my ex-wife. I stare at her in disbelief, thinking *You ended up here too, huh?* She shoots me a "the fuck you looking at?" glare. I laugh it off—that's so like her.

A paper bag appears before me filled with some sort of sustenance. I don't have the wherewithal to understand the concept of food and its necessity for survival, so I create an altar with the bag of milk—the softest expression of the feminine I've encountered in the depths of this metallic hell. I curl up with it and maybe lose consciousness. I'm going in and out at this rate. That's when I notice the sheets lying on the metal bed in the corner and how there used to be a man sleeping there. I connect this situation to the man in Yossarian's tent from *Catch-22*, and understand that by falling asleep in hell, he plunged yet deeper into its layers. To keep myself awake (or to help purge the toxicity of this nightmare), I begin cleaning up the cell and the trash that's been scattered about.

Next thing I know, I'm in a changing room, shedding prison clothes, and slowly coming back to myself. I'm finally being released from Hell (not that I understand why or what's going on other than the present moment). I step out of the changing room and a man appears besides me as I'm walking. He has a slight grin on his face. I can't tell if he's the angel Virgil or my future self, but he's the first person to acknowledge my existence that isn't a hellion. I look at him and ask, "Does it ever get easier?" He says something vague and incomprehensible, and it's lost on me. At the counter, he receives his bag of goods—what they took from him besides his dignity during the strip search—and he pulls out a pink Laffy Taffy. "Oh! Candy!" he says.

With a defiant look, I snap the pants open to fold them neatly into the paper bag. The snap is so loud, it wakes the guard up... "Wow," he says, as the emotion of my refusal to submit to this place is channeled within every motion I make. I retrieve my bag of stuff (I hadn't come in with anything really) and walk out toward purgatory.

As I walk down a long corridor, like the kind of tunnel you see at death, she appears quite neatly in the center of the hallway: Earth Girl. Seeing her standing there, I get the surreal feeling that I'm waking up from one dream and shifting into another and easily accept her arrival without any surprise. I am on the border of catatonia at this point, numb to all feelings but a smoldering, cold rage. She has only anger and frustration to offer me. Despite her heroic efforts to liberate me, I am unable to be grateful as she moves mountains to get information out of where I was arrested so we can retrieve the car: I had been driving unaware and have no idea where I ended up.

"This is exactly the kind of thing I was afraid of happening! This is why I kept trying to stop you from going out!" Her words pass through me. Deep down, I wonder if her fear is not what manifested the entire nightmare I lived through in the first place. (Talk about not taking responsibility for my situation.)

In the elevator, the employees of that detention center are talking about mundane things: sports games, the weather, parties that happened or will happen. The next thing I know, I'm in the back of a taxi cab. The driver has taken quite a lot of interest in me and my story, which Earth Girl explains at some length while I dissociate from reality in the back. Another blink, and I'm back at home alone—not that I have an understanding of what or where that means, nor do I have any real sense of self. All I know is that I'm alone, trying desperately to get people to wake up. I call my regional manager of the massage spa I work at and channel some demonic voice, telling him, "You only get one call; this is your chance. Wake the FUCK UP!"

Earth Girl is who I truly want to shake, to get her to see the Light, to have her experience the Love that's all around us. I am Robert Frobisher in *Cloud Atlas,* and I need to leave a fitting scene before I ascend to the next plane of existence. I am my brother who has been misunderstood for so long. I look around on her extensive bookshelf, realizing that every single book holds the key—the secret to reality. I lay them out haphazardly before I find myself in my spare bedroom where my massage table is, lying on the floor where I know she'll find me. I feel a liquid oozing out of my skull and accept that the deed has been done, and it's time to embrace Death.

On the other side of death is beauty; an incredibly beautiful woman fills my vision. She is vaguely familiar; all that comes to mind is that she is my ex-wife and soulmate—except a few hundred years in the future. In this life, I am a robot and am unable to move or do anything except be conscious of experience. She is talking to me animatedly, as if I were her only friend in this desolate future. What feels like several days go by, as the wind is the only thing that can move my soul and body. She continues coming back to see me and show me different parts of herself.

She moves to leave as my neighbor's dog has come around the back of the house where I find myself having this conversation with my mysterious soulmate—the only fountain of kindness I had been able to find since Water Girl gave me that beautiful hug in the mountains. She asks me to wait here as she returns the dog, but I leap up and dance around the yard in my boxer shorts, singing/yelling at the top of my lungs about Love and Truth. Bobby, the owner of the dog, comes up to me and starts to guide me back into my side of the duplex. As I do so, a Black friend of Bobby's gets out of a car in front of his house, which prompts me to shout, "Yo my nigga!" or something along those lines, to which the friend laughs with a beautiful smile. I've always found words to be harmless as long as love is what is behind them. Or as the cliché goes, it is us who gives words the power to harm us.

Bobby, who I am quite convinced is actually myself since I am my brother, eventually picks me up and carries me into my house. I whisper to him, "This is my favorite part, my favorite part," as I see that the movie of life is taking a different turn, and I want to let my brother "Arthur" know how much I love him. The scene changes again! There are about four or five Fire people looming over me in my bed. I feel myself shooting up out of bed before collapsing back down several times. I am hysterical, finding the whole universe as amusing as a cosmic joke, while also being terrified of the police officers that are here to take my freedom away once again.

To this day, I have no idea how they got permission to enter my house. I learned later that some neighbors had called the police on me because of my shouting, and the ambulance came after the cops to tranquilize me with copious amounts of haldol. The diagnosis was a complete psychotic break.

3

Descent into Chaos

So it Begins, after the Break

I wake up in Heaven. We have come full circle. I'm glad you got a taste of Heaven before Hell. Isn't that how the story goes? Yet, this is no parallel, for the Garden of Eden shows up much later.

There's no night and day in Heaven (or windows), which gives weight to the Eastern view that there's a bit of Hell in Heaven, too. I forget what fresh air tastes like. I've forgotten that I forgot. I also have plenty of chemicals in me doing God knows what, all the while trying to not be overwhelmed by every molecule of existence constantly stimulating me.

There's a puzzle on a table that I never can finish and a phone in an indent in the wall, which I call my father from sometimes. Besides that, red people that come in and take care of my vitality from time to time, and nurses in white who mill and seethe about the place, make up my world. All I know is that at some point, I'm being escorted from this place and an angel congratulates me for "such a quick recovery." I don't know what I am recovering from, but I have no concept of such things as past or future at this point; all I know is I'm getting into a car with a serious man, and we're going for a long drive. My mom and Earth Girl are driving behind us. It takes a few eternities to get wherever it is that no one told me we were going.

We arrive at a series of brick buildings that are one floor high. We're in some office-like courtyard and I get the urge to run, to enjoy this rediscovered sunlight and fresh air. However, I decide to trust the ones I'm with; I'm a fool who goes along with whatever harmony he's in. When I get deeper into the complex, I understand the truth on some level, that I'm being locked away again. I lose consciousness, as the sheer weight of the pain in that place knocks my Soul clean out of my body for a while.

I have a roommate now. He's an older man that gets stuck in loops and needs help cleaning the bathroom before he can use it. I have a copy of *The Little Prince* that Earth Girl has left me; I flip the pages frantically for the few seconds that I can focus to absorb some beautiful wisdom—usually from the Fox:

"Because you wasted so much time on me, you made me feel very important." -Fox[3]

Darlene brings me back to myself sometimes. She's a beautiful woman with a lot of Water energy, who assures me that she knows what I do for people. I wake up and look down to see her name on the journal I've been writing in, though I don't know how I got my hands on it. A man who is about my father's age goes on long walks up and down the halls and tells me to call my father.

A brown faux-leather journal arrives in my hands, along with a shirt that ironically says "Snake-Oil Salesman. Genuine Article." I take it for the humbling statement it is, but my mom wrote sincerely in the journal:

Dearest Arthur,
   You are my Butterfly.
   Your smile is infectious.
   And we are here for you.
   This long-sleeve shirt conveys
   Positively of you.
   Eu Te Amo,

---

[3] de Saint-Exupery, A. (2018). *The Little Prince* (I. Testot-Ferry, Trans.). Wordsworth Editions.

Mom/Alzira

The rest of the journal is filled with numerous insights/impulses that come to me and leap—sometimes furiously and sometimes elegantly—onto the pages. I notice a letter from Earth Girl, who apparently visited, but I have no way of calming down or being understood when I see her. The letter is an ingenious way to communicate; I skim through a lot of deep truths and insights that she wants to share with me if only I would listen. I hastily write replies in pencil under her words before I finish reading the whole thing. She's found an untapped reservoir of strength in her Soul going through this situation. She teaches me about emotions and how my mind goes much faster than my emotional response.

The visits with the doctor are pretty easy. He's a curt man who isn't too interested in reading his patient's moods, so he asks simple questions, which are simple enough to answer to convince him I'm sane and should be released after the seventy-two-hour involuntary commitment period. The counselor is a lot more sensitive, and her office has a nice atmosphere. She sees how much I really am struggling, but in true patriarchy fashion, she has little to no control over my treatment plan.

I'm visiting with her when they bring the dogs to play with the patients. I miss out on the healing powers of pure love. The next day, I enjoy the outside time in the garden—there truly is ample space, trees, nooks and crannies that let me feel as if I'm in another world, another dimension. The Garden of Eden at last. A place without cold, stone tile floors and without overworked government employees. We play a game where we toss tennis balls into a wooden board with cut-out holes. The breeze is strong and gentle; every time it blows, I feel it throughout my being and the balls get guided into the holes like magic. I enjoy the surprise on the caretaker's face as about eight patients in a row throw the ball perfectly. The Divine Wind is blowing, and I feel as though everything is in complete harmony.

The Ride Goes On

I don't have a proper segue here … I honestly don't have memories for how or when I got out of that place or the two-hour drive back to Raleigh. At least I got out after the minimum seventy-two hours and not a day longer.

I am shaving in my bathroom back at my apartment with Earth Girl. I am keeping the tradition of being as hairless as possible before interacting with my twin cousins that I love dearly. They are set up on Skype, calling me from Brasil. I see their faces as I talk animatedly, with one cousin having an interested, amused, and curious face while the other one is crying. I know she feels my pain and sees through whatever smile or excitement I may be showing. One twin seeing with the Mind; the other with the Heart—what a good pair they make, no?

Earth Girl rolls out our yoga mat for us to calm down after the call. After the first few poses, I slow down enough to my body's rhythms that I collapse on the mat. She gently guides me to bed where I black out. This Yoga experience, having such a profound and dramatic effect on my emotional state, inspires and empowers Earth Girl to want to teach one day.

I come to my senses in the early grey dawn. My Soul moves me to go for a walk. My mother, who is staying over on our futon, is too exhausted to protest and trusts me to not wander off into the aether. I go down the street, happy to be free and outside in the warm spring air. I open all the mailboxes on my walk, wanting them to know that the good news is here! A fresh Wind is blowing through the world, and all they have to do is open up and receive it to be renewed each day!

After I return home, my loved ones get ready, slowly but surely. I convince them to go on a fresh walk with me, and we tour down the same streets I wandered earlier. They notice all the mailboxes open and become concerned—especially since I bent one a little too much and caused damage to the property.

Yes, my behavior is eccentric, but is that so high a cost for Love? …To feel the Spirit of the Wind refreshing aching souls?

We visit the City of Bulls, Durham, and I am a ball of energy to everyone I cross paths with. Outside a restaurant for lunch, I begin talking to two beautiful ladies about how I am a massage therapist and I share the enthusiasm I have for helping people. They are amiable people, two sisters, and the one closer to me is the guardian who makes sure people are good people and stands facing the world for her younger sibling. My mother returns from the restroom and apologizes for me, but the ladies insist that I was no trouble at all and comment that, "He just needs his own business!"

The next scene is a lot more terrifying. I sit in front of an ice-cold doctor with piercing eyes. I can feel her looking for what's wrong with me, searching for exactly what kind of illness I have and how to label me. I am no longer my amiable, enthusiastic self, but a terrified child that wants to enjoy the sunshine each day and no longer be locked away anywhere. She is going out of town and does not have the ability to take me in as a client, but she tells my mother that I need 24/7 supervision and care.

We go next back to Earth Girl. I'm not in a good mood, and the messiness of our home affects me. I yell at her harshly to clean the place up by the time I return from my eye doctor appointment and leave in a rushed state of being. We venture to the eye doctor for a follow-up appointment for my Lasik eye surgery a month earlier. The symbolism of regaining my sight and a spiritual awakening within the same month is not lost on me. They assure me my eyes are perfectly fine, but show concern for my panic attack-like behavior.

I continue going along with the tsunami-like flow of the day on some less-than-conscious level, understanding that my mother is going to take me back to Virginia with her. My way of going with this flow is to pack all of my things in a huge flurry. The intensity of each moment nearly overwhelms me; I feel as if I'm going to be gone for a long time. I convey this to Earth Girl in once again not-so-gentle words or tones, and I see her break down and cry. The same neighbor who carried me into my home to save me last week is comforting her in his arms. He had gone through mental hospitals a few years back as well and understands what I am going through.

We drive north into the night, stopping at a gas station with a Five Guys restaurant. The brownie my mom gets me from the convenience store is full of sadness and makes me feel sick. I lean the car seat back and close my eyes, going into a sort of trance in order to channel the wisdom and answers my mother has never had the chance for questions she never felt ready to ask. She worries that she failed me as a mother, and that how she raised me wasn't good enough. What matters to me more is whether she will help raise me now.

The Hell with No Open Windows

I'm outside some clinic. My father is the first to arrive on the scene. He confronts my emotions and asks me if I'm not simply hurting deep down because of how my Tia is doing. He can tell my mania is simply me avoiding the repressed pain that has finally been unleashed into my awareness. Mania really is all about staying one step ahead of your emotions with your mind; that's why the more intense the pain, the more manic one gets! My Tia is in the hospital with brain cancer, and that's not something I can even begin to look at or process. Maybe he's right, but in this moment, that couldn't be farther from my Now.

I'm running around with my mother and father exploring the playground of the world. I do find an actual giant bronze globe that's hollow where the oceans are, and I climb up inside. I like the comfort of this space, the feeling of being in a womb-like structure, which is perfect for a rebirthing process. Emerging as a newly hatched phoenix, I fly around parking lots, fields, and streets with zooming cars I am confident will never touch me. I notice a man dying slowly to cigarettes, as I make my way across the street to the hidden safety of a grove. The grove is really the space between the bushes and the sign of some office complex, but I find a treasure all the same: a sign that says simply "PS" in bold, block white letters on a red background. The sign is small enough to hold to my chest, as I return to the other side of the street and give it as a gift to my mother.

Inside the office, I fill out paperwork and chat with the security guard, a man who I feel understands things on a deeper level. He tells me the story of how in third grade, the teacher asked a question (what question matters not) and everyone was coming up with all sorts of answers to it—even though it was clear they had no idea of the answer.

The security guard had said, "Maybe there is no answer."

I vow silently to never forget those words of wisdom.

I voluntarily commit myself to a hospital because people who seem to care insist this is the only path forward for me. Or upward. After I black out the rest of the journey, I arrive in the enclosed hallways of the fourth floor of INOVA, a hospital in Northern Virginia.

Ana the nurse is the first person here whose compassion douses the flames of my pain. I have a roommate named Adam, who wakes me up (or we wake up to the rising surge of dawn together, full of energy and passion); we brainstorm entrepreneurial ideas that we can tour the country with. We decided "Anything for a Buck" is a good slogan with which to use our unbounded energy to serve humanity in any way it needs at any given time. I take Adam's words seriously because the young Asian man whose anger scared most people away whispered to me that God controls the rooms, and I know being with Adam is kind of destiny.

My parents visit and bring me coconut water, which is what my body craves—I am in the process of melting all the excess Metal energy I have built up in my system and healing myself of eczema. I bounce around like Robin Williams and tell my dad every time he laughs that he laughs because it's true! For those of you with divorced parents, imagine my childlike joy! Both of my parents are in the same room again! I'm five years old, and everyone is together again! Family! This has the effect of both amplifying my mania in that moment and soothing my Soul. A silver lining is revealed.

Not that my delusions run so deep that I think it's some romantic reunion. But on a visceral level, some part of me is touched. I'd like to think I slept a bit deeper that night, for however long I slept.

I wake up into the waking dream. I run full speed at the window at the end of the psych ward: I-know-I-can-fly I-know-I-can-be-free-all-I-need-to-do-is-experience-the-fresh-air-that-lies-beyond-that-WINDOW!

BANG! I crash into the plexiglas, and it shoots me back! Yet, I feel nothing (it's a dream!). They drag me back to the room behind the nurse's station. Strong, immutable arms are holding me down—I don't know what's going on; just the restraining and I am terrified. The angel Rafel looks down upon me in his sky blue nurses' uniform, the one bastion of familiarity in this nightmare. I plead to him, "RAFEL! RAFEL! PLEASE!" He looks at me with a mixture of compassion and sadness, tears in his eyes. I know in this moment he is as powerless as I am in this world. Yet, he is an Angel, and *he does not look away*. They tranquilize me with a cold, sharp needle. Lightning sears me into darkness.

The Ties we Make

Andrew and I have formed a team. We are Bodyguards. He is a tall African-American with a lean build; I am a shorter Brazilian-American with a Chargers cap. Our salute is to look each other in the eyes and slap ourselves on our own shoulders while saying, "We are Bodyguards." Riley is the girl we have sworn to protect. She has a deep loneliness in her eyes and sits at a table all day, putting together a puzzle. She puts together the pieces slowly; people are drawn to her calm sadness, and she welcomes them and talks to them. One by one, like a saint out of the Scriptures.

Riley and I bond a little when I stay up with her—despite me taking the sedative Ambien. In the morning, she tells me how close we got, even though I don't remember because I was black-out awake (which is what apparently happens when one takes an Ambien and refuses to sleep).

I wander the halls at night, asking all the nurses that will listen, "How do I fall asleep? I've forgotten how to fall asleep." There's a nurse technician that reminds me of my twin cousins in Brasil, but my warmth makes her uncomfortable, so she's established a ten-foot boundary between us. I respect it when I remember, but it's hard when all I want to do is have everyone feel loved as much as the Universe loves them.

We help each other out for the most part here. I'm struggling emotionally in the common area, and Kieron yells out, "That's a badass shirt!" Kieron is a romantic like me and is always falling in love with new people. When doing arts and crafts, Kieron and I sit next to each other. He is sweet-talking a girl with all smiles and charm. I ask him how he keeps it all together, and he responds, "You just have to keep meeting new people." He's found his key to sharing Love in an acceptable way I sense.

I write in my journal a lot because insights come through to me like a waterfall that has nowhere to go but out, out into every place that it can flow into and every place. Whether it is received or not is up to the recipient.

Favorite Gems, Bizarre Scribbles, Excerpts from my Journal
What follows is my attempt to do justice to the writings that came through in my state of mind. Please keep in mind they are handwritten scribbles over the period of my 2014 hospitalization.

To: Fire
For: Water
Love: Earth
By: Wind
This Journal belongs to: Miguel, who saved my heart.
Greg who helped me
All who help me
"Read what you write" -Brother, Stuart

———————

Here's a clue
Create
Don't Destroy

———————

Don't let the seeds of evil take root in your heart

———————

You were right here the whole time ... happiness :)

———————

Happiness is everyone being their cog in a machine

———————

Rage against the MACHINE, not the cogs

———————

Land softly please I Love you.
~and it's a long way down.

———————

The KING is on the opposite COLOR space.
Build a Castle out of your Weakness.

———————

Suffering has a purpose, the Blade is refined in Hell.

"Do you believe in magic?" -Arthur
"Yeah. But it's not real." -Kieron
"I think
Feel it is ;)"

Am I your hero?

The doctors here are as intimidating as the woman with ice-cold eyes back in Durham. They are less scary because I have the shield of my acting mask and my desired goal of getting out. They are more scary because their judgement holds the keys to my freedom, and their power is that much more absolute. They know how to push my buttons. They do so to make sure I'm still crazy and unable to be released. The dance goes like this: meet with the doctors, they trigger me, and test my sanity; if I break, I miss my chance to have a calm discussion about being released.

I don't know what day it is, but I've settled down enough to know that I'm in a hospital. There is an outside world I can return to—even if I don't know the way. On the verge of my release, the doctors share how my parents don't think I'm better, and they won't let me stay with them. Since I have no place to go, the doctors argue they can't release me. My anger erupts forth, and I stand up from my chair, declaring, "I'll stay at a hotel or sleep in a field for all I care! I don't need their homes for my freedom!" My anger doesn't go past the breaking point. I'm still able to be present and show determination in my eyes. The doctors settle me back down, saying that they don't want me to sleep on the streets and that my parents will take me in after all.

Turns out they lied through their teeth to upset me. My parents never said anything of the sort! Dirty tricks like these is how I've lost faith in mental health system. The world tests our sanity enough each day WITHOUT gaslighting. What if it were mandatory everyone who treats patients had to experience insanity themselves first? True understanding can only be gained through experience after all ... but these aren't thoughts from back then ... I'll stop tainting the past with feelings of the present, because in those moments,

I was mostly carefree and happy to be released Alive. After being released, I spend the night with my father and stepmother; thanks to her dedication to feng-shui (not that she uses that word to describe what she does naturally), I have my first deep sleep that lasts through the night.

Finally...

Rest.

Adult Day Care

Now I have to go to something called "partial hospitalization" for a few days. It's one of those voluntary-mandatory things, and I guess the people are all right enough. I have a rough time sitting still through all our group therapy sessions. I blurt out the answers that people are going in circles looking for deep inside; they keep overlooking their blind spots. The answer is always right in front of you!

We pair up into partners for an exercise that involves us sharing our dreams for the future. I tell the girl that I don't have a future dream, but a predetermined Fate: a hell minion told me I was going to be president. She presents me to the group as "our future president" and the weight of that imagined burden—and the steep path to get there—almost crushes me.

On breaks, I go outside to enjoy the sunshine and fresh air. A second daycare group is often there, usually smoking. This other group is as curious about us as we are about them... Finally I discover the root of how the groups are divided: they are recovering substance-abusers. The wall of misunderstanding between us is high, even though we both go to the same place of animistic consciousness with different vehicles. "What are they experiencing without drugs? Are they crazy?" vs. "Why do they need substances to tap into life? Are they escaping themselves and feelings?" These are the thoughts I imagine for our perspectives...

The man at the sandwich shop keeps me in line and tells me to get my act together. It is nice that he cheers me on. He seems to understand what it means to be a man in this world.

An older gentleman in daycare lost all his money recently and shares the wisdom that, no matter what I do in life, make sure that I go into the business of Light and Love. He had made an enormous profit off the oil industry, but had lost it all in the crash of 2008; he hadn't really recovered fully from that and was in a rut. He assured me that if I invest all of my energy into a business that is for Love, I'd have no problem with the financial aspect of life.

He has keen eyes. He describes to me how he can see where everyone else in the group is getting stuck. He uses a metaphor of gears and machinery; people's beliefs are stuck plugs that are stopping the gear. We both want very badly to remove other people's plugs, but know far too well that it's not the sort of thing we're normally allowed to meddle with.

...Especially when we're also patients, considered insane, and not wise in any way...

Later, I learn that to interfere with another's path—with the way Truth is revealed to them—is not an act of Love. Often we are uncomfortable with another's pain, but to let them CHOOSE to see the Truth in their own Way is a great act of respect and Love. Take this chance to reflect on anyone in your life who particularly irritates or grates you with their inability to see what you see so clearly. Of course, we remind and challenge those we care about to reach their potential, but we must balance that with fully embracing who they are Now. Life unfolds for each of us in a miraculous way, so I've learned to trust that in others and focus on what the situation is revealing to me.

The doctor here is much nicer. She doesn't have a problem with my wanting to live a spiritual life: all I have to do is take my medicine. Go to as many workshops, retreats, ashrams, temples, or mountains that I have the stomach for, but take the medicine. That point was drilled into me very clearly. Take the medicine.

Take

The

Medicine.

Something in my soul is reluctant. I believe deep down that there's nothing wrong with me, that I am in fact a happier and more free person than I've ever been, so I don't understand this concept of needing medicine to go through life. Especially when it numbs me... Or I am numbing myself in reaction to this diagnosis... In my hubris, I deny the perception that I have a problem.

I wouldn't have such an issue if this diagnosis explained all my life and how it reached this point in some holistic way, but this label is the complete opposite from my teenage years. My last run in with the mental health system gave me the label of schizoid personality disorder (like a personality could be a disorder)—I never did get that. That label I embraced a bit more readily, as a way of empowering the mask of numbness I had chosen to wear to navigate this world.

Through that label, I found a whole forum of schizoids dedicated to feeling nothing, to deriving no pleasure from this experience called life—and with that, no weakness. We had a dry, sardonic humor and exchanged stories of feeling nothing and experiencing traumatic events offhand. We discussed the stones we used for our walls to become embodiments of isolation.

The Colder Depths of Hell

Flashing back to those times would be an incredibly long and arduous detour. Yet, I titled this book *Madness to Magic*. In some ways, the numbness and ice of my teenage years were more insane than feeling all my feelings at once.

I don't know when it started. It's hard to say when the world became more painful than I could bear, and the loneliness of existing fought against the yet harder cage of isolation. They say no man is an island. I say they didn't try hard enough. Perhaps it happened slowly over time, like how a mountain forms.

Perhaps a metamorphosis story is in order. Once, there was a young boy who lived inside his imagination and dreams. He saw his brother be put on very heavy medication for "autism," which made him like a zombie. This scared the young boy so much (he was already very prone to fear and would stay awake frozen in fear after watching a scary movie) that he locked that memory deep in his subconscious mind. Yet, he never forgot the lesson that being true to yourself and being vulnerable like his brother meant being misunderstood and hurt by this world.

The boy played lots of video games, which let him play with the imaginations and worlds others had created. Of course, he still liked to play sports and breathe in the wind, but this happened less and less the older he got, and the more his neighborhood friends began to move away.

In middle school, he discovered acting, which allowed him to put forth a beautiful mask in all areas of life. He used the mask to cover up his awkwardness and fit into most social situations. Inside, he still felt like an outcast on the outskirts of all the seeming merriment and carefree lives of his peers.

In high school, his thoughts lead him down yet darker paths. Once suicide becomes an option for the mind, one never forgets that it lingers there as a potential escape from the pain of this world. That whole episode mentioned earlier with handcuffs and Snowden occurred, yet it did nothing to set him on a brighter track toward a future. He falls in love ... or perhaps anchors himself to a purpose that might justify Existence itself. Of his many errors, the core one was his attempt to forge a mask that could itself be loved back. For surely he could not be loved for himself ... he could never be himself. Yet, this strategy leads only to more painful heartbreaks and loneliness.

My father wrote me this letter while I was in the INOVA hospital back in 2014. His gift with prose is something I have always aspired to. Perhaps his version of the story is more poetic and more accurate. Let it be a portrait of the audacity and foolishness of youth up to this point in the narrative:

<u>The Story of the Weester</u>

Once upon a time, in the hills of the kingdom of California, a weester was born. Three wizards of the realm took notice and bestowed great gifts upon him.

The Wizard of the Mind gave him the gift of power, the wizard of the Heart gave him the gift of communication, and the Wizard of the Body gave him the gift of peace.

Everyone who looked upon the little weester was taken with his countenance. His little face glowed brighter than a full moon rising over a calm lake.

As he grew, the beauty of his countenance was to open doors for him, the power of his mind was to avail him to great knowledge, and his articulate heart was to ensure him satisfaction. The three wizards were overjoyed, for they had outdone themselves.

.... But alas the stewards of his gifts did not get the message to the weester, and he did not learn the secrets of his gifts.

Along the way, his little heart was broken and not understanding the secrets of his gifts, he let the passion of his mind fill his heart and occupy his tongue, and he let the grace of his body mask his mind, and everyone overlooked his woes because they could not hear his sorrow and could not feel his pain for being blinded by the grace of his countenance.

... so everyone just assumed that he was the carefree, little weester who made everyone feel good and no one listened to him, and he felt betrayed.

You see, the secret that he missed was that you have to play with the gifts the wizards give with the tools that you have.

You think with your Mind, feel with your Heart, and act with your Body.

The power of his mind could only be known through his heart by those most trusted, and the grace of his countenance was the only available expression of his heart or his mind. Instead, he had used his countenance to mask his heart rather than express it and hid his heart from his thoughts till he was mute and manipulated his relationships with his mind to no satisfaction.

... and his sorrow overcame his mind and his body and his heart, and he longed for what he had never known but no matter how hard he tried, he sabotaged his relationships and darkened his heart, and the passions of his mind haunted him.

One day, the stewards of his gifts discovered their oversight and went in search of the weester to help him learn his mind, feel his heart, and accept the grace of his countenance.

They are hoping that he is still Listening.

-Terry Wayne Freeman

4

Initiation

Back to the Future

In retrospect, one might be able to see how it makes sense. Of course, the numbness of those years lead to the explosive emotional swings of bipolar disorder. Yet, at the time in 2014, with my history of distrust, I dismissed the radical changing of labels being forced on me. As if bipolar is something I've always had and always carried! I had no idea until it reached the infernal intensity of my twenty-fourth year…

Upon reflection, if we are to revisit such lands and not make our way fully back to the future of 2014, we will find ourselves back at the same nexus of experiences of feeling that was Hawai'i in 2009. I suffered a series of blows, traumas, and situations that lead to behavior I see now can be considered hypomanic. I didn't really have any support network to speak of, and it's a small miracle that I navigated that time without ending up in a hospital.

I leaned on the wonders of the internet and found an outlet for all my energy in the waves of reality and virtual reality. I discovered the wondrous intellectual game of *Mafia*, which appealed to me because it involves sharpening one's perception through the lies and false selves people present. I worked furiously to sharpen my sensitivity to deception, and went by the name *Fate*.

After all those branching realities in which *Fate* leads me to Earth Girl, in

2014, I am reintroduced to the glorious and dangerous tool of Facebook after the hospital. I post the truth that comes to me each fresh morning while dancing. I've completed the adult daycare and am at my mother and stepfather's house now. The emotional pain in the air doesn't lead to the same kind of sleep as in Tyson's, so I set my mind on new distractions.

I reach out to Earth Girl. The iciness in her response strikes fear deep into my heart. The fear of losing someone rises up in me to a panic. The fear of abandonment. I make it my mission to go back down to see her. I know my Fire can thaw her heart, and I want forgiveness for the pain I caused her in my extreme state.

Under the pretense that we are returning to gather all of my belongings so that I can live in Virginia for a while, we drive down to see her.

Wherever I'm Needed, Wherever I Want to Go

In my apartment—that place where my whirlwind of madness blew through—my neighbor shares that after I left for the hospital during my psychosis, their microwave went haywire. Weird ... I listen to my parents and Earth Girl's mom talk (who is visiting from Charlotte). They talk about mundane adult things. Earth Girl catches the mood of my inner child, and we sneak out for a walk in the sunshine. She starts collecting flowers and weaves them together. I'm happy to breathe in the fresh air and watch the Magic unfold, as the innocence I remember in her lights up my heart as a lighthouse for a weary sailor.

Gone is the iciness! The distance between our hearts is no further than the inch one must travel to arrive exactly where one is. We return home, her flower crown resting lightly on her head. I sit on the floor across from the parents. I feel struck with an exercise I learned in massage therapy school: we begin to do yoga.

Laughing Yoga.

I start guffawing—forcefully at first—but once the absurdity catches hold of the women, the laughter starts to feel more real. All this release is focused on my old stepdad, who finally bursts under the pressure and gives a bit of a chuckle. "That was weird," he says. They go back to their hotel to rest from the long drive.

Alone with Earth Girl and her mother at a restaurant, I open my heart and share my transformation. I let them know I've changed and that I am deeply sorry for the reckless actions that may have hurt her. I let her know that if nothing else, please take my money to support yourself and this new start. I have the check written out and hand it over. Earth Girl doesn't want my money, but they both do see the change in my heart. More like the settling down of the heart anyway ... all these changes feel like they've been in the works for more eternities than I can count.

She gives me another chance. My parents who drove me down here to pick up all my stuff are a bit perplexed, "So are you staying now?" What about the plan? Why are you changing The Plan?"

To satisfy them, they take some of my stuff with them on their way back to Virginia. I stay behind to take care of some logistics, such as reuniting with Eternity.

I haven't mentioned her up until now, have I? Well, one of the key experiences I had after coming back from Asheville was the realization of that one-inch shift ... That everything I loved and made my life awesome was right here all along. Eternity is my motorcycle, and she is parked on our porch, thanks to a makeshift ramp I made from Home Depot that allowed me to get her up there. It feels like I haven't ridden her all winter! I somehow convince Earth Girl's mom (who shall be called Mama-wen from here on) to let me go for a very short drive. Of course I go with no helmet for maximum effect and enjoy the freedom of the Wind in glorious spring weather.

Earth Girl is at work, so I have the full gaze of Mama-wen on me when I begin to play a game with my Fire brother from Latvia. We play "All Random All Mid" in *League of Legends*. In this game mode, the champion you get to fight with is completely determined by the forces of the Universe. Of course I get Yasuo, the Wanderer—my favorite champion—and it confirms everything I believe in: the illusion of chance. My Fire brother is a bit down. He has stopped feeling his emotions and wants only to exist in one of those sci-fi fabled states of "peace" and complete detachment. I remind him of his true nature. Of how he is the Stag God who carries us all with his incredible skill that he developed over the years. By the end of the game, he is doing quite well, much like when I watched Reck play Leona all those weeks ago. I'm pretty high on the feeling of victory and the symbolism of Yasuo, so I go to play again. Mama-wen's stern eye reminds me that I have productive things to be doing, like finding an apartment and other promises to make good on. I pass up on the game and go refuel with some lunch first.

We go together to the apartment complex of our dreams: Banyon Grove. The name is beautiful, as Mama-wen is also a sucker for symbolism. I tell the agent I prefer the first floor—I've always liked multiple entries for escape and ease of use—but she teaches me the top floor is the best place to be. No one's above you on the top floor.

The best thing is these apartments are brand new, construction being finished as I apply for the lease. The worst thing is this causes several delays for our move date, which goes from the end of April to mid-May ... to June. Our current landlord had already promised some of his other tenants that they could move into our place, so our delays are delaying his promises, too. Eventually we are forced to trade places with his other tenants in their 1 BR apartment for one month, which turns out to be literally in the backyard of our old place on a street we've never walked down.

The day comes for the absurd temporary move, and my duplex neighbor notices that I'm hunched over and not in a bright mood. Earth Girl caught me not taking my medicine and feeling happy. She got all worried and pressured me into taking Zyprexa again. It's the same medicine my neighbor was on a few years ago, so he understands how numb it makes me feel. On the other hand, his wisdom from a few nights ago returns to the surface. He stood on his porch under the lamplight and looked straight into my eyes.

"Is it really a prison if you hold the key?"

After the move, we treat ourselves to the local farmhouse-style diner. While I'm eating, I'm still in that depressed state. Earth Girl asks me, "Aren't you enjoying your meal?" My angry eyes glare at her, "No. I don't taste it."

Being a Taurus in heart and soul, this is apparently enough to get her to shift her views. She holds me on the floor of the "new" apartment, which is dusty, irritating my lungs, skin, and Metal Element all over again. She holds me saying, "I'm sorry if the medicine really takes away your ability to enjoy life this much. We'll find another way." I don't know why this doesn't comfort me as much as it should. I feel a bit bitter that it took more than my words to convince her I didn't need to take it or that it wasn't helpful. Then, are the words of a lunatic worth much to anyone?

Gotcha ;)

Practical Symbolism

I return to Virginia by train, seeking to buy a car because The Sex Machine is on her last legs. I'm wearing a red shirt and hang out with some of the AM-Trak employees in the dining car. One of them calls me Trouble. During one of the stops, I stand right on the white line that's not supposed to be crossed. Everyone else gives the edge plenty of room, not needing to rub up against it. There I was though, Troublemaker in Red, doing my stretches and enjoying the sunshine, which fell only near the edge. There is another attendant with a different perspective, who said, "Aww, he's not Trouble; he's got kind eyes." People see what they want to see or perhaps they see what is in themselves reflected. Afterall, Water is a clear mirror in its natural state.

In Virginia, I find a Black Scion, another dream car, with a beautiful spoiler and everything aesthetic that I've ever wanted.

Only catch is that it is a salvage title. I could go into another side story about how my manager sold me my first car in Hawai'i (which turned out to be betrayal incarnate), but for now, I realize that I learned my lesson when it comes to buying salvage titles.

Despite that, my desire for this car is pretty strong, but the only thing that stops me is how stubborn and greedy the salesman is when I try to haggle the price down with my father.

He teaches me that you have to be willing to Walk Away.

Next car I'm test driving is a Hyundai Tiburon, a style I've always appreciated with a hatchback that will fit my massage table. It's silver and has some checkered patterns on the clutch. Though I'm a bit rusty driving a manual car, I go through with the purchase of this clean titled vehicle. I drive it back to my dad's, and the whole car is shaking. This vibration fills me with anxiety and regret. I tell my dad I have a really bad feeling about this car and ask if there is any way we can return it and cancel the check. We go and pay the returned check fee first, getting into the bank right before the 5 p.m. buzzer closes.

The dealer isn't really fazed. They still have my check and simply give it back to me. They were a bit upset that the clutch smells like it's burning, on account of me not shifting gears all that well on the hill right before the dealership. In the end, it's a relief to make a mistake and to catch it in time before there are severe consequences.

The next model I check out is on Earth Girl's advice to get something practical, but since I feel the truth in the idea, I don't resist her for once. We arrive at a used car dealership where my dad, mom, and stepdad are all in the same fifty-square-foot area for the first time in … probably ever. They talk about adult stuff with the focus of me getting a car, so no real emotions or real-ity comes up. I end up going to a different dealer with my dad alone to check out a blue Toyota Yaris. We take it for a test drive, and my dad gets a really good feeling about this car. I trust a more seasoned Cancer's intuition (especially when it comes to big financial decisions like a car), and I start to feel pretty good about it, too. Especially with the smoothness of the ride and the minimalist design. The price is decent, too, and we drive out of there with my Yaris—complete with a Roxy sticker from the previous owner on the back.

I text Earth Girl; I tell her the car is a "Healcyon Blue" color. Healcyon is the name I've settled on for my business name—my vision.

She replies, " That's the kind of symbolism I can get behind <3"

The Holiday with No Name

In Latvia today, they celebrate their joining of the European Union. It is the first day of May. Their holiday has no name.

As many things of great import do not.

I return to my Union, taking the scenic route of 85 down to North Carolina with my new ride. The lessons from my father reach me on the road as the movement helps me think clearly. When I was a baby, the only way my mother could get me to relax to cut my toenails was to drive me around until I fell asleep.

My heart is Wind. My mind is Fire. The grace of my countenance is Water; these are the gifts the gods have given me.

Metal is a product refined by man, while the Wood Element is a product of nature. Through this juxtaposition, we can find our uniqueness. Through this synthesis, we can seek to optimize what we are. Metal is what I aspire to be—lead that can be transmuted and refined through Alchemy. Wood is what I am, rooted into the rhythms of nature.

I will be one with the Divine Wind. I will remind the world of the Wind. It is blowing.

A Phoenix gets caught in the Ashes

Stabilization is the name of the game back in North Carolina. Life turns out to be a lot harder than I remember. I always had a refuge in seemingly having an effortless life, being able to do things naturally without worry for things I didn't excel at. Of course this was on the surface; my world has been turned inside out. Now, everyday feels like an intense battle for my sanity with no one to teach me about grounding, balance, or anything of that nature. Most days, I am overwhelmed by the sheer amount of changes waking up demands. I am compelled to begin applying to colleges, feeling a purpose that is beyond what I can do as a massage therapist. Bureaucratic endeavors now seem to stress me out beyond measure. I find myself in an almost constant state of stress.

In times like these, I remember the ways that were once important to me, the shelters I had abandoned as the demands of life outweighed the value for our own peace. I remember my love for martial arts, discipline, and a way to practice being in my body. This leads me to Sensei, who teaches Genbukan Ninpo, the martial arts passed down from ninjas.

I arrived at his humble dojo next to a tobacco shop in Cary. The inside is beautifully crafted, and I am in love with the Kamidana (Shinto shrine to the gods) he has over the practice area—"I built this dojo myself. For two years, I came here to train everyday, and this place was only for me. Then out of nowhere, people started showing up and asking me what this is all about." He gestures at about ten students in the training area going through their own drills and techniques. "Now I've got all these students. Funny how things work, eh?"

He takes me to a back room that is set up as a traditional office, and I sit across the desk from him. In a rare moment of vulnerability, I tell him my story about why I am really at his dojo. About my madness, and that I want to have a structure/discipline to contain my power and flame ... He appreciates that I'm not "full of shit" like most people who seek training and agrees to be my sensei.

Training is only two days a week. However, the other days I struggle to learn how to meditate sitting on a rock in the park near where we live. Sensei tells me to use a voice recorder app so that I can get my feelings and ideas out while they are fresh and in the moment. I use it to channel whatever is coming through me; a lot of darkness comes out. There are gems of wisdom, too, as I try to align myself with the elemental forces of Earth, Water, Fire, Wind, and Space. These elements from the ninja's worldview help me navigate and stabilize the rapid internal shifts and newfound experience of reality.

Sleeping remains difficult. I wake up in the middle of the night possessed with the energy to write whatever comes through me; other times, I read old journals in an attempt to remember who I am. I call my mom who sings to me, allowing me to feel how scared—like a child—I am. She believes that life doesn't need to be this difficult. She likes the new me, it turns out, with my heart open and my tears streaming freely, as I feel all that I am able to feel.

Earth Girl helps in her own way. One night, she notices that I am taking in extremely deep breaths and says, "You don't need to take in so much of life at once." I really appreciate it when she says intuitive things like that; moments like these remind me why I fell in love with her. She's so much more than her beliefs about reality she happens to have at the time.

Another day, I am brimming with joy and excitement to share with her right when she arrives home from work, but she's not in the mood. She reprimands me for not being aware of her feelings and bombarding her with my day when she's had a crappy one. I figured sharing happiness was always appropriate. I struggle to understand the timing that is everything.

The next day, we sleep together in a rare fit of passion and I take a nap afterward. I wake up in a whole new world (the same feeling of waking up into a dream from prison), and we go to the arts festival downtown. I am insulated pretty well and surprised that I'm not being overwhelmed by the crowd. At one booth, we find a beautiful Chinese painting of a hut up in the mountains. The hut is across a great chasm with a river flowing through it. I feel that far apart from Earth Girl these days, as I try to sort out my feelings. Out of all the art we've seen, that one holds my attention, and the artist tells us the meaning.

In Ancient China, warriors did not fight and train all the time. This hut is a place of spiritual reprieve after a long and difficult battle.

Earth Girl explains to the artist why I resonate so much with it, and I purchase the artwork, the first time in my life I paid for art. We go back to the car to put away the painting, and her friend from work keeps texting her to come to the bar and chill with them. Earth Girl's phone has a variety of tones when she receives a text, all different sayings of Navi from *Zelda*. Today, every time she receives a text, Navi only says, "Watch out!" I get a bad feeling about the bar, but Earth Girl complains about my superstition, and we go against my feelings. Right when we arrive, a man tells me I look like Justin Bieber.

Something I have found over the years of trying to understand patterns is that whenever someone says, "You look like X" or "You look like my relative Y," it is a good sign that they are not seeing the whole of "you" or are not capable of it at this time. Walk with caution, dear reader, around these people.

Inside the bar, I try to numb myself against the cigarette smoke and the intoxication of those present. I stand by a plastic decorative plant—the only thing close to nature in the place.

A man in Earth Girl's group she's meeting with gets up to greet me and sits me down next to him. He says,

"I noticed you the second you walked in the room. Have you heard of the term 'Empaths' before?"

I confess I haven't, and he explains himself, how he is always trying to make sure everyone is in a good place or taken care of in the room. He says people like us very rarely come together, and he's taking it as a sign that because I'm a massage therapist that he should follow through on his application to a school. His name is Ray, and he shines more confusion into my life when he says, "You should take our meeting as a sign as well." I look down at his pack of Marlboro Light cigarettes and over at his "new" girlfriend with electric pink-dyed hair. I struggle to find meaning or what this is a sign of, but I begin to wonder if it is time for me to move on from Earth Girl and the painful struggle of our relationship.

I begin to hit my limit and become a buzzkill for Earth Girl and her co-workers. She leaves very distraught and confesses that it was like "living in a nightmare" having me there, disrupting the mood of all those people enjoying their indulgence. But what do I know about embracing nightmares?

I return to work at the spa. The manager I talked to with a demonic voice seems to acknowledge that I am in a better place now. His name is also Ray. He says that as long as I accept that I have a problem, then I am on the path of recovery. He moves me to a distant spa location out in Apex where he wants to keep tabs on me, citing that it's a slower pace than Raleigh. I sense that it's also better business sense, given that he needs therapists over there and has had trouble filling the time slots.

After a while, I see it's not such a bad deal since I hardly have anyone on my schedule, and there is a forest behind the strip mall in which I go for walks in. I alternate between three different spa locations a week. "I'm going where I'm needed," I tell myself.

Back at home, I take a walk after getting into some argument with Earth Girl and end up at the park as usual. There are kids playing basketball here (did I mention I'm not wearing shoes?). They invite me to play with them. I'm starting to have real fun! I get a sense that one of them is an angel, and the other one is very angry at something so he takes it out on his friend. I feel as if I can see into the core of their beings. I wander on, approaching a game of kickball played by adults. I don't know how to describe it... but they seem all drunk. Eyes glazed over in some reality that they've gotten lost in.

Right before I reach the game and get sucked in myself, Earth Girl appears on the hill leading up to the field. I get the same feeling I got when I saw her at the end of the tunnel leaving hell. I move from my dream into her reality, where she sits and sketches. I notice a woman, also without shoes, dancing lightly along the corners of the lake. I catch her eyes and playfully wiggle my feet in the air. *we're the same! Kindred spirits!* I think to myself.

She smiles back, which I take as encouragement to approach her. We have a nice conversation about her business of raising plants and coming to the lake here to recharge. She walks me back over to Earth Girl with a look that says, "O, he's yours, right?" As if to say, "Are you taking care of this lost soul?" Earth Girl confirms, which lets this fairy of a woman drift back into her own realm, no longer worried about whether she's leaving a fragile child alone in the world.

James Bond in the Hospital

Don't walk the same Path as me...
Only I was blown this Way
Please Listen so that you may
Find your Way
-Journal

The Path has gotten harder. More and more days feel like a struggle, and I've been trying to get into college lately. Something far in the future seems to be pulling me in that direction I decide on NC State—a local school with students who are apparently more laid back, which I learned from Wind Girl. Wind Girl turns out to be the girl from after I got out of jail, the girl who I thought was my wife's future self during my psychotic break. She says I was having a perfectly normal conversation with her and telling her about my experience getting arrested. I guess my human self goes on and on no matter who is driving...

Wind Girl gives the best hugs and sometimes I run over frantically through the woods between my old duplex and my temporary living place. I run into her just as she is approaching Bobby's. She gives me a heartfelt hug which slows down time, but then Bobby chases me away—scared that I'll freak out and draw attention to him. Attention is something a MJ dealer really wants nothing to do with it seems. As it turns out, he also is scared that I showed up at the same exact moment as Wind Girl because 'that's a bit too weird.'

I run away. Sirens blare in the distance. My panic attack deepens. I hide in someone's bushes. "They're coming for me, they're coming for me," I whisper. I cradle myself in my arms in an attempt to comfort myself. I don't want to go back to the hospital, ever again.

Later, I call my parents, who ask if I'm coming up for Memorial Day. I tell them I'm coming and not to let me forget, not to let me slip out of touch and fall into the raging current of Life pulling at my Soul from all directions.

In hindsight, my Soul was guiding my Life into a wave of changes that I didn't want to embrace. If life ever feels overwhelming, dear reader, with all the process of change and all the chaos that has entered your life, relax and rejoice! You find yourself on the edge of a miraculous new Way of Life. Finding that Life, afterall, is taking care of itself quite nicely without the need of anxiety or fears after all.

I try to take Eternity to a motorcycle shop. I follow Dan, the groundskeeper who came to clean up the yard, in his white van. The ride is invigorating me and I feel a rush of energy all over. I cycle through the five elements on my hand to keep control, each finger a different element. Earth. Water. Fire. Air. Sky. Earth, Water, Fire, Air, Sky. Earth water fire air sky. Earth water fire air sky. Earthwaterfireairsky EarthwaterfireairskyEarthwaterfireairskyEarthwaterfireairsky

The cycle builds up momentum. I tear off the chin guard of my helmet—I feel like I'm about to EXPLODE! My vision gets fuzzy. All I can do is to focus on simply the white van so I'm not overwhelmed. As we pull off the interstate, an ambulance whizzes by in front of us. I sense it's my ride to safety and I follow it to the hospital. Once there, I lose track of the ambulance and I ride through the parking lot trying to find a space. I rush and drive on the sidewalk because it's all so confusing! It's all so much! I see a sign for the ER and I drive right through it—right into the hospital through automatic sliding glass doors. I have enough sense to put my kickstand down before I collapse off the bike yelling to take care of Eternity take care of her! I'm helped into a stretcher and taken into the bowels of the system.

INITIATION

I'm left in a room in a bed for who knows how long. I eventually come to my senses and open up my wallet for my business card: "I'm Arthur Freeman, I'm a massage therapist." My business card comes in handy finally. A balding man in dark blue scrubs comes into the room to ask questions about me. He has a certain melody to him that flows through his whole body. I enjoy his fingers typing to the same song as his feet. He seems to be enjoying himself and rather pleased that someone is answering his questions fully, not giving him much trouble. Before I know it, I'm told to take my medicine and they let me leave the hospital. Simple just like that- no involuntary commitments, no accusations of insanity. I turn out to have the best defense for navigating the health-care system: a Label that says I know what's wrong with me.

The security guard greets me at the door and asks for my story. He says all the nurses and gossip has granted me a title: James Bond Jr. due to an entrance like that. He was kind enough to roll Eternity over to a parking space. Nothing got towed and no police were called.

What a nice hospital to have a break from Reality in!

Calendar Events Control the Future

I ask Earth Girl for help with selecting a new headphones brand so that I can listen to relaxing music and tune out the world. I'm at Best Buy, and she starts researching brands when a customer service rep approaches me. He takes me over to the headphones, and I fall in love with the brand Monster. I feel like a monster (or feel like the world sees me that way) and wish to wear that badge with pride the way my label protects me from mental hospitals. I fall deeper in love when he shared that the company that makes Monster is the brother company to the one that makes Beats Audio. My own brother has a pair of Beats audio headphones, so I know there's no other brand to buy—the signs have shown me the magical path of meaning to my decision.

I share my decision with Earth Girl who disapproves vehemently, discouraging my love for symbolism and accusing me of wasting her time to research a decent brand. Her anger shakes the Universe. Before I know it, a cop pulls me over in The Sex Machine.

The cops are friendly enough, but I express my refusal to let my car be searched. I know my rights now, and I'm not giving Fate another chance at having let some contraband magically appear in my car. Nothing is impossible.

The registration is way beyond expired. They confiscate my plates while I let the car sit on the side of the highway. Earth Girl is furious and won't be helping me, since she's at work with my new car, so I call up my good friend Writer Josh.

Writer Josh shows up, and that's when I get a notification on my phone for an event I had put in my calendar: "Get picked up by friend." I stare at the screen... I created this event in the past? Did I know it was going to happen all along? The madness that is reality sinks deeply into my Soul. I do not let it bubble up as excitement, given how those attempts have gone. I am done obsessing over sharing—reality simply is. More and more, I have learned that some moments are simply gifts from the Universe to you—a great secret that does not need to be shared or understood by others (yet here I am writing about it, heh!).

I ride home with Writer Josh, who believes that everyone has a novel in them. I remember the whole world I had created as a child and that I had started writing a fantasy book based on each of the Elements having a nation (Wind, Earth, Fire, Water). *Avatar the Last Airbender* discouraged me a bit, but I see now that my own version of the Elements is unique and worth sharing.

Defying Fate and Losing the Self

The day finally arrives where I attempt to go up to Virginia for Memorial Day weekend. I can't take my new car, which Earth Girl uses for her commute, or The Sex Machine, since it has no plates. Instead of taking the hint from the Universe to stay and learn to relax, I decide to make the journey with my motorcycle Eternity, who still has not been serviced.

I drive around 440—a loop that circles Raleigh—and my vision gets hazy as I pass the exit to route 1 North. This happens two times. I get frustrated at not being able to focus and get where I want to go. I stop by Cookout and eat a greasy food tray (supposedly good for grounding), and continue the journey north—this time through 95.

INITIATION

It turns out to be trying in every sense of the word. A few times, I pull over to lie on the grass next to the highway to pop some Zyprexa to hopefully help my awareness settle. In retrospect, Earth Girl's words of wisdom of "Seeing your parents doesn't ever seem to help [your emotional state]" combined with how it wasn't natural or in the flow to go ... well, it's too late to turn back now.

I make it to the rest stop just past the Virginia border, and I get off my motorcycle to take one step. Two steps onto the sidewalk, and then with my third step, I collapse onto the grass. It feels nice to lay there, even as I feel the Soul of the World drain out—apparently no longer feeling welcome in my rebellious mind—I cause a panic as people are wont to do it at the sight of physical distress. I worry a lot of people. The ambulance comes to give me some salty snacks to recover. I was conscious the whole time, so the fuss was all over nothing. Then again, I've always had a flair for the dramatic.

Richmond is my next stop for an old high school buddy. I arrive at his corporate building by driving right up the ramp to the glass doors (not driving inside this time!). Two people rush out to this. A graying man who is completely disturbed by my chaotic nature asks, "Who *ARE* you?" A woman receptionist takes him by the shoulder and gently says, "Now now, don't worry. He's all right." She leads him back to his office and returns to me with a knowing smile. "Come here with me. I'll show you where to park." She laughs after the man returns inside, telling me of his character and how he worries. I'm still not sure what she saw in me or my character that engendered trust so quickly, but a woman's intuition is never to be underestimated.

My friend has undergone a lot of life since I last met him—at least half a decade's worth (not that life can be accurately measured in years). He has cut his fiery Puerto Rican long-curly hair, but that's not to say his Fire had gone out. Merely focused, the way you turn down the gas on a stove so that the flame is more blue and less erratic.

He deeply cares about his corporate team, and I can tell his sensitive heart is ripe for bruising in the corporate world he's in. He's gotten a degree in finance and met a pretty girl that he's fallen in love with; that's how I always remember him—as the romantic. I appreciate that he's still living from his heart even in this often savage and bleak world. I learned that his favorite comic book character was always Spiderman. Something about Spiderman …about transformation? Weaving webs? …is worth reflecting on, but I keep it in the back of my mind.

Eternity wins me some cool points (her color scheme akin to Spiderman, with more black and without the blue) and after lunch, I'm back on my way north.

I sleep at my mom's and stepdad's, and Earth Girl's premonition comes true. She warned me that she knows how depressed I get around my parents—that being with them doesn't help anything. I settle back into a lower level of awareness I'm more comfortable with. Colors are less intense. The knockout roses are about all that can move my spirit.

I go to my dad's condo, a place where I feel I can relax but he's immediately concerned. "Where's your edge, dude?" Gone was the passion I had for a business. The Fire I had that burned brightly before I rushed back down to North Carolina…I had not completed my inner sojourn—my transformation process. Handling life at that intensity, at the Edge where it all unfolds, proved more than I was willing to sustain.

My stepmom isn't pleased that I had to make a harrowing journey on a motorcycle while Earth Girl enjoys my new car back in North Carolina. It also isn't lost on her that if I had gotten one of the manual cars I was attracted to, I would've had it with me since Earth Girl doesn't drive stick. Finally, I have enough stability to focus and to get my motorcycle to the repair shop for some much needed maintenance.

Leaving the shop, storm clouds brew from up above, and my dad follows me just in case I need refuge. I assure my stepmom that it won't rain on me, but she cautions me not to use up all of my luck this early in life. I feel fear on Eternity for the first time. Fear is one of the most overwhelming emotions to feel when you're feeling everything at about an eleven.

"Ever get that feeling … that this is the flight you'll never come back down from?" I ask my father —a former navigator on planes in the Navy.

"That's where faith comes in. You just know, and say to yourself: 'This is not how I'm going to die.'" My dad motions with his hands like an air traffic controller with a steady and sure gaze. I didn't realize my father had his own form of faith. The chain-link garage door recoils up, and in tune to its clinking, I feel like I'm breaking out of another prison, even though by now I've learned that they always let me out, given some patience. I salute my old man and rev up Eternity to take off into the sunset.

I wonder if I need a pretty girl at the other end to guide me into a safe landing. One day, I know I'm going to have to land all by myself.

Or crash softly.

I'm not hit by a drop of rain. On the way back to his condo after escorting me, lightning strikes ten feet in front of my father's car.

A Taste of Failure

Once again, I land back in Raleigh. My deeper instincts tell me that I need a place of my own to stabilize and sort through my experience. The Universe obliges my need through our landlord, who would let Earth Girl stay in the temporary apartment until the end of June while I move into the brand new apartment.

I ignore my gut, justifying it with compassion and the reasoning that I don't want Earth Girl to have to stay in that dusty, old apartment any longer than she has to. I go on about moving her in. The other problem is my arrogance—the day that I choose to help her move is the same day I have a practical massage interview at a new place I feel drawn to work at (the place is called Elements Massage). The day-to-day manager of the place is on board with all the elemental symbolism, and we had hit it off very well during the talk interview. I'm confident about my massage skills, so I don't even think twice about all that physical activity in one day messing with my flow.

I work on the owner first. I am not in a very relaxed state myself after having rushed around all day. It's a thirty-minute sample massage, so I try to get her shoulders in a better place. Oh! And of course it's not only one massage, but two sessions back-to-back I have to perform, which takes a lot more focus and presence.

The next person I work on is a fellow therapist, Neka. She asks me to pretend like she's a client. She acts like she's coming in for a simple relaxation massage and has never had a massage before. My hands are ignorant of whatever "play" we're doing, and I start throwing in every technique I have and go about ten minutes over time to address all the parts of her body. I respond to what my hands are feeling rather than what she has spoken. I miss an important lesson in listening.

She sees right through me not acting in line with her request and says I didn't pass because I didn't give her the massage she requested. Despite that, she sees potential in me though and decides to train me in her spare time. We work on Earth Girl, and I am awed at the way her fingers dance across the soft tissues. Her fingers seem to be boneless as she makes an instrument of soft tissue.

She helps me with my flow and teaches me about the power of Intent.

Intent is many things and is often called intention in these self-help arts. The point is to not do things mindlessly and to know exactly what and why you are doing any given action. This is of course invaluable when working on a client and helps therapists not get in a routine where they space out while letting their hands go through practiced motions. With intent, the energy of the massage becomes focused on affecting actual change.

Neka gives me advice for the next therapist I'm going to work on for my second chance interview: be very gentle. I am awed at her kindness and honored for her to see potential in me, so when the day comes for my second practical, I do yoga in the morning to be centered and relaxed.

I enter the spa with a soft confidence, riding the line between detaching from the outcome and knowing that I have something to offer.

I feel great about my flow on the older woman I worked on. Not trying to fix anything, not being absent-minded in a routine either. When she comes out of the massage room, she has a peculiar look on her face. One of shock, as if I had opened up a door to a new realm that she had never even dreamed existed. She says some cordial things and I never hear back from the spa.

The manager is confused because her intuition is usually spot-on when it comes to potential employees. I'm equally confused—I have never had a face-to-face interview in which I didn't get the job afterward.

I wonder what's in store for me instead...

INITIATION

Brakes are for Emergencies

I look up a few gigs on Craigslist because the downside to feeling your Soul all the time is knowing how unfulfilling a particular job is, or the toll it takes on oneself. The fact is that I'm the village Crazy of Massage Envy and sent off into nowhere land Apex instead of where I have regular clients in Raleigh. I come out of a "light" day of only two clients, which is about 2 and a half hours of massage. "Phew, that was a lot," I sigh, a little dramatic for even my tastes but I'm trying to express my feelings more. The front desk girls give me a look like I have nothing in the world to complain about. Maybe I don't, or maybe physical reality doesn't make the same sense it used to... Doesn't operate by the same laws, but who can I prove that to with mere words?

I nab a job doing chair massage for a Chiropractor at events. They go to offices and try to drum up business for their office. Soon enough, an opening appears and I get to be the massage therapist at the office as well. It's a nice part-time deal that gives me Freedom to sign up for events and also a bit of a challenge with more chronic/acute pain clients.

Another listing I apply for is a crapshoot... mostly because I don't have the three years requested experience at a place called "All Sports Muscle Therapy." I like the owner; he's got a decent philosophy, work ethic, and vision of getting away from the word 'massage'. I somehow bypass the required credentials because he sees me as a younger version of himself.

I meet someone who I look up to immediately. He's got about a decade of years on me; he's former army and doing about 30 clients a week with a double hernia. I'm amazed at his ability to work through pain and his thorough knowledge of the body. He's also humble enough to know his role as an employee and simply do his job. I consider him a Soul Brother, not that I'm quite sure why or anything.

So that's where I'm at. Oh, I am also taking some distance Summer School classes to get the required credits I need to graduate from that Community College I dropped out of to move in with Earth Girl. I figure with an Associate's, getting into the college I applied into would be no problem and it'd feel nice to complete something. As for NC State, my application got denied because my GPA was .1 too low for the Psychology major I applied for, so these classes would also help boost that into the range I need to reapply for the Spring.

I'm still working at the Soul Draining Job, but only on Sundays! Three jobs at once and two Summer classes... seems like a good pace to me!!

Earth Girl continues to spend more and more time on her career and networking. She frequents the bar next to her job and drives home drunk on many occasions. Tonight, she happens to have confirmed with me that she'll be home by 8pm and not stay out too late. 10pm rolls around and I'm calling her phone... no answer.

Midnight rolls around and I figure I might as well go to sleep. Trust in Fate and all that. No need to worry. Except I do worry. The anxiety hits me like an emotional truck—I've never been good at feeling this! My Mind shears with pain and Reality feels like it is splitting. I find myself spiraling as I lay on the bed in a futile attempt to relax.

She comes home in her bubbly drunk mood and I keep my feelings bottled up inside as I drift off...

The Pain of Parties

Once again, I land back in Raleigh. My deeper instincts tell me that I need a place of my own to stabilize and sort through my experience. The Universe obliges my need through our landlord, who would let Earth Girl stay in the temporary apartment until the end of June while I move into the brand new apartment.

I ignore my gut, justifying it with compassion and the reasoning that I don't want Earth Girl to have to stay in that dusty, old apartment any longer than she has to. I go on about moving her in. The other problem is my arrogance—the day that I choose to help her move is the same day I have a practical massage interview at a new place I feel drawn to work at (the place is called Elements Massage). The day-to-day manager of the place is on board with all the elemental symbolism, and we had hit it off very well during the talk interview. I'm confident about my massage skills, so I don't even think twice about all that physical activity in one day messing with my flow.

I work on the owner first. I am not in a very relaxed state myself after having rushed around all day. It's a thirty-minute sample massage, so I try to get her shoulders in a better place. Oh! And of course it's not only one massage, but two sessions back-to-back I have to perform, which takes a lot more focus and presence.

The next person I work on is a fellow therapist, Neka. She asks me to pretend like she's a client. She acts like she's coming in for a simple relaxation massage and has never had a massage before. My hands are ignorant of whatever "play" we're doing, and I start throwing in every technique I have and go about ten minutes over time to address all the parts of her body. I respond to what my hands are feeling rather than what she has spoken. I miss an important lesson in listening.

She sees right through me not acting in line with her request and says I didn't pass because I didn't give her the massage she requested. Despite that, she sees potential in me though and decides to train me in her spare time. We work on Earth Girl, and I am awed at the way her fingers dance across the soft tissues. Her fingers seem to be boneless as she makes an instrument of soft tissue.

She helps me with my flow and teaches me about the power of Intent.

Intent is many things and is often called intention in these self-help arts. The point is to not do things mindlessly and to know exactly what and why you are doing any given action. This is of course invaluable when working on a client and helps therapists not get in a routine where they space out while letting their hands go through practiced motions. With intent, the energy of the massage becomes focused on affecting actual change.

Neka gives me advice for the next therapist I'm going to work on for my second chance interview: be very gentle. I am awed at her kindness and honored for her to see potential in me, so when the day comes for my second practical, I do yoga in the morning to be centered and relaxed.

I enter the spa with a soft confidence, riding the line between detaching from the outcome and knowing that I have something to offer.

I feel great about my flow on the older woman I worked on. Not trying to fix anything, not being absent-minded in a routine either. When she comes out of the massage room, she has a peculiar look on her face. One of shock, as if I had opened up a door to a new realm that she had never even dreamed existed. She says some cordial things and I never hear back from the spa.

The manager is confused because her intuition is usually spot-on when it comes to potential employees. I'm equally confused—I have never had a face-to-face interview in which I didn't get the job afterward.

I wonder what's in store for me instead...

Brakes are for Emergencies

I look up a few gigs on Craigslist because the downside to feeling your Soul all the time is knowing how unfulfilling a particular job is, or the toll it takes on oneself. The fact is that I'm the village crazy of Massage Envy and sent off into nowhere land Apex instead of where I have regular clients in Raleigh. I come out of a "light" day of only two clients, which is about two and a half hours of massage. "Phew, that was a lot," I sigh, a little dramatic for even my tastes but I'm trying to express my feelings more. The front desk girls give me a look like I have nothing in the world to complain about. Maybe I don't, or maybe physical reality doesn't make the same sense it used to ... Doesn't operate by the same laws, but who can I prove that to with mere words?

I nab a job doing chair massage for a chiropractor at events. They go to offices and try to drum up business for their office. Soon enough, an opening appears, and I get to be the massage therapist at the office as well. It's a nice part-time deal that gives me freedom to sign up for events and also a bit of a challenge with more chronic/acute pain clients.

Another listing I apply for is a crapshoot ... mostly because I don't have the three years requested experience at a place called "All Sports Muscle Therapy." I like the owner: he's got a decent philosophy, work ethic, and vision of getting away from the word "massage." I somehow bypass the required credentials because he sees me as a younger version of himself.

I meet someone who I look up to immediately. He's got about a decade of years on me; he's former army and doing about thirty clients a week with a double hernia. I'm amazed at his ability to work through pain and his thorough knowledge of the body. He's also humble enough to know his role as an employee and simply do his job. I consider him a spiritual brother, not that I'm quite sure why or anything.

So that's where I'm at. Oh, I am also taking some distance summer school classes to get the required credits I need to graduate from that Northern Virginian community college I dropped out of to move in with Earth Girl. I figure with an associate's, getting into the college I applied into would be no problem and it'd feel nice to complete something. As for NC State, my application got denied because my GPA was .1, too low for the psychology major I applied for, so these classes would also help boost that into the range I need to reapply for the spring.

I'm still working at the soul-draining job, but only on Sundays! Three jobs at once and two summer classes ... seems like a good pace to me!!

Earth Girl continues to spend more and more time on her career and networking. She frequents the bar next to her job and drives home drunk on many occasions. Tonight, she happens to have confirmed with me that she'll be home by 8 p.m. and not stay out too late. Ten p.m. rolls around and I'm calling her phone ... no answer.

Midnight rolls around and I figure I might as well go to sleep. Trust in Fate and all that. No need to worry. Except I do worry. The anxiety hits me like an emotional truck—I've never been good at feeling this! My mind shears with pain and reality feels like it is splitting. I find myself spiraling as I lay on the bed in a futile attempt to relax.

She comes home in her bubbly drunk mood and I keep my feelings bottled up inside as I drift off...

The Pain of Parties

It's my twenty-fourth birthday! I've reconnected with a different friend from high school who also happens to find himself down here in Raleigh after finding God. I've met up with him and his Bible reading group for hilarious debates (and me saying apparently sacrilegious things), so I'm happy when it's just him, his wife, Earth Girl, and myself at a downtown restaurant.

After that, we go play laser tag—one of those "haven't done this since childhood" activities. We have some good fun and adrenaline pumping action until night falls.

Turns out, Earth Girl has a coworker who also shares the same birthday as me and also is celebrating it today. She says we don't have to go, but the empath in me wants to take her somewhere she wants as well ... my birthdays have never been historically about me anyway. My tradition for a while was to work on my birthday and not announce it to anyone.

We're at the party, and I'm having a decent conversation with a female coworker of Earth Girl's who is going through some transformative stuff. She's finally decided to work on getting to a healthy weight, and I'm delighted to hear that her husband has never once pushed her in that direction nor rejected her for where she was at. I wonder if I dare aspire to be that unconditionally loving of a man...

The turning point comes when I'm reaching my social limit for the day, and Earth Girl is in full swing having fun. She's near me when a coworker offers her a cigarette, a habit we quit together when we were first dating. She does it occasionally and socially now, but she still knows how I feel about it enough to ask me if it's okay to have a smoke.

I give her a look of "I'm not going to control what you do, but you know how I feel about it, and hey by the way, you remember it's my birthday, right?" My birthday wish, for my girlfriend to not kill herself with cigarettes ... hah.

She takes the cig anyway, and I leave the party. I don't tell her or say goodbye to anyone. I just go in my car, curl up, and wait for the world to change. She arrives in a bit of a panic, saying she'd asked everyone where I was and felt stupid at having done so. There's an angry vibe as we go home, and I go full turtle shell mode right up until we're in the parking lot outside the apartment. That's when she calls me autistic, infuriated that I have no idea how to deal with people, and storms up into the apartment.

I sit there, even more numb now, and even more petty. She doesn't have the keys—I know this—and it's one of those very rare days I actually locked the apartment. I take full advantage of this as I go for a walk in the summer night to blow off steam.

I get that feeling again, the one where I was manic in the field at dawn, but this time a lot less pleasant—that maybe I should disappear off into the night ... Keep wandering and see where fate lands me ... a Holden Caufield kind of angst. It's not until I'm on my return trip that I stop—for a long time—at a sign that glares at me.

In bold letters, it says: **Wrong Way**

It strikes me deep to my core. What am I even doing with this woman who doesn't believe in the soul? In magic?

I get back, and she's on the phone with Mama-wen, talking about how I barely talked with my dad the night before, and wondering what is wrong with her boyfriend. My dad drove down for his birthday (which was yesterday right before mine) and had dinner with us. He and Earth Girl went at it (she has a Fire Moon sign after all and is a really passionate woman), and I enjoyed observing the debate. The trouble is I didn't get up early enough today to have breakfast with the poor man before he returned up north... Yeah, maybe communication isn't our strong suit.

I unlock the door. She storms out to the balcony where I overhear more of my flaws and how bad an influence I have on her. The sad consolation is that I'm happy to see she's able to connect and open up with her mother emotionally in this way. Happy... Happy birthday to me.

The Denial of Help

I began seeing someone called a "holistic psychiatrist." My stepdad found her, and she's very expensive. I drive out an hour to see her and get put on some grounding vitamin supplements. The vitamins are very expensive as well; they were developed by people who realized pigs go insane if they don't get their dirt to roll around in. I guess they figured since humans are very similar to pigs that we need our dirt, too, so they put it in capsules and charge $110 a bottle.

I take them until I run out, but I start to lose confidence in them. Call it an anti-placebo effect, but I figure there's still a better way than spending all that time and money to be told to eat healthier and take a supplement.

I stumble upon Hakomi therapy. I read some of the philosophy behind it and the feeling of lightning bolts tingling through my whole system. "This is it!" I feel that I've found the modality I want to work with. To receive and to give. It seems to be a Daoist-inspired approach to therapy! I find a local practitioner and give it a try.

The session starts off well. I'm learning all sorts of new ways to experience my body and emotions. A strong emotion wells up. I'm asked to feel a part of my body that feels safe—turns out to be my big right toe. That toe "holds space" for the large emotion that's rolling through me. All new and strange concepts, but I'll roll with whatever helps at this point. She guides me to the massage table and does something called Reiki on me. She touches my left wrist (which has been touched hundreds of times in massage school and after), but I immediately burst into tears. Her touch landed on the emotional/psychic source of that scar, and all the grief my heart had felt in those days when it broke alongside my wrist bones.

She asks me, "Who are your tribe? Your people?"

I respond without hesitation, "My people are suffering."

I return home feeling quite refreshed, open, and clear. I can smell things once again and enjoy a night with Earth Girl, who is pleased at the results of this therapy. Bobby has something for me, but my soul beckons me to rest, relax, and enjoy.

At Bobby's the next day, Wind Girl is there when I come over and I'm happy I choose to wait. She helps me choose between two beautiful emeralds. I have trouble with indecision and overthinking all to hell; I am all caught up in "I want to make the *right* decision." She guides me to go with which one "feels" right, and so I lean toward my first impulse. I am relieved when she remarks that "That's the one that felt right to me too." She suggests I meditate with it, another new concept for me. Connect with a gem? Sit with it? While there, Bobby also gifts me a Black Tourmaline. I like how It fits quite nicely with its cylindrical shape in the palm of my hand.

All this to prepare me for the fall semester beginning at NC State University, where I'm taking a philosophy course and a theatre course. I didn't get accepted as a full-time student, so I can only take two non-degree classes at State while I take those two distance classes from the community college I mentioned to increase my GPA.

I get a call from my holistic psychiatrist. She's ready to drive the final nail in. She tells me that my Hakomi therapist called, and the two of them had a nice chat about my condition, mental state, and all that. They decided that no, it's better if I don't continue with the Hakomi and Reiki therapy until I've been stable for another six months.

It wounds me, but I don't cry. I wasn't used to getting any sort of real help from professionals (outside of massage) anyway. This deepens my hatred for the system and the liability game that mental healthcare has fallen to. I don't blame the Hakomi therapist because she has her own reputation to look out for.

This brings up a question for self-reflection: would I turn away a client whose mental state seemed unstable if I thought I could help? Earth Girl answers without hesitation:

"No. You would never do that. You would never turn away someone you thought you could help."

Would you?

Tripping on Ideas

The philosophy class at State is Existentialism, and it's everything I've ever wanted in an academic setting. The professor wears a different cosmic-themed t-shirt each class and shatters what everyone has taken for granted as reality. He engages everyone by having them put their views on the line and shows them how easily they crumble under the weight of philosophical analysis.

I imagine he has a lot of fun with his job. He particularly applauds me for pointing out, "We can't even be sure there is an 'out there' outside of our heads." A girl that's particularly sensitive to energy turns to me after class and starts talking to me as we leave class.

"I feel like I'm tripping when I'm in that class." I know exactly what she's talking about (not that I've ever "tripped" in the traditional way before) and am glad to not be alone with my feelings. We could feel the minds being blown in the room during each session.

My quest for healing takes me to try out a modality called "Freedom Bodywork." It's a style that is based on the teachings of Dr. Trager, a master who I always looked up to during massage school for his soft and gentle approach that continues to revolutionize bodywork today. I call up the originator of the method, Nancy Toner Weinberger, and introduce myself as Arthur Freeman. She responds, "Freedom is a very important concept to you ... isn't it?" Her voice alone soothes me beyond comprehension and puts me at ease. I feel waves of gentleness and compassion wash over me.

Shards of Time

The second time I attend the Philosophy class late in the week, I sit behind a philosophy major whose red t-shirt says in block white letters (same as the Wrong Way sign): "Only you have the power to unlock your mind." That image persists with me as I enter an expo called "Body Mind Spirit" at the fairgrounds. There's an overwhelming amount of stimulus, with a labyrinth of booths and pop-up tables covered in all types of cloths. I try to decide which speakers I feel like listening to, given there are four options at every hour (gah! choices!). I don't particularly believe in psychics, having zero experiences with them, but when I pass by a psychic whose name is Dr. Freeman, I decide to give it a try. It's very rare for Freemans to meet, after all.

She asks what I want to know or have insight into, and I shrug. I don't have any burning questions or things in particular; I'm simply here to see what happens. I'm the second one today like that, she notes.

She flips over majestic cards—angels, unicorns, dragons, and faeries leap off their artwork into my mind. The King of Air is at the center and I'm drawn to him like a magnet. Air. Wind. Freedom—my favorite element and the theme of my whole year thus far.

She says a lot of things that hit home, which surprises me. She mentions how easy it is for me to get sucked into people's worlds. I've never heard it put in those words before. Another line I etch deep in my heart on my wall of reassuring messages is:

"It's not everyone that has the ability to walk between worlds."

The speaker who was talking behind a curtain draws me in somehow. I grab a seat at a talk that's title didn't particularly interest me. It's called "Abundance Now, Blow the Lid off!" The mystic at the front is doing some prayer and calling in angels and all sorts of stuff. We get a golden bubble of protection from Archangel Michael and a lot of other energetic stuff happens. I feel a few sensations in my body that I don't understand. When we come out of the meditation, she shoots me a glance that shakes me to my core.

I pass a booth where a woman is sitting in full lotus on the floor meditating. The booth seems overlooked and passed by most people, but somehow they get my attention. They hand me a brochure on Falun Dafa, a Spiritual Qi Gong practice that's completely free and is practiced at Pullen Park once a week.

I feel a bit overwhelmed and am ready to leave the expo, but as I cross the threshold, a woman pats on me on the shoulder and says, "You dropped this, sir." It's the card of the woman who did the Abundance Now lecture. I take that as a pretty clear sign. I go back inside to sit down at her table, and she notices how I'm shaking a lot; she tells me that my aura is very porous. She calls in Archangel Michael's golden bubble again. I feel myself settle in and relax a bit, shoulders easing and calming down.

She channels some advice and says something about a spiritual hierarchy, which goes mostly over my head. I ask her how much I need to pay for her time and advice, but she says it's unnecessary. She asks me to take care as I set off on my roller coaster ride into the Unknown.

Wednesday: I look into the Falun Dafa lineage and see that it has a lot of teachings. Many of the "required texts" I skim start to blow my mind, such as there being "no such thing as healing" in that practice. I start to question my arrogance at being a massage therapist because there is some truth in the words, "Who can say who is healing whom? The chi doesn't work one way!" I get to the part where I actually have to PRACTICE and the complexity of the moves overwhelm me. It's a Qi Gong that combines chanting with specific tones and specific postures. It's all too much, and I tear up the brochure in a fit of frustration, saying, "No! I'm a ninja! Not some Daoist priest or hHoly man!"

Nighttime finds me at my friend's house having dinner with two fellow massage therapists. Time gets all sort of altered as we ride the waves of change. Sammi, my co-worker, goes from enjoying her food thoroughly to being disgusted with it. I am able to watch the micro-expressions on her face unfold in slow motion, how she is nearly ready to burst into tears behind her mask. Mollie, my spiritual sister, has a mind that starts to go into overdrive. Sammi looks at me in a moment of clarity and says, "Something's coming, and it's big." I feel the weight of her words without knowing the meaning.

Thursday is the day of my first session for Freedom Bodywork. I find Nancy sitting at a table searching through a butterfly-shaped key box. She's looking and searching through so many keys when I enter. We begin with some "Mentastics" (Mental+Gymnastics), which are designed to help your mind let go by resetting holding patterns of tension. On the massage table, I grow a bit frustrated and disillusioned. I don't feel like she's *doing anything* and don't feel the true benefit of the bodywork. I start questioning my decision to come here and spend my money on this when a concrete image flashes in my mind—*the butterfly key box*. I decide to trust this woman—this experience—and relax. Like a key clicking in a lock, my whole being lets go. I begin to enjoy all the movements of my own body and the soft touch of her hand as she rocks, shimmers, and elongates my tissues.

I get in the car and the emotional release comes on full. "It's ok to smile," I say through my tears, as I finally release so much seriousness and pain into the sky.

Later, at the dojo, I'm training with a nine-year-old. We really are present for each other and I mess with him by continually changing the rhythm and pace of my timing, as if I have time control powers. I can tell he's sensitive to these subtle changes, and he accuses me of messing with him. During a lull, I'm at a loss for how to engage with him. I throw out a timeless classic "so what do you want to study when you grow up? Want to go to college?" I could barely believe myself talking about college to someone his age. He surprises me by responding, "No, I don't think I want to learn anything else. I think you get what I mean." I was stunned that he was wise enough to not want any additional layers of mind and thinking added to his purity. After martial arts training, I ask Sensei if he ever had to go through an "initiation." He pauses to get my real meaning, then says, "You mean getting the *$#% kicked out of you? Don't even ask for it!"

INITIATION

Friday, my discipline begins to unravel as I go to a chair massage event for the chiropractor. I feel my intuitive senses heightened as I work on each person. I ask a larger man what he plans on doing for the weekend and he says, "A whole lotta nothing." The depth of Nothing becomes apparent to me then, and it feels nice. As if his entire being is a container for the Void, the true emptiness between each atom becomes palpable to me ... After the event, I'm riding down the elevator with Dr. Lance, who I confess a secret to.

"You know Lance is a nickname I used often a few years ago and it's a character in the first book I ever started to write. I've always wondered ... what it's like to be Lance?"

He turns to me with a wild look in his eyes and with a mystical demonic smile that sends me reeling and says,

"Actually, it's pretty fun!"

Outside, the event planner confesses that she likes ordering us men around and making us do things. She also tells me that Dr. Lance says I need to be "quieter." I feel that means that I'm not regulating my energy very well.

I go home for a whirlwind change of outfit in which I forget my uniform and arrive at All Sports Therapy. I realize then that my spiritual brother must have X-ray vision for when he massages people and it blows my mind. I work deeper and am more present with each of my clients that day. The owner notices a change in me and for the first time teaches me a technique: neural flossing. My inner world is in a huge turmoil as I navigate this new reality. I get tipped by a client but don't enter the information to actually receive it on the computer. Because what I'm offering is what the Universe offers to all freely, why should I ever charge for it? The questioning of my profession that started with reading some Falun Dafa text continues.

The owner has some more practical advice than Dr. Lance. He looks at my process of transformation that he can perceive, slows down to get my attention, and says,

"Hey—have fun this weekend, but not too much. You know what I mean, right?"

After arriving home, I go for a walk that takes me a very long time to come back from.

I'm feeling amazing because I am Alive. I decided to try a Tibetan Buddhist technique I read about in a book in which you reverse aging by going backward in time. I forget if you're supposed to spin clockwise or counterclockwise, so I just go with a direction. I end up spinning and having a lot of fun, as energy is flying off me in every direction. I end up spinning so fast that I leap off the ground like a helicopter. I do it again. Spinning up off the ground as my body flies horizontally, I land right on my ankle.

My euphoria is now co-mingling with a searing pain. I'm not sure if I've broken it or what, but I feel it as intensely as I'm feeling everything else. I don't have my phone with me and I don't really know who I'd call either.

Feels like this is my *initiation*.

This clear purpose forms as I continue forward on my walk, agonizing each step. Walking through the pain, stopping to rest when it gets too much, I inch forward as the day passes into twilight. I make it to a greenway and am glad to be off the main streets to be around nature where I can endure my spiritual test in solitude. I make my way up a very tall staircase—I mean everything seems very tall and grand in this state of mind—and enter the parking lot of some townhomes.

I stop to rest near some trash cans when a couple in a car drives up. "Are you okay?" They seem to have heard the pain of my soul and are offering what any decent human would offer.

To me, they are very far away, on some other plane, and I refuse to give in to my trial by taking the help of others. I don't stop to wonder whether the real trial is if I know how to receive help when in need. The pain gets more intense, and I start to use my cardinal sense of direction to head straight back to my apartment complex. Screw roads and well-traveled paths! I'm using the woods.

Entering the forest, the ground is too unstable for me to endure the shooting pain of my ankle, so I crouch down to crawl. I find a very tall tree that's fallen and put my belly on it. I make my way forward through agony, and a sort of primal energy begins to take over my soul. I feel like a wolf, teeth glaring in the light of a waxing crescent moon. I make it to the ravine—a staggering angled climb of about thirty feet of boulders placed here and there—below the street that leads to my apartment. I accept the initiation into the Earth Element as I make my way to the top.

In my apartment, I take a cold shower to cleanse off the pain and to numb myself. That's when Earth Girl comes home drunk on weekend reverie and after-work social drinks—so it must be nine or ten p.m. at night at this point. She comes into quite a scene: me taking a cold shower in the dark. Her buzz is killed instantly as she wonders what's wrong. I go to sleep somehow with "Bohemian Rhapsody" playing in my head, with various celestial orbs dancing about in my awareness of the solar system.

Galileo Galileo...

Saturday: A Day with Death

I wake up and Earth Girl lovingly calls me "Manic Fate" (she calls by my handle Fate) and has no intention of sending me back to the mental hospital. She tends to me with love and at least an attempt at understanding. I'm in a very poor condition with my ankle, but I am still overflowing with energy. I try to plead with Earth Girl to let me go to the dojo where I know Sensei will be able to help me regain balance. She insists I need to take it easy. With the flow of a goddess, she guides me into watching a documentary about deep sea creatures. I mean the really deep sea ... into the darkest depths of the world to mirror my descent into the Underworld.

The Underworld has a few common characteristics across cultures that are universal to the human psyche. Simply put, it is the place where chaos reigns and the light of day, order, and sense do not shine from above. "It is the place you are, when you don't know where you are,"[4] says a world renowned author and professor of psychology. We also find our hidden gifts, disowned parts of ourselves, and darkest fears nestled in its corners. The keys to navigating the underworld can be found in many videos, ancient texts, and guides. From this tale, I hope you can see at least what *not* to do by my history and to learn to trust yourself and others in the journeys below. One piece of wisdom I've discovered is this: make a point of visiting the underworld before it finds

---

[4] Peterson, J. B. (1999). *Maps of meaning: The architecture of belief.* New York, NY: Routledge.

you. Else it will catch you unawares!

–

Writer Josh shows up, as we had plans to meet that day. He takes me over to Wendy's where I order as greasy and as large a meal as I can, hoping this will ground me. Writer Josh is a bit down today because of how everyone is leaving their trash around work and in general. I take an incredibly long time to eat, and I get the feeling he knows something is up with me.

When he offers to take me home I decide to walk instead—three miles on my ankle? No problem. He tries again to take me and I turn to look at him and say, "Sometimes you know what you have to do."

And sometimes I don't know how stubborn I am being.

I take it slow—limping and using the guard rails as support—when I inevitably run across some litter. I start collecting it to do my part for poor Josh when a can of Monster catches my attention. That word—the same brand as my headphones—has appeared periodically throughout my life. Last time, it was the name of the anime, *Monster*, my ex-wife and I watched. We watched it in one last marathon as one of the last things we did together under Hawaiian skies ... I don't know if I decided one day to become a monster to confront people with their fears or if I never knew how to integrate the monster within me...

I see now that it is easier to be misunderstood and feared than to be seen and loved. In addition, how we humans view ourselves deep down creates the same situations to justify that view. This creates a cycle as vicious as karma.

I'm barely halfway into the first mile when a luxury black car pulls up to me. The driver offers me a ride—something about him compels me to accept. Maybe some part of me realizes how daunting it would be to limp those three miles for the rest of the day. When I'm in the car, I realize this man is Death itself. Death is my constant companion and never truly leaves my side. I am blessed to get to meet such a physical manifestation of this archetype.

I've always had a lot of fun with Death and today proves no exception. He ferries me back to my home, always on the border of Life—I mess with him a little bit on some of the turns. Waiting until that knife-edge instant of decision to tell him to turn.

INITIATION

Back at the apartment complex, I decide to roam around the buildings under construction rather than return to Earth Girl. She's working on a beginner level quest as part of an application for her dream job: designing video games. I undertake this as part of my adventure and feel as if I am in a giant video game that she has an omniscient observer view of. After convincing myself I am in Earth Girl's reality, I slip past construction workers who all have their own rhythm to them. A melodic, slow, and measured pace that gets things done ... they are also Earth. Making myself invisible comes naturally to me somehow, and I climb the empty apartment building to find myself inside a unit with stairs. A reading from Falun Dafa floats into my mind: "You have to keep climbing, you can always go higher." I take this literally and symbolically as I mount the stairs and find myself in a bathroom of an unfinished unit. There's nowhere higher to go from here, so I take the stairs of the main building up to an apartment that has a balcony. I begin to balance myself on the edge of the railing as I reach up to the highest part of the ceiling/roof ... and fathom for a moment trying to climb onto the roof. Some part of me is still sane enough to come down from this height, as my attention is drawn to the saltwater pool still being constructed. I throw some construction debris into it and make my way down.

The Water Element would be very refreshing on this hot summer day, yet the pool is still not complete. Barren, dry, and empty. A true reflection of my parched inner world...

After a time, I return to Earth Girl, who I find stuck in her creative process. I try to give her insights from the Universe, some way to organize all the information I've been processing and give her a framework to paint her quest on. "Truth, Love, Enduring! The three fundamental things, that all of existence has these qualities!"

It all comes out as unintelligible gibberish. She sits me down to play an actual video game, *Guild Wars 2*, so she can focus. I load up my character, Taiji the Ranger, and a NPC says cryptically, "You shouldn't go there yet. Why don't you stay around this area to gain experience first?" I have Taiji running into a wall, so the NPC continues to warn me.

"You shouldn't go there yet. Why don't you stay around this area to gain experience

first?"

"You shouldn't go there yet. Why don't you stay around this area to gain experience first?"

"You shouldn't go there yet. Why don't you stay around this area to gain experience First?"

What else can I do on this level then? I'm at a loss, and I roll around the floor on the yoga ball we use as a desk chair. Next thing I know, Earth Girl is taking a nap, drained from having to be present around so much Fire. I flip open a "random" page from a book, *Zen and the Art of Motorcycle Maintenance*, for some much needed Zen and advice. The words leap out at the page: "That's enough for today."

I don't listen.

I wander down the shopping center next to my apartment, arriving finally at a grass field next to an intersection. I pray to God that my brother may switch places with me, that he may experience the freedom and love of an open heart and not have to suffer so much. I have my Rainbow Reiki advertisement slip that I got at the expo because I like the colors. A stopped car at the light looks over at me (about three people in there). They all burst into laughter like I've never seen, and I figure I'm the cause.

I feel that I'm a fool … The mad jester here to take others worries away through any sort of release…

I cross the road and find myself sitting on the sidewalk. There are lots of ants. They are all going in such a crazy haphazard pattern … Chaos. I feel just like these ants as I rise to return home. It feels very far away. Only one block of linear distance but light years away in reality … As I walk up the street, an ambulance is driving down the hill. I immediately sense "There's my ride" and go out into the street to meet it head on.

The ambulance screeches to a halt, and the EMTs get out to check on me. They're convinced I've had way too much to drink, and they assume I went to the NC State game that day and had partied hard. Without me realizing it, I'm suddenly heading with them somewhere. I see one of the male EMTs look off into the distance; he seems to me to be communing with angelic guides. He turns back to me and says, "I'm really glad you came with us, it's

INITIATION

the best decision you've made all day." Another of the EMTs is female with pure green eyes like Wind Girl's ... I feel comforted, especially since I have the hairband of the actual Wind Girl around a flap in my wallet. The fresh air by the vent in the ambulance helps me stay stable as I go on my epic journey to who knows where.

I'm on a stretcher being carried, and a male voice tells me to get ready for the "flipsy upside down backsy," which involves moving me from a stretcher onto a bed in some dramatic fashion. I lay there for a while, coming back to my senses. I get up with my Rainbow Reiki flyer, and the nurse tells me to use Reiki on myself to calm down and relax. A few eternities later, I'm in a hospital room and a man in a black shirt is talking to me. I figure he's also Death, and I assure him that I know him well and remind him we have a lot of fun together. Being unable to function, they leave me to myself for a few more lifetimes. I feel my fourth dimensional self stretching back through time, all the way back to that demonic smile from Dr. Lance. It feels like a continuous series of afterimages with each slice of reality a different version of myself, yet all the same chain.

After blacking out for a while, I finally notice a shift in my body. I feel a Yin energy going down and expanding through my legs, and with it a feeling of ecstasy and pleasure. I come down from my high into a very serene and beautiful feeling. I find a sitter to my left. Unlike the angel sitter, this one seems to be the face of the Void itself. Something is troubling her. With my long hospital gown and newfound sense of self, I channel my inner Socrates.

She is running into problems with her daughter, and she's also very exhausted. Finally today, she had been about to rest when they called her into work. I empathize with that and begin to share my insight into her worldview. She says, "I feel like I should trust you ... But..." the hesitance never gets fully cleared up. An assistant to the doctor arrives and is happy to see I have enough sanity to carry on a conversation. I tell him of my bipolar diagnosis and ask if I may use a phone. I get my phone to charge in the meantime so that I can call Earth Girl, whose number I never memorized. Perhaps my sense of peace comes from the ease at which this hospital will release me: no involuntary hospitalizations here. I have my diagnosis and it serves as a shield, they know what's wrong with me, and so do I—so why keep me? Earth Girl arrives later with her flowery energy—she was very worried. She called my father apparently, but for now, hey why don't we make some pancakes? She makes me the most delicious pancakes, and I eat them on the floor of our bedroom. I go to sleep after that, or rather pass out from the overwhelming day...

Deeper into the Void

I wake up a maelstrom and remember only packing haphazardly as I feel the impending presence of my father's approach. He's coming to get me; he wants me to come chill out with him in Virginia. He teaches me how to walk down stairs on my messed-up ankle. The trick is you step down with your good foot first, then the injured one. We walk arm in arm down the stairs in the world's slowest three-legged race; he had recently injured his left ankle in Romania.

On the drive, I'm talking up a storm. Completely oblivious of the toll it would take for him to make a nine-hour round-trip journey. I even wrench the wheel for him doing seventy on the highway, swerving us into another lane. With his patience having reached its limits, he scolds me with an anger I have seen only a few times in my life.

We pull over at a gas station where I begin to text Earth Girl. Her responses are long and come so quickly, my sense of reality starts to break. My dad brings me back with a piercing "SHHHHH!" as he goes to fill up.

As we continue driving, I tell Dad of my Mom's words of "wisdom" after watching **Oldboy** with her and Earth Girl: "Life is a prison. We make our own prisons," she said. He turns to me and touches me with the gentlest hand I've ever felt from him. "I am so sorry you were told that."

After the long journey, we arrive at nightfall to my father's condo in Tyson's Corner. His wife, with an extremely anxious look on her face, approaches me with a miniature viewfinder—that has a single picture. She demonstrates how to use it by holding it up to a picture and swaying her body as if she were in the scene. I take it in my hands and press it against my eye, seeing a beach with the child-selves of my brother and me. I use my second sight to transport myself to that beach, feeling the ocean breeze and the salty sun air.

I feel that I can physically merge with the viewfinder, as all boundaries have become fluid and energetic with my new state of awareness.

My stepmother takes it back from me and says soberly, "I know what this is. We need to call the hospital." My dad is exhausted and yet still protects me from that Hell; he is sure that I can relax here with him. We sit down to have dinner and I watch my face in slow motion as she looks at a bottle of Naked juice. The look of sheer terror, as if a ghost were present in the bottle itself, slowly emerges on her face before she fixes her mask back on. I begin to suspect that my father is either Time, Death, and/or God. I excuse myself to take a very long warm shower in the dark of the bathroom. This further worries my , but the water feels amazing. I let it wash away all the madness of the road and pain of my Soul. I sleep on the same orange air mattress that I slept on so well after I got out of the hospital in April. The waxing crescent moon hangs in the sky.

???Day

I wake up while still dreaming a few hours later. I wrap myself with a white bedsheet to go on a Socrates mission around town. I take my Black Tourmaline with me, an ancient crystal that fits in my palm and becomes my lightsaber. I roam the streets, making my way to an empty parking garage. I use the blue button on the intercom to call for help. I ask for my father. They pretend to not know who he is, but everyone knows who God is deep in their hearts. I have a coy smile on my face as I walk away, climb a staircase, and come out over a garden. I feel attached to the crystal in my hand. I remember words from Falun Dafa, about how humans have all sorts of mortal attachments not fit for cultivation. I let the crystal tumble from my hand onto the concrete below, where it splits into two pieces. I pick up the smaller one, still burdened by mortal attachments after all.

On my return trip, I wander aimlessly on the streets when a cop on patrol slows down to check me out. I tell them to call my father, but they don't seem particularly interested in my situation. I appear a mere sideshow for their amusement, especially since I dramatically let my weapon fall to the ground so I would be of no harm—my lightsaber of course. I have since found a black trash bag, which I carry with me to gather the filth of the world and take it where it needs to be. I find a great walking stick that reminds me of Earth Girl. A mile long circle of sidewalk wraps around my father's apartment and I somehow remember where I am. During one lucid moment, I look up to see a great Sign: Red Hat's glowing man in a red fedora. I let the stick fall, unaware that one day Earth Girl will indeed work for Red Hat—all as foretold during my waking dream.

Making my way to a parking garage, an older version of myself appears. Perhaps I should say mySelf, for I don't recognize any difference between us. All that separates us is distance in time. He's an older gentleman and a security guard, and he tells me a few stories about his love of fishing. He lets me rest in the breezeway where the Wind won't reach me. Without the Wind to blow me here and there, I drift asleep for a few Eternities. Waking me up is a younger security guard, who has all the compassion in the world. He gets me a packet of peanut butter M&Ms for breakfast and goes off to do his duties. After returning to my senses, I head back to the condo with the black trash bag in tow. The trash bag also contains my Socrates sheet, and I leave it right under my dad's first floor balcony; I am quite certain that he will look straight at it from the balcony upon waking.

The stimulation of the apartment and the fresh day sends me into a whirlwind of activity. I grab my cell phone and leave the apartment without putting on my shoes. My brother picks up on the second ring; he talks to me as I walk around, touching various stickers on cars to send him the symbolism and energy contained within. Before I know it, the police arrive, as I apparently look threatening and suspicious walking around with no shoes and touching cars. They put my hands on the hood of the car, which is searing hot. I feel the energy of fire enter me. I'm afraid I'm going to overheat. Yet, I don't dare move them or complain. I look at the Korean officer and plead for his understanding—surely he understands the Chi and the flow of things in his culture? He does not. They search in painful slow-motion through my entire backpack—damaging things in the process.

My father arrives, the White Knight that he is, and begins to talk some sense into the officers. After some smooth talking, I am whisked away on a car ride deeper into the unknown. At a stoplight, a young man crossing the street on his skateboard grabs my attention, and I open the car door to yell, "NICE SKATEBOARD!" My dad does not share my enthusiasm. We arrive at an unassuming building, the same playground with the giant bronze globe statue. I don't recognize it in my current state and continue to do cartwheels in the grass. My father tries to talk some sense into me. He believes that this is being caused by the stress of my aunt passing away and my other aunt having brain cancer. Speaking of cancer, my father and I were born one day apart at the end of June and both call the "Week of the Empath" our astrological home. That said, projecting our feelings onto each other comes like second nature as our two oceans collide, so supporting each other emotionally is a challenge, despite our bond. This pains me every time I let it come into my awareness, so let me continue.

Inside the clinic, Andre remembers me and I remember him. The clinicians that actually decide my fate are not as familiar with me, however, and the screening process takes place with my mother and father inside a single-windowed room. My feeling of panic begins to rise, as some part of my consciousness recognizes this process and what is about to happen. Then they start dropping the truth: commit yourself to the hospital voluntarily. "You are not okay." I know going to that place will not make me okay—has never made anyone okay—and I refuse. I refuse to go the same way I went last time.I refuse to trust the system.

I don't like this confinement. I don't like this prison. I want to GET OUT! I stand up on my chair and open the window behind me, which is the size of a framed diploma. I put my fingers through the bug-wire mesh and it comes apart like butter. I feel magical while tracing the rectangle and opening the portal to my freedom. I step out with one leg, but I have to do the splits to get the other one through.

The process takes so long that half the staff have gone outside to make sure I land safely. I let go deeply in my hips and make it through the portal. An eerie sensation washes over me, the feeling of impending doom, while enjoying the scene that is playing out in front of me. I imagine this is the calm before the book of Revelation in the Bible. Everyone stands about ten feet away in a sort of protective circle of sanity—or control. I wander over to the parking lot and see a motorcycle. I feel the freedom of that motorcycle. I also know that I am not going to have that anytime soon. Despite not being lucid about the situation fully, I feel that deep down. A wizened older woman is the closest to me in the circle, and she talks me through the situation. Through her wisdom-filled eyes, I know I must endure what comes next.

The police arrive and handle me roughly, handcuffs and all. I am taken to the hospital where a very long procedural process takes place. I am handcuffed to a bed as police officers take shifts to watch me, as if I were some threat to the entire world. They are competent enough red people and have a more down- to- earth philosophy than me. They are not there to be helped by me like the watcher nurse back in North Carolina was, and our back and forths are not truly engaging enough. I grow restless and move around as much as the handcuffs allow.

Finally, I am taken up an elevator to that ominous fourth floor of Heaven where the angels are. Sure enough, the first angel I see after I step out of the elevator is Anna—my old nurse. She drops her hands in a sigh, her spine collapses in defeat, and her face makes a pained "Oh no Arthur ... you were never supposed to come back!{ expression. I lift up my shackled hands and shrug, "Yeah, it's me. Yeah, I did it again."

The sheer pain of it all fragments my Soul, and I lose lucidity.

5

Rising Wind

Love in Moments, Piecing Back Time
I wake up nine days later under a full moon that I can't see. Here are some lucid moments I had during my nine-day dream:
Moment 1-The Trial: There's a man having coffee in the room next to the dining area, and he's pretending he's not an official of any sorts. Next I'm in an art studio, where a mock trial is being held. Problem is, the trial is real and I am unaware since I was saving up my lucidity for the courtroom. The "judge" asks me to sign a paper and then asks me a pivotal question for my sanity:
"Are you being forced to sign that paper?"
I look at him with defiant eyes, "Yes." [I don't remember this part at all.]
That seals my fate. I am committed to the hospital for thirty days involuntarily. A prison for my own benefit, or so they would say. I don't remember signing the paper, my father tells me about this scene later. I do remember walking out of the studio, and my father clasps me on my shoulder. He laughs a dry laugh of absurdity.
"Welcome to your path," he says.
Moment 2-Who I Am: I'm walking down a hallway when a girl I'm falling in love with asks me what my favorite pokemon is. She's convinced I'm a Meowth, but I channel my preying mantis arms and say, "Scyther! Scyther!"
Moment 3-The Girl: In another scene, I'm kissing her and she is telling

me how she doesn't like the way everyone looks at me like I'm some insane clown. I tell her what they think doesn't matter. Only that she sees me clearly.

Moment 4- Reality: Next, I'm playing the only song I know on the piano, "The Song of Healing" from *Zelda* and she's leaning against me. It's her time to get out of the hospital. We're having some moment of closure and farewell. I confess to her that I have Earth Girl outside of this place and that our love could never last. The mood shifts, and she confesses she has a boyfriend as well.

Now I wake up or rather shift into an awareness that is more ordinary and linear. I realize that it's been nine days since that Labor Day Weekend Initiation ankle Injury. NIne days since I went down the rabbit hole … I have a journal with me, which lets me know that Maria was the girl's name and that she was not a hallucination.

I wrote her this letter:

Maria,

I once walked a thousand miles on the beach of life. I've always been seeking something, not realizing the lapping of the waves at my feet was all I needed. I'm done worrying about the footprints behind me and what tomorrow will bring. I just want to stay with you forever. You'll see the signs, and if you always believe I'll always be there.

You'll feel me on the Wind,

Link

She responds in a clear bright handwriting:

You'll always be my hero, you are

Sora and I am your purple keyblade ↵.

You're my mario

-Princess Peach :P

The next three entries:

I just came to run by the between places, to warm myself by the flowers, smell the roses in each moment & know happiness.

The clues are there

Dear girl,
Definitely missing you, thinking about you, it <u>sucks</u> being without you.
You make this world a better place. Don't feel super bad though, it's just bullshit. I'm looking for a therapist to make an appointment. Food here is lulzy, makes my head spin. I feel like I've lived here for ten years of the Horse.

<u>Reiki</u>
1 Kyo dake wa Just for today
2 Okuro na Don't be angry
3 Shinpai su na Don't worry
4 Kansha shite Be Grateful
5 Gyo wo hage me Work diligently
6 Hito ni shinsetsu ni Be kind to others
Mikao Usui[5]

The next pages have my signature collection, assigning people archetypes so that I may be able to navigate this world. Among my favorites are the mystical nurse, Jon (who I call Mr. Sandman), and the diplomat, Yuri. I write Link many different ways, trying to integrate that persona and all the elemental versions of it into myself. I have various notes and plans to get out of here, as well as affirmative messages to myself.

    The hardest part is that I'm here with people I remember from my last visit six months prior. I get the haunting feeling that they, too, are stuck in a loop—in and out of the hospital. Our lives are like the insane live fiction of *Catch-22*, forever going on airplane missions we may die on … I remember Andrew, and we become bodyguards once more. He still thinks of Riley, who does not grace us with her presence (we are glad she is free). There's a Native American girl who always calls her sister on the phone—though I'm not sure her sister is real.

    I'm not sure my own brother is real either. I start to go full schizophrenic,

---

[5] Usui, Mikao. (1999.). *The Original Reiki Handbook*. Translated by Christine Grimm. Lotus Press.

looking back at the past, wondering if he was always in my head—have we ever been in the same room without family? How come we never went to the same school? Have we ever been in public acknowledged by others who wouldn't know my condition? Was my roommate Bobby real? It's suspicious that I'd have a roommate named Bob twice ... maybe they never existed? HOW CAN I TELL FOR SURE WHAT IS REAL AND WHAT IS FAKE?!

My dad takes me by both shoulders, looks me in the eyes, and asks, "Where is Stuart now?"

I pause.

Looking at him like I don't know why he's asking such a mundane question, I say,

"He's in Boston ... in the Coast Guard."

Later, on a different visit in another room, I share with my father the realities of my fellow inmates. He remarks that, "Haven't you ever thought they are just plain crazy?"

I pause.

I ask him, "What does that make me then?"

I refuse to let his faith be channeled into me alone. I am not separate from the other cases—we are all in a toxic pool, taking pills to numb ourselves into compliance with a corrupt environment. Not all equally of course; there's a girl here who was once on twenty-three medications at the same time. An unheard of brew and dosage of conventional medicine's attempt to control states of consciousness beyond all Western concepts of reality.

My mother no longer visits me. On one phone call, I come to the sad realization that she has given up on me—she resigned to my thirty-day sentence. I feel deep in my bones the withdrawal of her belief. She'll let the system handle me: she trusts it (as she trusts in God, it dawns on me). At the moment, I don't see the pain that she is unable to bear by seeing me, or feel the love in her prayers she makes without fail each night (she hasn't told me that she did this, but in my heart I already know). All I feel is the complete abandonment of any and all the support I've ever had. Abandonment. Earth Girl feels a million miles away, but I don't think about her much.

That's a question for reflection, is it worse to be abandoned to

yourself...? For people to give up on trying with you, tired of watching your endless cycles of pain...? Be left to your own devices...?

...Or to be abandoned to a system? A cold machinery that works on charts and symptoms ... as if somehow Love could make its way through those gears... (it did, it always does).

The former, perhaps, is a loss of trust in the suffering person's ability to free themselves. A loss of patience for another's path. The latter feels like a loss of trust in one's own ability to care or that their love is insufficient for the well-being of the sufferer. Of course, when are things ever so black and white? What seems best to me these days is to find that grey area where you don't abandon those you care for, but you don't get involved past a certain point either.

A tricky balancing act.

"Checkmate;" –Fate

Earth Girl is being evicted from my apartment— a deal with the devil that I apparently made during my blackout in any attempt to appease my captors. My stepfather was quite content to blame my manic episode on her use of marijuana. Being the fighter that she is, she replied that perhaps it's the trauma of growing up and being raised with zero emotional intelligence that is the real cause of my episodes. He threatens to evict her in response, and she removes herself to cut all ties with him. Even if I wanted to call her, I never memorized her number. I call my ex-wife a few times, but remember none of the conversations.

In my room, I have a piece of cardboard paper that I assume I made in some group art therapy. On one side, I have my name signed in cursive, *Arthur*, and on the other is a bold **LINK**. In the course of flow on this highway to hell from Hell or beyond Hell, I go to my room several times a day to flip the cardboard paper over and channel a different side of myself. There are things Link can handle that Arthur simply can't. There are times when I feel heroic and able to ease the pain of the other patients, but I don't remember whether I was Arthur or Link during those times. Perhaps *Shadow Link* is a more accurate term, with glaring red eyes and the hatred that only a rejected aspect of oneself can feel.

On several occasions, I am promised that I'll be getting out soon, but somehow the doctor evades my attempts to meet with her. I've been written off as a thirty-day patient and no hope is given to those cases. The nurses involved—the angels I remember from my last visit—are mostly encouraging. This does not help my case as hope is not what everyone chalks it up to be. Hope is a demon that tempts you with some brighter tomorrow—some moment in time outside of your experience where things will be "better." That moment never comes. Hope remains a seducer away from the only thing that is—*now*.

Now hits me like an angelic choir. I remember standing at the south window, after my hundredth failed attempt at proving I am sane and balanced enough to get out of the hospital. I realize that there is no getting out. There is nothing else. There is simply "just this." The music of the spheres echoes softly from distant planes.

From now on, I am happy to eat the food that's provided to us and to spend time in silence with the other patients. Another patient goes into a fit, screaming, and has to be taken out. Inside, I think to myself, *They're missing it! They're missing it!* I play the games we have access to and get to toss the big bouncy ball up and down the hallways. Sometimes I slip out of the moment when the nurses tell me that the doctor may be here soon or that I may be getting out today. However, I know my mindset has really shifted when my mom tells me that I may not be getting out today and I say, "That's okay. There are more people to help here!" I go back to my "work" of being present with the other patients and sharing moments with them. One of my favorite duties is to get the energy flowing and people uplifted by dancing to music videos! "Happy" by Pharrell is really popular and I feel happy dancing with the whole world and giving myself permission to BE happy :)

Being Present with Pain

Magic begins to emerge as the melody of the present moment. I sit by the window facing south—the closest experience to outdoors this place has—and watch the windsocks dance in the air. A graying gentleman is next to me with his East-Asian wife, and together we create a sanctuary of peace in this madhouse. Everyone rushes up and down the corridors here and there, but we windwatchers sit in silence. The older couple remarks at how culture has changed and how it seems we've lost this simple truth. I begin to wonder about the old man—why is he here again? Why does he not get to rest in these moments at home with his wife? He simply doesn't know who he is sometimes and forgets things often. But he remembers this moment—and this moment is all we have. To me, he is an exemplar of sanity. He also knows "exactly where I'm going," as he uses his finger to point upward. Upstairs is mentioned here and there by several nurses, and I begin to think it's some sort of code for the next level of Heaven. I wonder what that's like…

I talk to a group of interns dressed in red. They stand a bit removed with hesitant looks dressing their faces, as if insanity is a communicable disease. My charm stat is high enough that I can approach them and they feel a bit more relaxed (also with piqued interest since I used my Fire powers to stop time and see their name tags before it should've been possible). They ask me, "Why are you in here exactly?" Speaking with them, they feel like I'm a normal human being—perhaps a bit extraverted—and that's the point I want to make, dear reader.

I want to cut clear through the illusion, stigma, and discomfort surrounding mental illness. I confess I do not have sufficient research into the neurology or physiology involved with feeling "uneasy" around mental patients (or neurodivergent people, or those with disabilities, etc.). I can only offer my own insights and conjecture: perhaps being in proximity to those persons offer too clear a mirror for us at our own very real fragility. The fragility of the mind is especially a haunting thing to witness. Yet as these brave interns have shown, beyond that discomfort, we—the "mentally ill"—too are human. Perhaps we are simply more sensitive than others to the polluted water of neurosis in our society and are on the frontlines to show to others how bad things have gotten really. If you would just talk to some patients on their terms, you, too, may begin to wonder why they're locked up.

Anyway, I hit it off with the intern from Roanoke, Virginia, a real country gal. She can appreciate the moment, slowing down. She sees that she had some ambition to come "make it" in the city, but now misses the quiet simplicity of the open fields.

Later, a woman who goes to shock therapy (yes, they still electrocute people) for her depression is out in the hall with me and another Wind brother. We intuitively know what must be done—not that we exchange so much as a glance to acknowledge this. We are playing the game where you toss bean bags into a board with holes, and I get five in a row landed. The Wind is with us and we somehow get this luck transferred to the depressed woman. Her face lights up slowly but surely as she gets more and more bean bags in the hole. The surprise on her face—that this is life! That this can feel good—is priceless! I believe this is worth more than a 1000 volts of any shock therapy, but I'm a fool in a mental hospital, so what do I know?

I have a new roommate. He's a manic-type like me and we don't cross paths very often. He tells me bluntly that we won't ever see each other again and nothing personal, but we don't have to get along. Later in the hallway, he's shouting and wrestling with the strong nurses. I ask a female angel if I was like that during the dark days—if I was ever that violent. She assures me, "No. You were never like that." I am glad I didn't give trouble to angels who have no control over the orders handed down from above.

If the present moment is so beautiful, and also all we have, can't we stand to be a bit kinder to one another? Gently remind each other of what's real?

Breath of Life

Today is harder than other days—especially when it seems like I'm on the verge of getting out. Freedom ... the closer it is, the harder it is to enjoy what you have in your locked world. Alan, the nurse that I notice, has been giving me less and less Zyprexa and starts me on only Lithium (in psych terms, no more anti-psychotics, only mood stabilizers), even though my prescription from the doctor says otherwise. He is one of my favorite angels. I ask him what the pin on his lapel is for as the dove catches my eye. "The dove is the messenger; on the day Jesus was reborn." I ask for a razor to shave, and Alan assures me that I need to be seen as an adult now and to keep my mustache. I ask if I can be of help. If they need a massage therapy program for the patients, he grabs me by the shoulders and says, "Don't even *Think* about coming back to this place."

The doctor tells me I'm not being released. She has an artful way of doing this—by not seeing me. If I don't see her, I can't get out. If I don't see her, she doesn't have to face my sanity or pain and tell me that I'm still stuck here despite being lucid. My mother arrives—I have told her on the phone I'm getting out, and this time it's real. She is hesitant to encourage my belief since this has happened many times before and I still have plenty of time left on my involuntary commitment sentence. Alan assures her that I'm not delusional; this time it is for real. I notice how he works at a slow pace, gently taking his time. I get a strong feeling that he is doing some paperwork behind the scenes or arranging for things to work in my favor when normally only the doctor can release me.

He begins talking to my mother as time slows down—he comments that she reminds him of one of his past loves. I began to wonder if all the male angels here were in love—and this work is their way of honoring that Divine Love that happens between all who dare to open their hearts. Darkly, I imagine if it is a punishment as well—to be sent to work in Hell for failing the hearts of women. As Alan fills out the paperwork, I can't suppress the feeling that I'm somehow getting away with something—an illegal between the lines/cut the red tape act—as I get on the elevator. I've tried to sneak on this elevator before so I fear they may stop me at any minute. I wonder if there will be some prank and I'll be taken off. The clay-colored doors close as if into a tomb.

I emerge from the elevator into a fascinating world of color and life: plants. I notice the green of the plants—real or fake it matters not—arranged around this lobby like area. We visit a little market shop, and I notice the intensity of my gaze makes the cashier uncomfortable. I have not yet learned how to dim the light so that it does not blind or burn.

On the car ride home, I see the sky—The SKY! That luminous blue sphere that stretches from horizon to horizon and as an endless window! I look up from the highway and there's this huge expanse of blue with clouds drifting through it. And there are birds! BIRDS! Hawks! Circling, drifting, soaring, loving: beautiful creatures of freedom. We get to a Costco gas station and I have to use the restroom. My mother allows me to go off—brave soul that she is—on my own in public to use it. I look across the black expanse of asphalt and think, *Really? I can go all out??* I begin to sprint. Long, awkward strides, feet slapping the pavement in a chorus of freedom—I begin to fly. I flap my arms—I'm by no means at a cruising altitude—and I fly through the air all the way to the entrance to Costco and the restroom.

At my mother's home, I <u>sleep</u>—so deep I scarcely remember myself. Forgetting who you are is one of the key ingredients of being alive, as outside of your head (or outside of your perceived problems and little "self") is a wondrous world. I wake up and listen to music. I really hear the music—feel it— in my entire being. I dance not to get through the pain or to lift the spirits of those around me. I am *danced* by the music itself. Nothing could be more joyous than a Free Soul dancing alone with no one watching. The dawn shines a gentle reminder that I have made it through the Crucible of Transformation, and that

I am *Free.*

II

Magic

6

Rainbow Dance

Innocent Magic, Dark Magic
My mother takes me to church, and I recognize I am here to be of service. I write "Link" on my name tag so I don't confuse all my personal problems with the work of God. My good Soul friend sees me, and I remember him at once from the last time I got out of the hospital. Back then, he said simply, "It's all about up here," as he pointed to the sky and one's connection with it. He's limping a bit—a sign that all of us have gone through our own rough times this month. He reminds me of service and how he helps behind the scenes, and his wife looks at me with more than her eyes. She knows it's time for me to go through what's called a chrysalis—something you need a sponsor for. I sign up as Link and don't think much more about it, since it is many moons away. What matters is the Sunday school children and how I get to spend time with them and hold space for them as they go through their craft projects.

Back at home, I see children playing outside in the neighborhood and join them. They look at me with the same eyes as my friend's wife and let me play with them. Other children join, apprehensive about the teenage-looking person, but I had earned the approval of the ringleader of their merry band. "This guy's okay," he reassures them. He's not the oldest, but he's got the sort of authority that comes from the Soul and the others recognize this while someone outlines the games for us to play.

His older brother is a dark Jedi. Everyone confesses their true spirit to me in one way or another. The Dark Jedi notes our mock playing and says, "I want to see someone get hurt," but is not challenged by any of the children and senses the strength of my Soul enough to not contend with me. He circles the cul-de-sac on his bike as a shark would.

A girl is there who shows me the chains strapped to her Soul, and how her father has instructed her of everything that's dangerous in this world: there's poison ivy, snakes, spiders, strangers, sickness, bees, and death at every corner of her awareness. I see his fear snake through her and the apprehension in her light blue eyes of how to be in this world. A boy who wears orange and is considered "autistic" is a true gift to the circle, and I am able to see the Light in his eyes, the purity of his Soul. His brother knows there's nothing wrong with him, but confesses that their parents don't sing the same song.

We play all around the backyards with our plastic swords, and I take up my lightsaber against the darkness—still proudly wearing my rainbow name tag "Link." I stand on the edge of a deck's railings on the second story, "walking the plank," when the Dark Jedi sees his opening: he pushes me off.

By then, I had learned to Fall, and I rolled on the grass with the lightness of the feathers the angels gave me.

The Doctor is Always Right

The adult daycare awaits me again. I return to stay at my father's in order to be in proximity to the place. The nurse there remembers me from earlier in the year, and she has a beautiful ladybug pin on her lanyard. The ladybug smiles at me, and I feel comforted as we go over my history. I wasn't fully present for the intake process last time, but we review my answers, and I smile at the Light and Love my past-self expressed.

"Wow, I said that?" I ask, surprised at the love that comes through when I'm unconscious. Perhaps, I was merely overwhelmed with love and could not handle it.

The nurse and I then discuss the nature of time; she remembers what her physicist father described it as:

Time is like a loaf of bread—the whole loaf already exists. With our limited perspective, we go through this loaf one slice at a time.

She feels moved to be in the presence of someone reminding her of the totality of what is. Feeling safe with me, she talks about how her intuition saved her from being crushed in a rockslide when she suddenly called off a hike at Great Falls. After plenty of Nurturing Ladybugy Nurse agape, I'm taken to the Doctor Who Remembers Me.

The day continues with a beautiful bang, as I say to this battered psychiatrist who knows the hardships of fighting in the darkness of depression and madness:

"You were absolutely right, doctor. I should've taken my medicine."

"What a way to start the day!" she says, her spirits immediately lifted. She turns to her co-workers. "Did you hear that? I. Was. Right." With an easy smile on her face, the look of one finally being listened to, she takes me into her office:

"Arthur, we're happy to see you because of what you bring to the place. It's gotten heavy around here lately. But we don't want to see you either! We know how hard it is on you to go through [Hell]."

As we walk to the group therapy session, she tells me that I remind her of Johnny Depp; I stagger around with my best Jack Sparrow impression. She laughs and says that perhaps this is my role in life.

To be a breath of fresh air.

Cartwheels

"Is that ... Cartwheels?" someone whispers to a woman in the group. She nods, and I am confused as to whom this comment comes from and concerns.

During the next break, I learn that during the Nine Day Dark, I would do cartwheels—which I see as me spinning off excess energy into the four corners of the world—up and down the halls of the hospital. It seems I did a number of other disturbing expressions of madness as well, which earned me some sort of reputation with this woman who I don't remember at all.

She regards me with the politeness that comes from thinking someone is insane and now is challenged to see them in a different light.

I struggle with the patience to listen in groups, as I see everything and nothing at once and want to comment on everyone's views. We learn about a dialectical type of therapy, which sounds a helluva lot better than cognitive behavioral therapy (CBT). Having a conversation with another human is a lot more refreshing than thinking we are all machines that need an updated program.

To each their own, eh?

There are two girls in this group about my age. Well, one calls herself a grandma because that's how high her emotional maturity got after spending an intensive retreat two months in Utah. She looks at my green folder that I labeled "Zen Freedom." She remarks, "Those are some great words," in a way that reveals she's a seer who looks from the center of the Universe. The other girl is a dreamer—she lucid-dreams eleven hours in a row and wakes up tired—we all have a crazy time together.

After a week of daycare, I get permission from my dad to hang out with the seer. Our parents drop us off—like we're in high school again!—to hang out for awhile near a mall in Tysons. Our combined energies amplify our madness, as she remarks a strong sudden craving for alcohol, and I run around jumping up and down off parking garage ledges. Maybe there was some wisdom to not getting involved with other patients after all...

At night, I call the teacher who showed me Freedom Bodywork because I missed our follow-up appointment. She's offering back-to-back weekend workshops for the first two levels of training in the method: learning to treat the body prone and then supine. I sign up for both so I can learn how to bring freedom to the full body—only my adult daycare program's duration is on either end of the first weekend and 230 miles away in Charlotte. I'm told to definitely not drink alcohol and stay on my medications—Zyprexa and Lithium.

I ditch the Zyprexa immediately, taking the train down to Cary; I make some conversation with a high school girl who is returning home. "Cary ... is the most boring place in the world. Nothing ever happens there; it is completely safe." Privately, I think of how nice "boring" sounds after all the drama of this past year ... I arrive to see the aftermath of the storm I brought through Earth Girl's life. Apparently, during my nine-day blackout, I had bargained her off, agreeing that she should be kicked out of our apartment since she wasn't technically on the lease. My stepdad had been convinced that her smoking marijuana around me had triggered this manic episode, and their heated e-mail exchange led to him using his co-signer privileges as leverage to evict her. My mother and father agreed that she was "not good for me" and summarily removed her from my life without my conscious consent—even though it was possibly what fate had decreed for quite some time and I had not the willpower to follow through.

We drive over to see my spiritual brother, who had some proposal for me he wanted only to share in person. At this point, it was clear I was "no longer employed"—if that's the correct term for letting an independent contractor go by our shared boss. When he greets me, he inquires where I have been and what happened. I feel ashamed and unwilling to open with the direct truth, so I hedge around the rough time I went through with vague language.

He picks up the vibe of the experience and reflects. "So you had a character-building experience."

"Yeah. Heh, character building."

Re-equipped with my car, I drive down to Charlotte and focus on the Freedom Bodywork class and learn how to be more gentle, relaxed, and at peace in myself. I try to embody the wisdom of Dr. Trager in the hopes that life can be a smoother ride with more ease and play.

Water Girl lives here, and I try to contact her to share all that I've been through since our time in the spring. She's not available, so I spend my downtime trying to find a spot to sleep near some parks in the chilly autumn air. An officer taps on my window (that's happened quite a bit in this tale, hasn't it?) to tell me the park is closed. I tell him that's fine, and that I'm not in the park. He offers some sympathy and tells me of a Wal-Mart parking lot that I can park in to sleep at where the law won't bother me.

The bright lights are all that bother me here. I end up getting a hotel for the second night, calling Dreamer on a whim and seeing spirals of purple as I fade into slumber.

Back in Virginia for a single day of daycare (which was not mandated but I feel obligated to complete anyway), I say my goodbyes to the good nurses.

I also ask if I may be of service—if they need a massage therapist on staff, as nurturing touch is an essential key to the healing of mental illness! They tell me to reach out in a few years, or better yet, to focus on being of service wherever I find myself.

Let me stress this last line now for where you may find yourselves: truly, there is work to be done. Often when we come through the other side of some transcendent experience full of madness and meaning; we begin to want to give more to the world. Often we can struggle with a vision or if we "should" plan some great idea or work to implement into the world. Often still, if we focus simply on our immediate surroundings—our present moment experience—we could clean up a bit more here and there. This "cleaning up" or improvement of our small microcosm will in due time spiral out into greater works and amazing momentum of healing the world. Without starting nearby, we ensure that any grounds made further out there are less sustainable and perhaps only temporary. I suggest such a pause now that you have finished this little segment.

In the words of wiser persons, "Clean up your damn room first."

Shaman Camp: Illumination

Part of the whirlwind of activity before I ended up in Hell was signing up for Shamanic Initiation ritual all the way up in New York's countryside. I was drawn to it because the name of the company hosting it was the Four Winds Society, not that I had a clue about what shamanism was. I make up for that by binge-watching the anime, *Shaman King*. The essence of the show is that shamans from all over get to compete to be the king who is allowed to make their dream a reality.

Well, the week before said initiation is a class called "South Wind," which is where this lineage begins its instruction, as it works its way around the Four Directions. In said class, I would learn how to perform *illumination* of the chakras, which would be my first introduction to energy work. Problem is that it's expensive, a week long, and I'm terrible at making decisions. Did I mention it also would mean I wouldn't be present to help Earth Girl move?

She's found a townhome and a roommate situation, but we're still living together until the end of the month.

I'm still struggling with this decision of whether to take the workshop or not. All that travel for a two-day initiation seems a bit silly, but I don't like starting things (the program in full would be seven-week-long classes total) that I'm not going to complete all the way. On my way home, something compels me to stop at a Bass Pro; Earth Girl has been looking for some boxes to move in.

Context Flashback to the first time I got out of the hospital earlier in the year: I was downtown in Raleigh, roaming around and wanting to get the business card of a bail bondsman should I ever get arrested due to a storm of fate again. I saw a motorcycle and I missed riding Eternity, so I went over to check it out. Remember also that I felt nearly every symbol was the Universe speaking to me directly: the motorcycle's decal shined brightly. The decal said:

Go Pro. Be a Hero.

I took the words to my heart to mull over ... be a hero? Be a professional hero? Get my business on point? (No, I had no idea that a GoPro is a camera at this point.) Flash back to the present.

Bass Pro Tip

I talk to an employee and he says, "Yeah we got tons of boxes." The gentleman says that he'll go get them from the back and have them laid out for me. I wander around the store briefly ... and right in front of me are some cameras and that same sticker: "Go Pro. Be a Hero." There's that sign again!

I look up, straight up, and see a real sign. Hanging from the ceiling of Heaven with four corners of glory is a white sign that reads simply in bold black letters:

Illumination

Lightning bolts start shooting down my spine and throughout my nerves. This is it! This is the sign! Magic!

I take my boxes and my clarity back to the NuNest (for as long as Earth Girl remains, it will be the NuNest ... I don't know what it'll be after she leaves). I sign up for the workshop without any hesitation.

Earth Girl is furious that the week of the workshop overlaps with her move so I won't be around to help. I figure that it's better if I'm not around for the whirlwind of emotions and pain that I bring.

Can Magic be Taught?

I first make my way to Virginia Beach, where another survivor of the mental health system—mentioned earlier as Dreamer—wants to hang out with me. I enjoy the brisk waves of October and climb up a pile of sand a few stories high—scaring an excavator driver on the other side of the sand mountain. He starts shouting something as I flee down the dunes like a child. A giant statue of Neptune towers over us like an emerald statue of liberty guarding the sea. His gaze reminds me of the primal waves of emotions that have carried us through the hospital and to this very shore. The words of my father echo in my mind, "Life is about riding waves." Dreamer graciously offers to pay for a hotel room for us; we have a magical time that happens when judgement and the harsh gaze of western psychology is absent from our togetherness.

In the backcountry of New York, I am up for a week of healing, deep conversations, and Shamanic training—essentially learning how to "Dream the World into Being." Despite all I have experienced this past year, I find myself being very skeptical at all this notion of healing, energies, chakras, and whatnot. The Lithium I continue to take daily and programming of the culture runs deep I figure. We are asked what we are looking for in our circle of about thirty students, and I say, "I'm here looking for nothing." I write Nothing Shaman on the first page of free space and inside that, I write Freedom Shaman. Probably not much of a difference between the two anyway.

This is what sticks from the first day's lesson: Shamanism is a path of Spiritual Freedom. There are no rules and only one agreement: when Spirit calls, you answer. When you call, Spirit answers. I like nice and simple things and the freedom of amorality. In my Daoist studies, the concept of external moral guidelines was seen as a lesser, untrustworthy form of virtue. Be true to your own nature and true virtue will happen on its own; rules are only for keeping those corrupt in line through fear.

We practice a few healing practices. I keep complaining about how I can't feel anything—especially my body. I'm completely disconnected, and it surprises my partner that I'm so "in my head." Turns out it's the safest place to be after going through a lot of pain, so who can blame me?

I meet many interesting folk, like a South American man named Francisco who is my partner for reading each other's lives through a rock we hold in our hands—the practice of "psychometry." Closing my eyes and trying not to overthink things, I share with him what I'm sensing, a lot of travel here and there all around. It doesn't feel very insightful. I mean he flew here from South America after all, but he surprises me to share that his work indeed has him traveling all the time. When he reads my rock, he shares that he feels like I came through a lot of darkness, almost like the bottom of a spring being compressed and finally being launched free. Seems accurate enough but still too vague to impress me.

Later at dinner, I sit with him as he teaches me about relationships:

"Be careful about opening up new cycles," he says. I know what he means. Not that it could change my behavior simply by knowing. I've always followed attraction and the hope for love wherever it leads. Always willing to take the risk of opening my heart. Perhaps "careful" is a word I have a particular aversion to.

I call Earth Girl and tell her about how awesome this place is.

"Oh great, and when were you gonna start to care about my day?"

"I'm sorry, I just have so much joy and happiness I want to share first!"

"Look, that's great and all, but I'm going through a stressful time here. Work has been extra, and my mom's going through some things."

"Aw, I'm sorry. By the way, I had some insights about your mom, about karma and how she can shift things back into balance…"

"I'm not really in the mood to hear about karma from someone who's had life handed to them on a gold platter with a silver spoon."

I stop her. Then, with exasperation and tears, "Please, if nothing else, you can't say this has been easy for me. I've been blessed in ways you weren't and never had to worry about food or shelter, but please—don't ever say it's been *easy."* The duality of our upbringings was always a point of contrast. I took for granted my material security, and Earth Girl didn't even seem to know it was possible to not have an emotionally nurturing home environment. I'm oversimplifying here, but...

My feelings seem to reach her through the Void.

"Well... that's true. I'm sorry."

At the picnic table on the third day, I get a chance to open up and talk about my manic episode and hospitalization with the group. I'm received with understanding and am told that it got labeled as a manic episode because they don't know what it is. This rings a chord for me and I feel like I'm in a safe place—where I'm not crazy. Where I am accepted for the wildness of my heart.

Speaking of my heart, it's been six winters since I began using the phrase, "There's nothing colder than my heart," to keep myself warm in the winter. A mantra of numbness as a defense against a cold and unforgiving world. Today, I woke up after a frigid night of camping in the New York autumn with tears in my eyes; I hear myself say, "I've stayed warm because of my heart."

Experience the Journey

I use the momentum of waking up with dawn to attend a yoga class being held on the Omega grounds. The teacher guides my hips into what an actual down dog feels like, and I realize how far I have to go. During Shaman class, I add on the page of Nothing Shaman "Lightning Shaman" as a more tangible Element (yet so ephemeral!) that resonates with my path.

A particular moment takes place in a cafe where I see Alberto Villoldo, who is the creator of this entire training organization and prolific writer/teacher. He walks out the door as I hesitate to ask him some questions about journeying—the skill that drew me the most to this path—and I miss my opportunity. I look at him intensely out the window of the cafe. He comes to a halt. He looks up at the sky with a curious glance and then turns around and comes back inside the cafe. I take that as a sign he has "felt" me and ask my questions about the journeying practice as soon as he enters. He is slow to answer, but gives me a "keep at it, and that skill will take off before you know it." His simple encouragement would prove useful in the coming months...

In the leisure time between classes, I reflect on the direction I want to go with my life. I focus my energy on starting my private massage practice—finally—as I had been given a tip from Soul Brother about a new yoga studio in a great location that has a room for rent. I commit to renting the room out and building a clientele. Zen Bodywork is the name I have been using. I bring up my fear that I'll fall back into old patterns or won't be as productive without the structure of a job to my new shaman friends, and Francisco assures me that "Life always flows."

Never the Same Twice

What follows the workshop is the Shamanic initiation ceremony. I sit around the fire with a few other souls. One talks about how his training through the Four Directions has gone and how he's going again through the South, West, North, East classes. He draws out a spiral path that continues to deepen through the same pathways. I counter, fresh from having my head filled with Falun Dafa literature, and say that I'm aiming at the "straight-up path."

He looks at me with a wary glance, not at all underestimating my words, but really wanting to get me to feel what that means. "Good luck with that straight-up path," he says.

The next day, we sit in the large conference hall and listen to a lecture by Alberto. I go into a semi-trance and see swirls of energy being drawn to him, and actually see his aura. I don't know what to make of how it seems everyone's energy is being drawn toward him in that way. The Q'ero Shamans perform a divination ceremony for us, casting tea leaves. The spoken prophecy smacks of generalist advice, and my skepticism remains on high alert (which probably didn't help my mental state for the ceremony in which the Q'ero Shamans bless each of us one by one with their mesas). A mysterious British man had forewarned me it was quite the experience and how he felt "he was naked up there" on stage. For me, when I approach the shaman, all nervous and unsure of how to hold myself, it feels like I'm simply tapped on the head with a bag of rocks, as the shaman mutters in an ancient language. So much for my belief in "magic," huh. I've come to learn my cynicism, or perhaps my demeanor in general, always tends toward the missing element in the room. In this room of believers, perhaps I am the one seeing it all as a giant Kool-aid party. Yet, I'd like to believe some part of my Soul participated fully...

The final activity pairs me with a partner for a brief dialogue about how we intend to move forward with our lives. My partner is a woman who wants to open up a "rite of passage" type venture in the North Carolina mountains, so she takes me living there as a sign. In response, I mention my own vague intentions, "I want to become a Master of Wind and Fire."

"You already *are* that!" she implores, yet I don't see how that could be so.

Perhaps that same "some" part of me listens...

Deja Boo

Southward-bound, I stop at my dad's apartment in Northern Virginia. Before continuing my trip, I'm pulled over by the police. The taillight my dad warned me about on the way to New York is the reason, but to make it worse, apparently I fit the bill for a drug runner: "out of state plates with a history in the area." The officer calls some dogs in, and my trauma starts to come up. I refuse to let them search the car, having learned my lesson, but that doesn't stop the narcotics dog from jumping into my open window.

The cops start to search, thoroughly saying that the dog gives them probable cause, as I have an extreme deja vu—not the dreamy kind but the scary kind where you see a situation that has the potential to go as south as it did in the past.

I talk with the cop about his life to ease my anxieties, assuring him that there's no drugs in the car and they won't find anything.

He shares some pretty dark stories about being a cop—"stuff the public doesn't know we do. The other night I had a call into a house and found a guy hanging from the rafters. It's hard to deal with sometimes."

I tell him about being a massage therapist, and he confesses he's been thinking about a career shift—and massage therapy might work for him. I start to ease into the synchronicity of our conversation as the other cops finish their search.

"You sure you don't have anything or haven't had anyone smoking in there recently?"

"No officer, I really haven't."

"Huh … that's concerning. These dogs are well trained to not make mistakes."

I smile inwardly, feeling as if none of what happened was a mistake at all.

Life Always Flows

My sojourn ends at an empty apartment, the blank canvas my Soul's been yearning for. Normally people go on spiritual journeys and have to integrate those insights back into their day-to-day life. Here, I am blessed by having no work and no routine; this also turns out to be a curse. I go on walks through the woods across from my apartment to try to find some calmness in the river and the sounds of the forest. One of the first episodes of *Shaman King* has Yoh, the young shaman, staring at a river for hours. His soon-to-be friend, Manta, watches him and waits for him to move, yet more hours pass. At last, he stretches his arms up and, with a great sigh, exclaims, "Ah! How great it is to be one with nature!" He goes back to watching. Manta boils over, furious that he can somehow stand there doing nothing for so long! I notice both characters in myself as I attempt to watch the river for more than ten minutes…

While I have no outward routine, my mind still goes through the same restless patterns. Meditating comes as slow as my shaman-in-training partner mentioned: start with five minutes a day, small and slow. The process of my mind reaching out to grab anything and do anything to avoid being watched … amazing.

I watch yoga videos and follow along. There I have something to focus on, something I can "do," even though I'm a beginner of beginners and have not learned to relax into the poses. Either way, some sort of balance begins to form in my life as I take better care of myself.

I wander into Barnes and Noble one day and gravitate toward the Tarot cards they offer there. The Wildwood Tarot ... a Celtic origin deck that speaks to me with its featured cards of the Shaman, Wanderer, and Sun. Symbolism has always provided me with much guidance, and now here it is in a structured way with intelligent design and archetypes!

Near my new studio, I meet a homeless man outside Hayes-Barton Church named James. He tells me that Arthur is in the Bible, though I've never heard of that. "Arthur is a finisher of faith." In return, I remind him that if he can't trust himself, how can he trust anyone else?

Bushido
"No chains can hold me,
I am Free
No sword can end me,
I am a Soul
No light can blind me,
Beauty's within
No darkness can smother me,
I am the Light
I seek Nothing,
I find Everything
I die for Eternal Love.
Gentle and easy like Water,
Free and swift like Wind,
Warm and carefree like Fire,
Strong and loving like Earth,
Gaze with wonder at the Sky."

I wrote about what my path means to me as part of therapy. *Bushido* means "Way of the Warrior" in Japanese and is more often referred to as the Samurai's code of ethics. Of course, I am all about a personal path. It's a simple exercise you can take time to do: What is your "way" of being a warrior? What principles or values guide your actions? What does integrity, strength, courage, or virtue even mean to you? Even now as I write this, I learn that my way shifts and develops over a lifetime—as it should be. Who

I was when I wrote this poem is vague enough to still hold true, but I have come to ground my *Bushido* in a more solid way.

I don't know if talk therapy is helping—there's no obvious breakthroughs or shifts in perspective that I can notice. I take Earth Girl for a session one time and afterward, she gets out of the appointment like a renewed Soul. "That was amazing! Everyone should have therapy!" She further insists that it's helping me out a lot.

10/21/14

Today is the day I confront my Duke psychiatrist, whose cold eyes brought up so much anxiety for me a mere six months ago. I stand up for myself and tell her that I've run out of Lithium and **I do not want a refill.**

"That's incredibly dangerous and foolish. I do not recommend this course of action."

"I know what I have to do."

My confidence wanes a bit as her harshness and cold demeanor dampen my courage. "I only hope I'm not making a mistake."

"You are. One that will end up with you back in the hospital."

A strong sense of defiance rises to meet her. I will not end up back there. Sensing an impasse, I get up to leave.

Her tone softens as she shifts out of a professional role.

"Take care of yourself," she says, and it was not an empty phrase.

I leave with the feeling that deep down she believes in me, that I can go beyond medication into a new world of stability and peace. Perhaps, my confidence lit a spark of hope in her cold and methodical world.

My next appointment is with my psychologist, and I talk about the Flurry of Fire and all the changes I'm ready to make and am moving through. The depths of my loneliness teaches me what Earth Girl tried to teach me: being alone is much different than being lonely. A fire rises within me, as I share with my therapist that even if I am the only one in the world who loves me, that would be enough.

Autumn Dreams of Winter

I dream I am walking down to a fishing pier. There's a man with a hook for an

arm, singing softly. His eyes are lined with wisdom of the ages, and a cheerful smile. I wake up with his song in my head,
  "Oh the tears we'll bring
  Oh the years we'll sing
  This man's story
  Oh the winds we'll fly
  Oh the skies are high
  This man's story~
  Oh the fires are bright,
  Oh the times are right
  This man's story~
  Oh the waves are sure
  Oh the rains are pure
  This man's story~
  Oh the stones are cold
  Oh the young are bold
  All our stories~
  Oh my sweet destiny,
  Oh my the love I've seen
  This one's story~
  Is there nowhere to lay my head?
  Is there no Earth to make my bed?
  This one's story..."

NC State gets revisited, as I still feel drawn to higher education. I agonize over which major to re-apply with and feel overwhelmed by the options available. Anthropology seems interesting, especially for my budding interest in Shamanism, but I don't like the course requirements too much. I read my best friend from high school's Facebook profile (a rare activity for me). I notice that he majored in philosophy. A classic competitive fire wells within me, as I realize I still consider him my rival. I let the impulse flow through me as I decide here and now to apply for philosophy without doing any more research or dwelling on the subject. After all, didn't I read all those books for fun? Camus? Nietzsche? The Tao Te Ching? How could I have forgotten philosophy's place in my heart?

When I receive the letter of acceptance for the spring semester at NC State, I shift gears from the massage business I am working on to school.

My dad stops me mid-charge. "What's your goal? Why are you doing this, really?"

His way of support is to challenge me and make sure I'm clear on what's going on at the heart of the issue.

"To make connections," I come up with on the spot, as I do not have much respect for the academic rigor, nor certifications, that come from school. I've always been able to coast on minimal effort and never really have seen what I'm missing out on. People on the other hand– social groups, young people with some passion in their hearts—now those I see value in. I have no idea who I'll meet or have any sort of plans for that thing to happen, but that's never been my style anyway.

The end of November and the time comes to put The Sex Machine to rest. She's broken down on Earth Girl on her way to work. I go to help her get a used car, since my credit allows her to get a decent loan. Sex Machine sits outside her apartment for a few weeks before I finally get a guy to come junk it.

I send her off on her final voyage to the scrapyard while the man who comes to pick her up—David—talks to me for a bit. He shares how he lived in Hawai'i for a few years, living a clean and simple life. He also majored in philosophy and is really happy having his own freedom. "To be getting paid for doing your own thing, isn't that the best?" His words bring me a lot of encouragement for my chosen major, and way of life!

In December, I look forward to two blessings: the Way of the Shaman workshop with the Foundation for Shamanic Studies and a trip to Brasil.

In the Way of the Shaman Workshop, I deepen the ability to journey shamanically for all sorts of spiritual healing purposes as well as divination. I don't remember Michael Harner's definition for journey, so here's my attempt: a journey is a spiritual sojourn across the Veil, where one's consciousness interacts with the Spirit World. People may say the experience is fabricated by the mind; I say the experience is created by our mind's attempt to interpret the experience of the Spirit World through our nervous system. I've met people who completely and fully "go to another place" like a lucid dream. As for me, I have always been aware of my body to some degree, as my body (somatically) experiences and processes the journey for me. Of course, I'm not "fully here" either ... as if that should surprise you from reading this book thus far! Hah!

Other participants are having trouble accessing altered states or trusting that their journeys were "real." I had practiced diligently (not that it is something achieved through effort, don't misunderstand) after returning from the workshop up north. Perhaps, I simply had more motivation than others to escape the reality I currently faced (which is also to say that this practice helped me return full circle to the imaginative worlds and creativity I had enjoyed growing up). As to whether my Soul was actually traveling to other realms and experiencing other planes of existence, or I merely reawakened my imagination, who can say? The aim of this book is to find magical ways of looking at our madness, not to prove any sort of metaphysical theory. Whether the faeries in your mind are real or not is up to you—I'm enjoying my friends and the adventures we share!

The community of practitioners itself is a rich part of taking the class. To simply be around people who see each other for their gifts and respect the reality of a rich inner and psychic reality ... It's circles like these I wish I had discovered in the first months after my hospitalization, and it's gratitude over having them now and the confidence it builds that I will indeed be "just fine" off my medicine.

We were asked to bring a rock for divination and I chose one from my nearby forest. I second guess myself a lot and am unsure whether I see a dragon in my rock because one is there or because the teacher had seen one in his example.

The teacher's wife says, with quiet confidence, "There are dragons in this room."

When I journey to the Upper World to find a spirit guide, angel, or teacher there, it's with surprise that a present version of myself appears in another body. I ask myself why I am my own guide, and his reply is:

"You wouldn't listen to anyone else."
Apparently, that isn't so uncommon.

Saudade

It's been eight years since I visited Brasil. Eight years since I learned that there is a Love that can pull anyone out of the darkness. My twin cousins showed me that Love (which I now know is called Agape) and it was able to pierce through the depression I was in at the time…

That's a longer story, as right now I'm going to Brasil to visit my *Tia* Elza. She's in the hospital with glioblastoma tumors. Deep in my heart, I know that this is the last time I'll see her, but I don't tell my mother that. Hope is a beautiful thing… sometimes I think it exists to keep us afloat until we've become strong enough to swim. Maybe that's why the power animal that came to Elza during my prayers for her is an ostrich. And death… Instead of focusing on how it affects me and the loss, I try to see how it's a homecoming for the one involved.

I also spend my time focusing on life. The twins introduce me to their long-time friend, a girl named Hannah. She is very interested in me, not in a romantic sort of way, but in a sort of "I didn't know someone could exist like this" way. I can tell she understands and speaks English, but I find it cute that she pretends not to in order to borrow my journal. The one I quoted before from the mental hospital, actually. She is fascinated by my poems and the depth at which I had fallen for a girl (Maria…) so quickly. I am happy that on the other side of the coin of death is a young girl who begins to learn more about herself, love, and the world. I like to think I was in the right place at the right time in many ways.

My mother goes to see her sister every day, but I manage only two visits. I can smell the radiation on her, and it's painful. She can barely form sentences and doesn't often remember who people are or anything about herself. A miracle occurs when the choir from church comes to sing with her and in that moment, she returns to herself. She sings and is the full light of God shining on this earth. It's a beautiful hymn. I fight back tears for no reason other than I think the sound of weeping would distract from the music. I try to massage her legs and get some circulation going for her as I notice that she has trouble putting weight on one foot.

I go to the roof of the hospital for some fresh air. It's a flat roof that has no railings, no barrier from certain death. I'm on the ninth floor. I'm on the edge of the roof. Everything goes white.

I think about a lot of things on the trip back from the hospital ... like why my dad wanted me to see Rio as a dump ... Also about the pain in my Tia's eyes as she asked me to please pray for her ... I hold my cousin's hand on the bus for an eternity and feel her heartbeat. It's always the touch I forget I need so much. It's always the Love, which is the heartbeat of Brasil that I forget when I leave. Brazilians, in my experience, have a much different relationship with emotions and touch than White culture in the United States. Here is a place where you can have your heart on your sleeve as a way of connection, not as a weakness. Here you can cuddle with your friends, kiss your uncle on his cheeks, and laugh at every sunset. Of course I forget this when I leave; it's too painful a loss for me to handle.

I figure this way I don't feel *saudade* as much. *Saudade* is a portuguese word that you have to feel, as translation doesn't do it justice. Maybe you're feeling it now ... reminded of a loved one whose smile you still hold dear.

"To love another person is to see the face of God."

-Les Misérables[6]

Back at home, I face the fear of loss in another way. A beautiful yellow mixed dog stays one tier below my cousins' part of the home. Her name is Kelly, and I fall in love. I haven't let myself have a dog for many reasons, but the main one is deep down I have never faced the loss of my childhood dog, Kaloh, being hit by a car. Especially because she died after escaping the house after I opened the door ... I have always felt like it was me who pulled the trigger.

---

[6] Boublil, Alain. Schönberg, C.-M. (2012). *Epilogue*. In *Les Misérables: The Motion Picture* (Motion Picture). Universal Pictures.

Worse, I gave up on searching for her.

I go on a walk with Kelly and somehow she gets away from me. I go chasing her down, the terror of life repeating itself pushing me onward. The nightmarish feeling comes up again. I refuse to let Fate have its way. My cousin and I eventually pincer her, and she lays down through the sheer force of my exasperation bearing down on her. Relieved, I sober up and vow to be more careful.

On the long slow days of summer, I lie on a couch that smells like my vovó to escape the heat. I listen to Amanda Palmer on my iPod, a gift from Earth Girl, and her book called the *Art of Asking*. Who knew how difficult it is to be vulnerable! What courage it takes to ask others for a hand! Later, I find myself on the beach of Isla do Governador ... The calm smell of the beach at night lulls me into a gentle state ... We leave footprints in the sand that I'll always remember.

It's my last day in Brasil. I hold my Tia's hand and promise her I'll come see the Olympics with her in Brasil in the summer. The tears behind my eyes betray that I don't think this will happen. I go out on the roof again. I'm still terrified. This time a gentle breeze carries me to the edge before I can think. I stand there and the fear is intensified, but my True Self comes to meet it. I find the trust in myself for life to keep on living. How long have I been getting in life's way?

Back at my cousin's house, I give my little blond cousin Kevin a comic book, *Vagabond*, that I found for 1 rael while crossing a bridge. I eat some brownie cookies and then have to say goodbye to the twins. Karen doesn't stop crying, but I smile because I know I'll see her again. I don't have the same foreboding loneliness of eight years ago, where the ocean between us was as impassable as the walls of my heart.

I return to my cold fortress in Raleigh. I order Nepali cuisine to reunite with Earth Girl, who is out having a beer or two. That turns into eight hours of waiting, a cold dinner, and me having only the waning moon and stars for company. *Saudade~*

Light's Rebirth

My father visits for dinner with his wife to celebrate the Winter Solstice. My dad's a Celtic at heart, and we enjoy the turns of the wheel together. We discuss a new potential major for me: the cultural aspects of mental health. After all, it's that people simply need an environment to be themselves rather than drugs to fit into what is!

For Christmas, I ride out to Charlotte with Earth Girl to see her mother and father-in law. A blue jay smiles at me on the road after we leave. In Charlotte, we have a festive dinner. Earth Girl's mother is the shining ray of hope for me in this world, an example that there is compassion that can shine through no matter how many blows life has dealt you. Her husband shares that when he was younger, he was convinced he'd live forever...

On the ride home, Earth Girl and I talk of deep matters. I open up to her about Shamanism, power animals, and all sorts of lessons from my time alone. She gets excited with the ideas and wants to add them to her rogue-lite she's designing. She's always full of a million ideas that are fresh and awesome. When she says that we're different enough in our ways of thinking and worldviews to have a lifetime of engaging conversations, I feel a warm glow of optimism.

A Cold End to a Wild Horse Year

College starts. It's much the way I remember it being when I was in community college four years ago. My English teacher's enthusiasm for stories radiates rays of hope for a meaningful semester. She uses the myths and stories of all sorts of cultures to reveal the magic of this world we live in. I like to visit her during her office hours solely to have meaningful conversations. One visit, I explain my thoughts about how immortality in Daoism is misunderstood by scholars. With the class, she shares this nugget of wisdom:

"Are phones and screens really the problem? Or are they simply the physical expression of what we're doing with our minds all the time? It's not as if we've changed that much from one generation to the next."

One night, I overcome my social inertia and venture out to a meetup group for the first time. They call themselves "The Church of the Earth" and are a bunch of pagans. With me getting into Shamanism and my Celtic roots, I figure it's worth seeing. It's been ages since I sat around a fire anyway. There's no one my age and the night is chilly, but I enjoy being around a few other weirdos. I take my leave and drive back to my lone dark castle on the third floor of Banyan Grove.

As I drive through the parking lot, I see Earth Girl's car coming the other way. My mind races to conclusions: "She came to see me!? She left after seeing I wasn't there!?" This optimistic version of reality turns into a u-turn when I catch up to her. She pulls off to the side in a parking lot after seeing me.

Drunk and eating a salad she got from Harris Teeter is how I find her. Her intent was to get some food and hadn't paid a second thought to see me. She wants to eat healthier, but the problem is she's drunk and the salad isn't fulfilling. She voices her desire for some greasy "things and wings" from Zaxby's. I find it pretty amusing going from health salad to fried fast food but hey, what the hell, I'm just happy to see her. She's bought the remade *Majora's Mask* for DS and running into me inspires her to change plans and curl up with me and play video games rather than go to a party where her friends are waiting.

I drive her over to Zaxby's, giving her some light sass about the unhealthy food. The mood shifts, and she calls me a buzzkill. She claims she doesn't want it anymore, even though we're almost there. "Take me back to my car." The dark mood pierces through me.

"Look, I was kidding. Come on, let's get you some wings and things…"

"No. I'm done."

I take her back to her car, but I am overcome with a terrible dread feeling of "She isn't going to want to see me again, is she?" I can handle a lot of things, but the hardest for me is when things change—losing someone who is right there in front of me. That psychic pain of feeling the timelines of reality shift by my own hand no less. We went from a chance wonderful meeting and hanging out to an angry goodbye? I plead with her to lighten up and not leave.

I'm standing outside her car, the silver Yaris I co-signed for her, and she's in the driver's seat. I'm praying to myself to find some way through this situation.

Instead, something more instinctual moves me and I get in the car with her. Her reaction is explosive: she leaps over to the passenger side and gets hysterical—"GET OUT FET OUT GET OUT."

I have no idea what's wrong. In my mind, it's our car really—but she's panicking. She starts calling numbers randomly; she even calls me!

Now I'm in a bind.

I can't let her drive like this—not only drunk but now with out-of-control feelings.

She calls her friends who are at the party a few blocks away.

I breathe and blank out in this living nightmare, as still as possible.

They arrive. Beats later, a police officer arrives doing his patrol.

I explain the situation, having little help I'll be understood. A girl is crying and shocked in a car with me standing there—what else does it look like? My two ex-friends console her, while the more professional one of the pair gets the full story from me. He listens patiently and I'm grateful. One of the ex-friends drives her car, and they assure me they'll take care of her.

I return to that dark castle. Or maybe it's my mood that darkens the whole sky… There's one week left in the Year of the Horse until the moon fades to black.

I am stressed beyond belief—I know she won't want to ever see me again. I feel her friends justify their hatred of me and convince her we need to separate. They have all the proof they need.

I am all alone, terribly alone, as an island in a sea of regret and sorrow. It's Valentine's weekend, 2015.

I wrestle with dark thoughts—with the bitterness of a man who feels deeply unappreciated. Some inner demon tempts me to take the car back—since both our names are on it—and to see how far she manages without my help. She doesn't want my help anyway, right? I'm a demon anyway, right? Well, I figure I might as well act in accordance with how I'm seen.

Love exists in my heart. It won't die so easily. It beats back the urge with a firm declaration, "I will not take back a gift made in love." It's this dedication that saves me, but the dark thoughts torment me unceasingly.

I auditioned for a play the week before and received a role. Today, ice and snow are still on the ground from the weather yesterday, but I ride my motorcycle to the university because it makes parking so much easier. I go to get fitted for my costume, and a blue jay squawks at me intensely. I have no idea what he's saying.

I'm driving to my massage studio afterward, doing a session trade for a haircut I had received. Behind a white van, my mind goes to that madness incident where I channeled James Bond. The whiteness of the van lulls me into a stupor ... I figure I'm about to die. Following closely, the snow in the middle of the road comes into view too late as I go straight into a mound. My bike loses traction and goes sideways, my right shoulder slams into the pavement.

I start laughing. The dark thoughts immediately get transmuted into light—I see, I see! The ambulance comes. The EMT asks me if I want pain meds. I refuse. I want to feel the pain, I want it to be my penance.

I'm wearing my favorite black shirt, but the doctor wants to cut it to get to the clavicle, which is clearly broken. A selfie sent to Earth Girl is my way of saying, "Please help, don't you care enough now? I have no one else." She doesn't care, doesn't budge at the cry for help, and tells me to take a taxi home. The cab driver plays a quiz game and if I can get answers right, I get the ride free—I get a few right but don't know that AC/DC is Australian.

The year of the Horse ends. With it ends all of the misfortune of that year. What's beautiful is the transformation of misfortune into fortune, of dark into light. Beauty and pain mix together as medications numb me to sleep.

Under the Moonlight

Before I broke my clavicle, I walked out of an informative rehearsal to auditions. A Delhi girl with moonlight skin—an aberrant white sheep of her family—starts matching my stride to my car and making conversation. Inside, I wonder who she is and why she is still talking to me, but outside I project charm and suffer her gladly.

We notice the moon is full together. She takes notice of everything with her peacock tattoo. When I tell her my name is Arthur Freeman, she doesn't believe me.

"Fate's a much better author than me," I confess in response.

Her nickname is Sun—"like the great ball of fire"—and she is the emanation of turning madness into magic. She mentions the last time she did this under the moon with an audition, she got the part, so she wonders if her luck will take the same pattern.

We both get cast as members of the Chorus in a modern version of the Greek tragedy of *Antigone*.

Picking up a Fallen One

The day of my surgery also happens to be the first day of rehearsal that I can make. My father and stepmother drive down to shuttle me to the hospital and post-anesthesia haze back to my place. I know they won't sleep on my futon and will try to make the return trip to Midlothian in one day, so I assure them that Earth Girl would take care of me for the rest of the day.

I hadn't exactly asked Earth Girl for this blessing. To me, this fell under the category of "basic human kindness," given the circumstances. Earth Girl sees it differently. We have a history of co-existing peacefully and it's not like I'm asking for her full attention, so I feel confused. I offer to go to rehearsal to give her space to do as she pleases and perhaps calm down.

She drives me to NC State, whose mascot is the Wolfpack, so it's no surprise that the first male I get close to will be called Wolf. This has more to do with his own animal qualities and spirit than the mascot, but the synchronicity is hard to ignore. I enter the rehearsal hall and our wonderful Triple Pisces (her words not mine) director takes one look at me and asks in more polite language, "What is up with your energy?" I tell her of my surgery—yes I clarify, it was earlier today—and she politely kicks me out of rehearsal to go rest and stop being crazy. She sends Wolf on this task, whom I meet for the first time.

I climb into his BMW convertible—Ulva (may she rest in peace)—and he asks me where to go. At this point, I could theoretically go home to my dark castle instead of testing my luck with Earth Girl, but I don't want to be alone nor do I trust strangers with knowing where I live. She also lives closer to campus for what it's worth.

We don't get very far. At the corner of Morill Dr. and Western Blvd, noxious car fumes overwhelm me, and I leap out of Wolf's car—getting on all fours on the chilly sidewalk next to the road. (To this day, the story is contested whether I vomited or not—I know I did not; I needed some air.) Wolf drives me to the parking lot where I get out at a vague spot to also protect Earth Girl's privacy. He wishes me well with great concern in his eyes (and also seeing right through the fact that I didn't direct him to my own home) and that is the murky beginning of a real friendship.

Earth Girl is still not pleased to see me, as I didn't give her much space or time. I take a break to call my mother; we talk for a long time and that's when I learn how acutely the energy of another person can affect one's body. I don't know if it's my relationship with my mother or that her love grounds me back into my body, which is currently riddled with painkillers and anesthesia. I go outside into the bushes in such a flurry that Earth Girl comes after me and watches me vomit. As if a switch was flipped, her entire demeanor changes. Perhaps it was the verifiable, tangible, earthly expression of pain that was needed to reach her, but she began to treat me with kindness and nurturing feminine energy.

My broken clavicle is used as part of my costume in the play *Antigone*—where we are survivors from a war. I am part of the Chorus. Together, the four of us form the elements. I am Air. Sun is Water. Wolf is Fire, and the fourth member (unnamed for the purpose of this story) is Earth. The companionship and community of theater carries my pained and lonely soul through the separation from Earth Girl.

The wheel turns, and as spring warms, so too does my heart thaw. I have a long way to go, but I'm moving forward now. I fall in love again and break my heart just as quickly, but this isn't the book that will go into such stories, even though Eros can be said to be the truest form of madness indeed!

Burn Away the Stigma

The hot summer of North Carolina beats me down as I canvas door-to-door to save the Parks for the Public Interest Research Group. I raise a lot of money, make a lot of money, and burn out as quickly as the love I mentioned. Walking the trails near my apartment, a blue heron startles me into wakefulness. Later on, I am drawn to seeing my first woodpecker. The red stripe on its head captures me. When I'm looking for a massage therapist later that weekend, there's a woman who is the spitting image of a woodpecker! Her hair is dyed only at the top, a bright streak of red. We hit it off and she allows me to rent her studio per client for the few I still see.

Between Heaven and Earth[7] stares at me from her shelf. This book deepens the five-element theory in a way that was much more thorough and scientific than the introduction of the Qi Gong workshop in the mountains. The questionnaire reveals I am still very much a Fire type, but this was related more to the directional experience of my energy rather than the actual element of flame—such as that which burns. This book uses the sun to describe the five element phases: the core of the sun being the Water Phase, with Wood Phase being the expansive direction from the core, Fire Phase being the outer limit of the sun, Metal Phase being contraction toward the center, and the Earth Phase being the axis, which is center that all the other Phases balance and rotate around.

This diagram shows how the elements interrelate, with the circle showing how each element generates the next one in line, and with the star lines in the center showing how each element controls the others. This book said your main personality type is actually a three-element relationship: your main Element, Element that influences your main Element, and the Element you influence.

---

[7] Bernfield, H. (1992). *Between Heaven and Earth: A guide to Chinese medicine.* New York, NY: Shambhala.

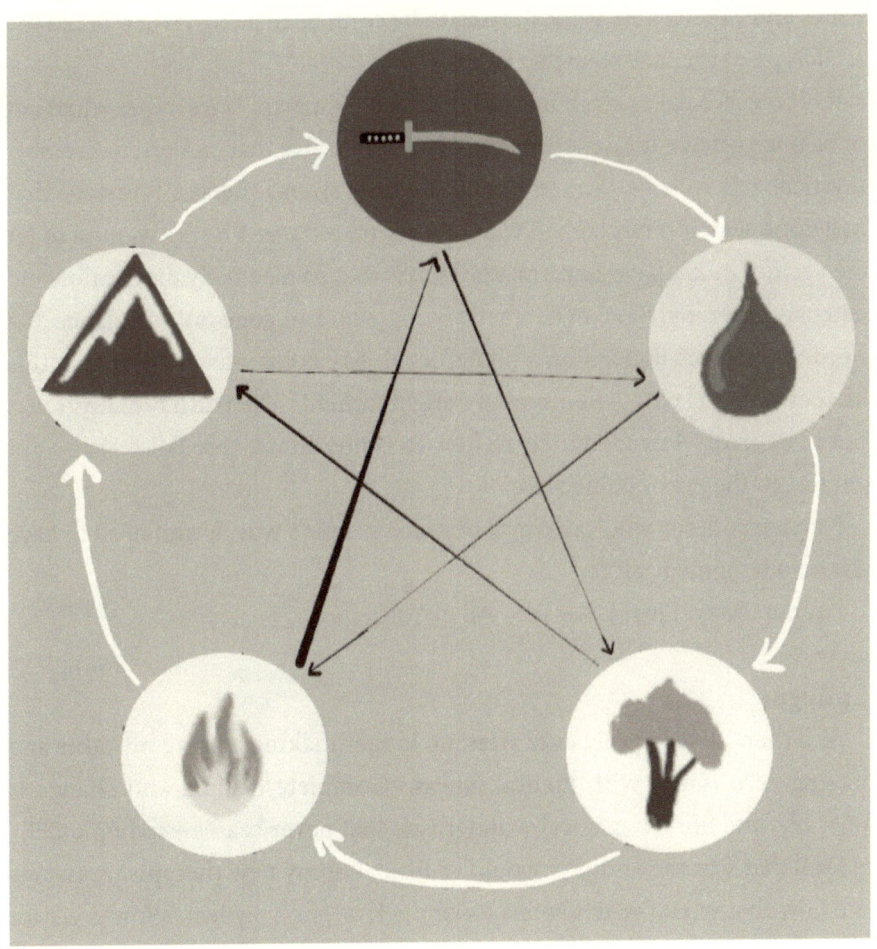

Image Credit by Stuart Freeman 2022

As a Fire-type, I have to be mindful of having a strong Water Element (core) energy which keeps me from expanding into an unstable state (too much Fire). This book helped me understand that my Fire had been very low for a very long time, which meant there was nothing to keep my Metal energy in balance. My Metal energy was overactive, leading to my dry skin, perpetual sadness, and rigid discipline that choked the joy out of life. A lot of my health issues and experiences were starting to be confirmed as real when I read the archetype of the Fire element: Wizard.

It hit me as hard as black ink on paper can hit a man: "Fire-types when out of balance often experience manic, expanded states that can often resemble mystical experiences." So clearly put. So little stigma. I was a Fire-type that had gone way too far, blazed way too hot on a flame I never wanted to let die again. I didn't have some mental illness that needed daily medication and extensive therapy; I am an energetic being who had gone out of balance and needed to be rebalanced on a higher level. My error was in confusing this bliss and "high" with some sort of enlightenment. The truth remains I was out of control—I needed to learn how to center in my core (Water) and not get lost in the joy of being alive.

I am a wanderer who can travel between people's worlds and need to have my own to come back to.

I'm not crazy. I just Love You. All of You.

Epilogue

And then I live happily ever after, no longer making glaring mistakes and having zero issues with mental illness. Complete healing and change is possible, and life is a magical wonder ride that never ceases—so hop on!!!!!

Well that was the ending I would've liked, but my new therapist reassures me how that would've deflated a lot of readers who may feel "Wow great for him, here I am still on three medications struggling through each day" or something.

If you're one of those readers, first of all, reach out to me. Find my Youtube channel, Healcyon, where I have plenty of content to help you make small changes in your thinking and lifestyle. I believe in you, in the depths of your beauty and power, that you can uncover! Second of all, know that isn't how the story ends. The rest of this book includes more misadventures in Japan, Peru, and China, and how I pursued even more dangerous ends to make sure that I was not living a life of fear. My brushes with the mental health system continue as I learn more about what it means to live with respect to the reality of being bipolar.

Second of all, my journey isn't quite finished. As determined and confident as I was to never visit a mental hospital again, we'll see how the limits of my soul are challenged in the following chapters!

7

Dao of Adventure

A Path with Heart

We left off in the summer, right before finding a beautiful clear path and practice that stabilizes my mind.

As 2015 (a Wood Goat year) continues, I appreciate the Shamanic path for its ceremonies, rituals, and ability to journey for all sorts of spiritual purposes. However, after reading the *Secret of the Golden Flower* by Osho, I am able to come full circle back to Qi Gong. Qi Gong is a Taoist practice based on those arts! It looks incredibly silly in retrospect, but I assure you, dear reader, that at the beginning of this book, way back in Asheville, I had made no mental connection between Qi Gong and Taoism. My excuse is that it was taught in a very scientific way, with some new age references to "Source or God" thrown in there to appeal to Westerners. Taoism was never mentioned, but this is a weak excuse because of course all the arts of Qi and Chinese Elements are related to or are rooted in Taoist philosophy! Even the most casual of practitioners or students knows that! The perhaps more accurate reflection as to how I missed the connection was that I was not yet ready to see it. Thankfully, I was guided to Osho's book at the appropriate time, who made it quite clear and blatant to me about the internal arts based on Taoism.

After practicing the methods described in the book, I had a very vivid dream and felt they had accomplished their purpose. I know having a live teacher is preferred, so I began my search! Summer was consumed by seeking a daily spiritual practice, as well as some impromptu getting together with either Sun or Wolf sprinkled in there. Throughout summer break, I researched a bunch of different traditions of Qi Gong to get involved with. Well, research is a strong word. I scroll through a couple threads on the Daoist forum "DaoBums," where people with my particular search had already asked pertinent questions.

My personality has a paradoxical problem of liking a wide array of things, in addition to taking what I get into seriously enough to dedicate myself to it. The sheer number of lineages and practices of Qi Gong (not to mention energy work from other spiritual traditions!) makes analytical thought useless, so I go with my trusty "follow my heart" way and my infatuation with the name "Stillness-Movement" and all the balance it promises. I set off on a road trip adventure to Terre Haute, Indiana to experience an in-person workshop with Grandmaster Michael Lomax. No, he's not Chinese, but what does that matter? What's real is real. He trained under a legend in China if you are concerned with such things anyhow.

I could describe the magic and power of the clinical Qi Gong and all we did that weekend. The purpose of this book is not to try to convince or argue for the reality of mystical powers. However, I'd be doing my fellow "mental patients" a disservice if I did not assure you that what you experienced in altered states cannot be completely swept away under the rug of illusion or madness. Even after all my experience with madness, I remained skeptical at the mere thought you could "project q'" (emit it from your hands) and have it have an impact on a client without actual contact. Suffice to say what I felt and saw was too real to ignore and that was sufficient for me. Did I mention Michael also trained under a Cherokee medicine man and had added many Shamanic elements to the lineage?

Here it was, the convergence of my own paths and interests. Still, my relationship with commitment is rocky, and I returned home indecisive and anxious about choices and decisions.

Magic of Three—Before I left for that trip, I was doing laundry old school style outside the ES King Village Apartments. On a laundry line was a preying mantis; I have never seen one before in the flesh. On the way to Terre Haute, I stopped on the side of the road to pee in the woods. I came out of the tall brush with a preying mantis on my solar plexus. Finally when I started my fall semester, I found a preying mantis had climbed all the way up to perch on the side mirror of my motorcycle. Spirit had my attention, but what's the message?

I couldn't use my book *Animal Speak*, which is my go-to for symbolism of nature. I had lent it to the therapist I was renting a room from, but when she returned it to me, I sat down right there to open to my destiny:

Praying Mantis (yes dear reader, in case you were blowing your circuits; my typos were intentional. It was not until I saw this entry I realized how it was actually spelled. Symbolic in all the ways)—**Power of Stillness.** Lightning bolts went down my spine! Stillness, as in Stillness-Movement Neigong! I called Michael right then, and he showcased his Heyoka abilities by taking the opposite cadence of my slightly manic-speaking pace.

"How ya doin' Arthur?" he drawled. I told him I was ready to sign up to the clinical Qi Gong certification program right then and there. Having a daily practice and doing it are different matters, but this is where my seriousness came in handy. Michael asked as a show of good faith to practice Stillness-Movement for a hundred days and then decide by the end whether it was worth it to continue. A short year ago, I could barely stand five minutes of meditation, and now Michael was asking one hour each day! I struggled with my mind and its constant assertions that "You might've put the timer on silent! What if it never goes off? Open your eyes! Check!" and used my pride to stay with it until the end of the hour. It got easier as the months went by.

Floating Bridge to the East

In September I see a praying mantis, a large female one, with a broken leg outside of my classes. Curiously the mantis was nibbling on her own leg! The girl of my dreams looks at this as well. I notice her gaze and and my attention blinks back and forth between the mantis and her, who we'll call Lotus. Some powerful synchronicity is afoot, but I don't actually even talk to her until a literal hurricane (Joaquin) of synchronicities had us together outside of class in October. She is Japanese, which adds weight to the synchronicity because I am scheduled to study abroad in Japan in 2016.

Born to Japanese parents and growing up both in Osaka and the US, Lotus is a unique blend of Japanese perseverance, patience, appreciation for nature, and Stillness combined with American individuality, self-sufficiency, and relentless work ethic. Unsurprisingly, she is a Gemini and embodies a beautiful paradox. The first time I invited her over I pulled a Tarot card for us and it said "Reunion." We both felt like we had known each other for much longer than this lifetime. I savored the Miracle that was our coming together for a few months. I fell in Love with the way she would eat toast, taking each bite like a delicate kiss. I fell in love with how she would sneak behind my back to wash the dishes. We would have a playful competition over who could help the other more.

Our connection is smooth and easy, yet it falls into confusion because of the unclear status of my dynamic with Sun. I was made painfully unaware how difficult it is to manage connections, how to have healthy boundaries, and how poor I am at conflict. Surely all of this ties in with my poor emotional regulation and mental condition. I escape all that confusion to take a whole continent and Pacific Ocean's worth of Space. Yet with all that Space came the challenges of being in a new land with no support system or familiarity.

I go on to have wonderful adventures in Japan, some solo and some with Lotus (who joins me after her Spring semester in NC finishes), which is worthy of a short story all its own! I am remiss to not include it here in its entirety because of the depth of Magic that I experienced in the mountains of Japan and in the kindness of their people. Indeed, I experienced the lows and struggles of mental health being far removed from all that I had called home and all the systems I had used to stabilize myself.

You Do Not Suffer Alone

Others were not as lucky. On one Friday night, I slid back into my reclusive ways and turned down an offer to go drinking in downtown Osaka. In the morning, I get up too quickly from my desk and spill water all over a Fox drawing I had colored in. It feels like a terrible omen, which my mind jumps to draw dots between that and my turbulent long-distance connection with Lotus. I am in a funk all day, until a fellow study abroad student calls me that evening.

A fellow exchange student, Tommy, jumped in front of a train Friday night and took his own life.

I feel shaken deep down. My unique mix of arrogance and self-hatred jumps to the conclusion that if I had gone with them Friday night, I would've known—sensed—his inner turmoil. Pain recognizes pain. I wasn't that close to Tommy, but the death reverberates throughout the student body.

The teacher in the first class on Monday asks us to say a few words about Tommy. I am unable to speak with the torrent of emotion coming through me. I get up—slamming my chair back—and storm out the door after proclaiming "you want to know what Tommy meant to me? He was someone I had the chance to help, to be there for. And I didn't." Overwhelmed is an understatement. This is all too much. I failed him...

I go on a walk to my go-to nature spot—the waterfalls of Nigawa behind the school. I impulsively take up a short stick on the walk through the woods. My mind makes that stick out to be Tommy. At the edge of the cliff, across from the waterfall, I brood and feel the churning of emotions like the waterfall: grief, loss, heartache, shock, rage. In an act of desperation, I decide that somehow jumping from the rock I was perched on to a dry rock on top of the waterfall would psychopomp Tommy's soul to the "other side." In one motion, I get up to leap across—not wanting to hesitate or overthink the danger of my attempt—and my legs give way! The wracking pain of grief unsteadies me. I lose my balance.

I fall...

down...

...the waterfall.

My back hits the water. My pain is lifted up by angels. A quick (and relatively painless) transmutation compared to the motorcycle crash in 2015. I hear them singing "You Raise Me Up" and I start laughing. A miracle that I survive and did not land on the rocks below the surface. A miracle the community did not suffer two tragic events in such a short time.

At the memorial service, we are all somber and grieving in our own way. His mother flew out from Washington State to be present and experience the worst news a parent can get. Yet, over midway through the service, she exclaims—"Enough with the sad music already!!!" She knew Tommy wouldn't want us crying and moping all over. It was time to lighten the mood and soberly accept the reality of what is.

[Since that time, I took a Shamanic workshop on psychopomp and how to properly assist souls in crossing over. I am happy to report that I was able to visit the train station where Tommy died and led his soul to the gates beyond in the Upper World. I say this for the people reading this that knew him and care for his Soul. For others, whether this was all in my imagination or not, do not concern yourself. Again, this is not a book to prove Shamanic realities.]

Abridged Adventures

More could be said about Japan—so much more! After graduation, I climbed all three of the Holy Mountains [Haku-san, Tate-yama, and Fuji-san in that order] in one week by the grace of Spirit and thanks to all those who helped me get where I needed to go. One family even interrupted their afternoon drive to take me back up to Haku-san, and then circle back around to pick me up after I retrieved a necklace I lost! I faced loneliness, friendship, and hardship. The ascent of Fuji-san was shrouded in rain and mist. Lotus herself got a spell of altitude sickness, so we retired to one of the mountain shelters for a few hours before making the final climb past the clouds. The sunrise greeted Lotus and I in an eternal moment of beauty. The Climb is what makes the Peak worth it.

I took with me the depth of Service and Harmony of the beautiful people I crossed paths with and I know it will always be in my Heart. That and I finally was able to put the ghost of my marriage to rest on an island north of Hokkaido, which left me feeling more clear and light than ever before. It took fasting for 6 days on only water and some electrolytes. Attachments really can be that Deep, so don't underestimate how long it takes to let go of things… (perhaps again I am more stubborn than the average bear!) As always, be gentle and patient with yourself. Gentle and Patient.

It's just Life

Yet, I crash back into my fall semester literally the day after I return from Japan in 2016, not having any sense for what the word "integration" means. I struggle through my relationships where my fractured self continually hurts all those around me. Part of the bipolar life is not having a healthy "ego" or personality. I face the reality of that as I am pulled in many directions at once. The one person who refused to pull on me emotionally was my Lotus, who diligently tries to teach me the difference between actual flow and going along with the demands and desires of others. In other words, she helps me forge an actual backbone much at her expense. In her words, "She kicked my ass," and it badly needed it.

My struggles with balancing spirituality (which was the antidote to all my problems of course!) and living in this world at the time are summed up best by these two anecdotes from my senior year:

I had been making a terrible habit of putting Lotus last on the priority list, simply because my priority list was dictated by whose emotions were the loudest and whose needs begged for attention. I agreed to meet up with Lotus at a talk named "Spiritual Escapism" being held at NC State.

Yet, I arrive at Pullen Park with the wind blowing the leaves all about me, Sun, and her friend Sol. We had done a cool group meditation together, and now it was time for me to head to the talk. A gravity seems to hold me in place as I find myself unable to simply say, "I'm going to this talk, goodbye." The interaction continues to get dragged out more and more, and I don't walk away. I don't use the word "gravity" lightly. Like the sun, Sun has a pull on me that is difficult to describe.

Later on, Lotus forgives me too easily and says, "That talk was *for you*," drawing out the last words to emphasize how guilty I am of that escapism. The words settle in my chest as one more regret.

One more friend is worth mentioning whom I got really close to during our time together in Japan. I'll call her Voice, who seemed able to see right through me and analyze me with precise language. She is the one who called me about Tommy's suicide. Suffice to say, it was a frighteningly accurate combination when she and Lotus discussed me. "It's like he thinks caring for people is a bad thing, so he adamantly refuses to show that he does," Voice mused. Apparently, I was that transparent to her powers of observation during our weekly walk and talks home from the campus in Nishinomiya.

When I run into Voice [of Reason] at NC State's Entrepalooza event while she was working a catering job, I ask her cryptically, "So what's going on with you?" with the meaning "It's no mistake we've crossed paths today, so what do you really need?"

She responded, "You act like everything's written in the stars... It's just Life."

8

Jungle of the Soul

The Power of Groups and Dreams

My senior year at NC State, I really took advantage of the free counseling that is offered to all students. I joined group therapy in the fall and the spring, and was fortunate enough to be placed with the graduate students due to my status as a non-traditional student. The larger bandwidth of a group adds for an accelerated healing process, not to mention all the potential clashes, triggers, and informative interactions that can come up.

In my first group, I received very quickly the feedback that I wasn't really "participating"—that I showed up for the group as a sort of sage or philosopher, only to give advice or to go into lengthy stories to illustrate points. My old belief from childhood that I was an outcast and outsider, and that my role was to use that perspective to share insights came up. My main lesson was that I was using that role to avoid vulnerability, and what it takes to show up on the same playing field as everyone else.

The second group's highlight was the immediate conflict with the person across from me. Always note who you are sitting across from in a circle, as they likely reflect some opposite polarity of your awareness. This woman couldn't stand me in fundamental ways. What infuriated her the most was that my mere existence as an empath offended her. Said another way, my ability to feel what others were feeling and understand them (perhaps not know them fully—of course not) based on very little time together caused friction between our worldviews. What surprised the therapist was that we continued to keep coming back to the group and worked through our conflict, until a cathartic last session in which some of my past was able to help her process her own more clearly.

The final introduction to group work goes by the quite apt name of "Circling." Dream Circling to be precise, an intro to which Lotus and I attended. We all sat in a circle and I got to share a dream of mine, as I have always been a dreamer. I simply never knew what to do with dreams unless I had a strong intuition about what it was telling me. Until this circle, dreams had always been like a memory or series of images sometimes with a little emotion. When I shared the dream into the circle, it came alive and I could actually feel, both emotionally and sensually, the whole story unfolding! Everyone in the circle shared what they felt experiencing the dream (as if it were their own), and it was startling the level of insights and how much of my inner/outer life was reflected in the short dream. It made a deep impression on me, and I've continued with Dream Circling to the present day.

Return to the Land of Heart

This next story arc begins in Brasil, the start of a three-month-long adventure that is my graduation present in 2017. Despite all the external awesomeness that implies, my inner emotional state continues to be a stormy mess. One can think of mental illness as sort of inverse meditation. People often take up meditation to be able to find happiness despite external circumstances. Mental illness often looks like being miserable despite wonderful external circumstances.

I know I missed Brasil as soon as we arrived at the airport on Ilha do Governador. Spontaneously, we are approached by a man who, in true *jeitinho* fashion, is making a living doing currency exchange at a great rate. We do this off-the-books exchange, eat some delicious stroganoff (pronounced in portuguese: su-tro-ga-naw-fee), and I reunite with our beloved heroine Kelly:

Perhaps I have not done the Brazilian way of life justice. I have a sudden impulse to be an ambassador (being half-Northern European) between these two cultures. *Jeitinho* is a term that I have written a blog about, but the short version is that it refers to the easygoing attitude, the "it'll work out somehow" mindset with which Brazilians approach many things.

Calmness is Always Needed

We take a day-trip to Barra da Tijuca, a scenic beach that grants scenic views of Rio in the distance. After finding a nice spot and settling in, my brother displays how wonderful it is to be a Leo. He's eating some of the food we brought, and I watch as he methodically makes a cracker ham and cheese sandwich. Then I watch as he makes and eats every last one we had packed. One after the other. I can't help but admire his single-minded focus! After my mother's anger wakes him up to what he's done, he walks over and apologizes to each of us in a solemn manner, as if he had wronged the world itself!

In the ocean, I'm learning to surrender to the waves that I did nothing but fight as a child. Not fight in anger, but always playfully! Yet, the struggle was real and the symbolism of enjoying the punishing waves that I threw myself at time and time again is not lost on me...

Here in Brasil, the waves are not playing either. My cousin and I are in the waves, and a riptide begins to pull us out farther from shore. The atmosphere shifts and the danger is very real. I have always been blessed in these times with my own single-minded focus; all else is tuned out and the only reality is bringing her back to safety. Calmness breeds calmness. My concentration seems to ease the panic that was setting in as she holds on to me. Slowly but surely, making use of the rhythm of the waves, we make it back to dry land.

I'm left to wonder at the contrast between my usual inner turmoil and the perfect calm I feel when faced with a real situation. Is it the reverse for most others? Do they enjoy peace day to day and then when things get serious, they panic and get overwhelmed? Surely it is not so simple ... yet the mere thought makes my daily struggle bearable if it prepares me to be centered when it counts.

Celebrate Yourself

One of my cousins is getting married. I borrow some nice clothes and take a rare selfie that I put on Instagram. Most of my photos and philosophy of social media are focused on showcasing beautiful places and experiences. What do *I* have to do with it?

Yet Lotus comments that it's her favorite photo yet and explains, "It's a photo of you, celebrating you!"

What a thought... celebrating me? It has taken me much longer to integrate this type of wisdom, and I am far from the self-fulfilling ideal! Here's hoping this seed planted takes root in you, dear reader, and that you see yourself as a unique gift to the world worth celebrating.

Sitio

I share my heart pain with Lotus, a pain that I don't quite understand, and she immediately suggests that I go lie down in a clear river! Sensing the shamanic wisdom that she naturally embodies, I find my chance sooner than I could've hoped for.

I'm at a retreat outside Rio, a place where my cousins and their friends from church go at times to connect with nature, God, and themselves. I wander off after we make it to the river to cleanse by myself and do some Qi Gong. Pain leaves my body as the beauty and power of nature moves me. The magic in nature cannot be disputed! Find what the forests, rivers, parks, stones or even the trees near your house have to offer you, dear reader. In time, they will reveal much to those willing to listen.

Throughout the day, I notice Jaguar and Puma symbols, which I vaguely remember has something to do with Jesus Christ. At night, the energy in the air is tense. Everyone seems to be triggering each other and not getting along. What breaks me is when my cousin says, "I just want this to be over and to go home!" Her frustration touches some tender part of me; in my heart, I want people to enjoy and feel the beauty of what is right here! For her to want to fast forward? To miss out on it all? Heartbreaking!

So, I stand up in front of a group of Brazilians, with Lucas being my excellent translator. Moved by some unseen force, I feel called to share my story. I've always felt this sort of thing is egoic as hell (do you perhaps understand part of why it's taken so long to finish writing this book?), but the call is stronger tonight. I share my experiences of the mental hospital, the ones most fresh and real, and a few of them are moved to tears. The story reaches a climax, and the effect I wanted to have—to get them to *feel* this moment, to not miss out on ever-present Love—comes out in their eyes. The atmosphere shifts, and we all *remember* why we are here.

To love each other.

Love pours into me through their eyes, and I sleep deeply that night. The profound sense of a traumatic and painful experience being of use to others ... well, it makes it all a great deal easier to accept.

I returned from Sitio to read an e-mail letter from Lotus titled "Letting Go." She shares her growth, her sorrow, her pain, and her genuine wishes for me moving forward. Her letter offers unconditional love and true friendship. "Enjoy Peru!" she finishes.

Pain and desperation wash through me as I feel her pulling away from me. Despite all the beauty in the letter, the part about never being able to be in a romantic relationship with me again is a spike in old wounds. Some part of me wants to love her as much as I've been able to with others this trip. To have her be with a more relaxed and open version of myself. I let the Bible fall open to a page of the Divine's choosing and see the line, "Wait for God, he brings Courage."

Unfortunately, I am impatient as hell.

Outcast Aside

The perfect storm is brewing, yet I trust the winds all the same. I spend my last days in Brasil in leisure with my family, savoring the moments with my cousins that I can. I promise Lotus I won't reach out until she does, but she continues to be on my mind and I struggle to distract myself with webnovels. I leave my cousins with my laptop because technology is ridiculously expensive in Brasil. (My cousins often fly to America with discounted airline employee ticket rates in order to buy new phones/computers). With a lighter physical burden, I take flight to Lima. I spend a few hours during my layover touring the city. I finally arrive at my final destination in time to sleep.

During my first day in Peru, I find myself in Iquitos where three Great Rivers (Amazon, Nanay, and Itaya) meet. After waking, I convert all of my dollars into soles. I find some free tourist information. The lady offers two paths: a long walk to see a lot of wildlife or a boat ride to a butterfly garden.

I chose the *mariposas* (or *borboletas*) and found it interesting that animal names differ so wildly from Spanish to Portuguese. I secure my cell phone in a zippered pocket before taking a bumpy motor car ride down to the river port. The driver is very friendly with me and even gives me his number to ensure repeat business on my return trip. My first brush with the rivers connected to the Amazon. The twenty-minute boat ride is noisy yet all the passengers stay silent. I arrive at the port that connects to the butterfly garden.

Instead of following the main road, I use my broken Spanish to zig and zag through the brush jungle where dirt paths abound. I eventually find my way to the garden where Nick, the English speaking volunteer/savior, greets me and guides me through the reserve. Originally only a butterfly garden, the fateful arrival of an abandoned baby jaguar in a crate led the garden to evolve into a refuge for all sorts of rescued animals. Their newest arrivals are a couple of monkey brothers who could be seen wrestling with each other at various places outside the mesh net as we walk through the garden.

The blue morphos and tiger butterflies stand out starkly to my eyes. The owl butterfly who camouflaged with its golden eye in plain sight is also quite attractive. Then I run into these little guys:

Ocelot brothers came next. They lounge in a relaxed way that reminds me that I am here to take it easy. My only responsibility is to enjoy myself and explore these worlds. My mind learns that toucans can die of starvation in as little as six hours without food and the slowness of anteaters and how they could survive in the same jungle as jaguars.

Today, that baby jaguar is an adult by the name of Pedro. He graces me with his presence, and we share a long gaze. Jaguars sleep for seventeen hours a day on average so for him to be awake during my brief time at the center is quite the blessing.

Nick is a kindred spirit and human-animal at the center. He offers me a lot of advice in wandering around Cusco. I admire his wanderer lifestyle and how he works/studies/volunteers his way around the planet to experience all the diverse richness of our world. We exchange instagram information and bid farewell.

I wander around the island after having a bit to eat. I pass some fences that probably are a boundary of some sort, but the road itself is open, and I go deeper into the jungle along wooden walkways. I make it to what looks like a giant fishery as well as a farm of some sorts. A man in a hammock startles awake at my approach and inquires about my trespassing. I play my ignorance card well (there really weren't any glaring signs after all?) and tell him about my travels. His mood softens immediately. He shares that he was on his way to South Africa when he got delayed due to "mysterious bureaucracy," while also mentioning how he only stays at this property of his about 1-2 weeks out of the year. He is a Floridian college professor after all and a busy man.

I catch his drift that this is a special and synchronistic meeting, but he further surprises me by sharing how rare it is to meet "good people." He offers me a stay at his estate should I ever need down time or to enjoy the healing presence of the jungle. He has local people he employs as one of his "good works," and says that I can tip them for cooking and cleaning but otherwise it would be free to stay for me. Stunned, I receive his email address and make my return trip to the river boat.

Back on the Iquitos side, I find my motor car driver taking a nap. He's a bit upset that I did not call him or return by my predicted time! He drives me back to the hotel where I am to meet my fellow explorers of the Great Unknown. As fate always has it, I meet a man from a different part of North Carolina and one from Georgia. What an incredibly small and vast world we live in!

The Stage is Set

My morning starts off with breakfast and Scott from Georgia. While we are talking of the mysteries and various spiritual topics, I overhear two female shamans in training. They seem to be at the cusp where they realize that they can connect and hold space without drinking Ayahuasca (the sacred drink that Shamans of this region use to reach altered states of consciousness and do their work). They now realize that the Mother is always with them.

When we get up to leave the restaurant, I am compelled to say something to them.

"Thank you for all that you do; it is incredibly beautiful and rich work to hold space for others."

Their response is positive and they are left feeling an angelic start to their day! Next, I meet Kinga from Sydney, who thaws a bit after some conversation. John from Spain likes my sunglasses and he thought I was sporting a new style. That style being that it only rests on one ear since the other half of the frame had broken off.

A fitting look to match how I feel like everything I touch breaks.

To round out my first group of people is Greg, who has a pleasant and amiable energy, and Vlad from Canada. We all clamber into a van to make the trek deeper into the jungle, only stopping for a nice meal where we get to meet Shakira the dog.

On the moto car ride to the port, my phone falls out of my pocket. Lost to the urban sprawl of Iquitos. In my journal, I write:

"I miss most [my photos of] Pedro the Jaguar haha. Real connection with Nature time."

I get the sense the universe is serious about wanting me to disconnect with no backup options to reach out to the outside world...

The boat ride through the Amazon is long, but the sunshine is pleasant and the vibrancy of life is pulsing all around us. The small watercraft is dwarfed by the immense Amazon River. I can't help but wonder at what mysteries travel through the deep waters. Ceremonial sounds and laughter greet us along with wild dancing of the villagers in the afternoon sun.

Meeting New Friends, the Plants of the Jungle

After we are shown around the center and the Maloka (indigenous word for house, here used as the sacred space for ceremonies), I discover my roommates to be Gen from Japan (でもはでしたくない[8] and John from Spain. We eat our first meal off the grid. All the meals here are friendly for the *Dieta* for Mother Ayahuasca. I feel awesome eating simple and clean meals. Oh, the wonders of being provided food and shelter!

In the Maloka, we are introduced to Johnny and Jivan of the Mastes tribe. They begin the ceremony for Nunu. I am allowed to self-administer the powder up the second nostril…. Whoosh! My head clears, my eyes gain vitality, and I feel centered in my third eye. I wake up in the night with arms feeling notably different. They have a relaxed quality to them, flowing with energy that makes them feel more fluid and at ease.

Morning comes. With the sunrise, I am greeted by the distinct feeling that I have arrived back home. I feel as though I have awakened from a long dream and had been living from afar up until now. I don't know what my Soul has been up to, but I'm happy it has returned to me (or that I have returned to it?) here in this magical place by the river.

Kambo is my next medicine ally, which happens to be a poison administered after burning a wound into my arm. I am overcome by a hot flushing feeling rather quickly—I vomit (from now on, I learn to amicably refer to this as "purging") into my orange plastic bucket. Feeling a lot cleaner, I have lunch and deep conversations with an Australian and a European. "You'd be surprised at how much opening up to others is part of the process," we are advised. I am also warned at lunch not to eat white rice before an Ayahuasca ceremony, but I've always thought that it is digested quickly and I dig in.

While opening up to my fellow travelers, I am inevitably met with the incredulous glances of "You have never tried [hallucinogens] before? Really, this will be your first time?" I never thought of them as something to "try," and the mere thought of them always terrified me. Funny destiny would lead me to this experience in its own mysterious way… Truth be told, it was *because* I am terrified of them that I choose to walk this path to the hidden depths of the Amazon.

In the afternoon, our first voyage into the jungle takes us to "monkey island"

---

[8] However, he doesn't want to talk in Japanese [with me]

where we ride around on our boat and see monkeys swinging and smiling through the trees. I see loads of fish—and also kingfishers—and the beauty moves me from head to toe.

The evening settles into the jungle air like a blanket. We have our peaceful hour of reflection and silence to prepare for Ayahuasca. I do my Stillness sitting practice and focus on facing the fear that I came to work on: madness. I felt compelled to embark on this journey on the off-chance that all the drama I'd been causing in my life, all the rushing around to change constantly, and all the obsession with esoteric symbolism was simply a way to avoid losing my mind again. I can't help but wonder if I merely didn't have the courage to face and live that new way of life—that intensity of awakeness after the first manic episode. I fear that I diverted myself into exploring all sorts of "side paths" that the Dao De Jing mentions. I am about to find out.

The *maloka* is lit by candles as the shamans sit in a row in the center. We are called in groups of threes to take the sacred brew. I drink mine in one gulp before I can think twice and return to my mat lined along the outer ring with the others. Gripped by uncertainty, I let the energy move through me as I lie facedown on my mat and embrace the earth. I sit upright to vomit thoroughly and then lie back down prone to relax. Shifting into a familiar state of awareness, my insight comforts me. "See? This is the state it takes you to. You've been here before. There is nothing to be afraid of." So it turns out "losing control" isn't what I'm afraid of … Ayahuasca teaches me the depth of relaxation—and how the world keeps on spinning without my constant involvement or attention. Relax! Enjoy! The goddess Earth spins on her own time and she has nothing lacking in her—save perhaps the appreciation of those she serves (yet like true mothers, this does nothing to impede her love).

Next, I find myself in the bathroom for some very intense purging. Like I am reaching deep into my intestines to pull up something … white rice! I laugh out loud at the wisdom I ignored and that's when I begin to see colors—red,blue, and green as the foundational pixels of this whole reality. Yet, I am not here to speak fully and candidly—for this is not a book about Ayahuasca or the experiences I had with her. Indeed there are mystical states and places that even the best poets aspire to describe, but one must venture for themselves to those lands.

The next day we process our experience with Shaman Willard and do some yoga to help "wring that last bit out of the towel" as a fellow participant describes it. A near akin metaphor was used by Earth Girl many moons prior when she described why she did mushrooms from time to time. Best way I can describe it in my own terms is a "psychic cleanse."

I peruse a tome on astrology, the *Secret Language of Destiny*, which outlines the "path in life" that shows up in our charts. The magic hits me like a gong, as my path is named the **Way of Freedom**! I take the advice that I need to learn to enjoy shattering my self-limiting beliefs and mindset through guts and determination. Shattering! I am filled with rage at all the ways I had taken my stuckness to be "law" and obedience to things. For a path is not a straight road but an ever flowing see-saw between comfort and expansion. My comfort zone being none other than authority, dogma, and systemized rules! I take my feelings to the retreat's punching bag. With each balled fist, I seek to blow through all the endless tape I had suffocated my heart in. Doing what was right? Pah! I am no more than a coward terrified of the boundless freedom of the unknown.

Real Fears

My second Ayahuasca ceremony leaves me with a deep insight: my real fear is not of madness, but of being authentically myself. Of being seen. Of the harsh gaze of others at my fragile and timid heart! I relax until I purge. Then—sitting upright—my vision begins to dissolve into another place—

Pain shoots through the *maloka* as lightning, when a fellow participant (let's call him Marq) screams "HELP!" He's lost and afraid. I snap back to the maloka and focus my attention on him. He is taken out by the staff behind the bathroom where I follow.

"It's going to be one of those nights," says Dolan. "Find your center," he advises me.

I feel like I'm in the hospital again, I feel like I'm with another patient who cannot be reached—I want to bring Marq back to himself, to this place. Yet there is nothing for me to do; it is not *my place* to do anything. "He's in good hands," a woman soothes. I pick up my fan and begin to wave it at myself, which helps me stay present. The conviction in my heart becomes the shape of "if Marq doesn't know where he is, I'll know where I am. I'll be right here, I'll be the missing piece of this puzzle!"

I look down at my business card to keep myself centered, for—and this is the best part—I had chosen for my subtitle "A Way of Freedom " to describe Healcyon! Synchronicities abound! One always knows their pathbooks are not required in the slightest.

Yet Marq howls in the distance, and his pain still reaches me. I begin to have regrets because I saw him go up to drink, *saw him*, after listening to him earlier in the day say, "I don't think I'll drink tonight." I see the patterns as they unfolded, at how his belongings were all over the place when I arrived and all that symbolized he was at the edge of going too far.

Looking down at my card, I remember my full name and begin to relax. This happens at the same time that Marq is returned to the circle, and I feel all is in its place. The *icaros* start, and Willard sings my soul clean. I sit down and refuse to lie down during this session, thinking, *I will not sleep through life.*

Rei Arturo

As we process the night before around breakfast, a girl from LA remarks with fear in her voice, "I ... feel like I'm still tripping. I haven't come back yet." I tell her to trust the process, cliché as it is, and not give in to fear. During the circle, she shares her realization that "Ayahuasca is a *hell of a drug* and really dangerous." The facilitators stop her to say, "You will never hear any of us call her a drug. She is medicine." Perspective is important, but who can say who is right? We are taught she is called the "Vine of Light," even though in the following years I learned that it can be translated as Aya-Huasca or "Road to Death." (Huascar is the Guardian of the Underworld in Q'ero Shamanism, and shouldn't I have remembered that from New York?)

After that, there is a bit of a market set up in the *maloka* with all sorts of Ayahuasca-inspired works of art. I began to talk to Odirico, an excellent salesman. He strokes my ego by calling me "Rei Arturo" upon learning my name. They teach me that jaguar is the king of his jungle, and I am drawn to buying a wall hanging from Odirico that helps me connect with Ayahuasca. I have enjoyed bringing back portals from overseas over the years. Today, I take time to read *You are a Badass* to allow some self-love and recognition into my heart. I reflect on what it means to be me ... to be a king. The quote that comes to my mind is from Alexander the Great in the anime *Fate/Zero:* "A king is one who laughs the hardest."[9] I always admired him, yet it is not without irony that Alexander shows pity to King Arthur (Saber, a woman) in that show. As her way of kingship is that of a martyr ... Perhaps my admiration comes from my poor attempts to find Alexander's regal enjoyment within myself.

Yet, as I am reading *You Are a Badass* by Jen Sincero, I am not without trying to change my habitual ways of thinking! I write this brain-rewiring exercise:

I say Yes to my adventure. I am willing to put work in to change my life. I say thank you to all that comes, grace. I put myself first, no longer acting out scripts to seek others acceptance. I am original, unique and important. I will not give up. I choose Freedom, to enjoy my path. I surround myself with positive people, encouraging, on their paths. I serve those who need help finding their way, Offering Freedom. I am a Badass with an interesting life. I love my life and who I am.

[I'd like to fully acknowledge how easy it is to say those words and to write them down. Living up to them has been a whole other story. I don't want to give the impression that my life suddenly changed after all that! Yet, where else can we start? First, the wise ones tell us, we must have something to aim at. This is key to the magic of living a true life.]

Due to some miscommunications that led to me not getting a ride from the airport, the hosts of the Maloka offered the Sapo ceremony to me free of charge. Sapo is the Portuguese word for "frog," and that's how this resin we were about to inhale is presented to us. We sit in a circle in the daylight of a smaller Maloka and I had the unfortunate position of being fifth. This let me

---

[9] *Fate/Zero.* Directed by Ei Aoki, Ufotable, 2011-2012. *Crunchyroll*, https://www.crunchyroll.com/series/GRJQ04Z3Y/fatezero.
  Series - Streamed

watch the extremely varied reactions to the medicine and gave me some time for anxiety and second thoughts to emerge ... especially when the participant next to me seemed to go through Hell and back only to emerge seconds later and say, "I want everyone to know ... that I won," as drool lapsed from his mouth. I come to think of him in time as "Ice-Man," simply from the way his aura and demeanor impacts me.

Without giving myself time to think twice, I inhale the smoke and within seconds, a wave of energy knocks me over. Wave isn't a strong enough word. An explosion like a shotgun blast kicks me onto my back, as energy courses through my body and moves me around wildly. Next thing I know, my vision is coming back and I'm standing up near the center of the room and the woman facilitator is guiding me to sit back down with her hands. (I learned that I had been fighting the air with various martial arts moves. "Someone's watched too much Dragon Ball Z," I overheard later.)

After the ceremony, I bask in the sunlight, looking out at the river with a mysterious smile on my face. "What the hell did you see?" someone asks. I slowly piece back together my ego personality and mind. Seeing a Hawai'i t-shirt on Scott helps me remember some of my past. Lots of people have visual experiences or want to have them, so what you "see" is an important question. For me, it was all feeling, sensation, and intense awareness. I keep my silence.

Walking to the village, I pass a scene out of a dream—or a nightmare. Hanging from a clothesline are three and only three towels. A Rose. A Peacock. A White Tiger. All inexplicable references to Sun. A feeling of inescapable karma begins to dance on the periphery of my awareness...

On top of all this is yet another Ayahuasca ceremony, the Third One. The full moon is ascending into the sky. In my preparation for the ceremony, I take some protective puffs of "mapacho," a medicine plant I haven't described yet but is tobacco, which has a strong masculine presence that is versatile and "can do anything you set your intent with it to do." A little unnerved deep down by Marq's experience from the previous night, I smoke some in addition to my usual ritual of Stillness and preparation. My intent for this ceremony is to clear trauma, center me, and power.

The experience is one of relaxation, letting go, and I feel a lot of weight being lifted. Yet, when the ceremony ends, I have not returned from the Spirit World fully. I drape myself with a sheet, Socrates style again, and wander over to the kitchens where I find the shaman and his girlfriend. Gifted with the vision of Ayahuasca, I could see clearly their dynamic and how unhappy she was. I sit down on a chair as the medicine man attempts to bring my soul back into my body. A song plays in the background, and my words ring with power as I stop their worlds "Wait. This song..."

"What?? What about the song?"

I pause, unsure of how to connect my intent with my next action, and choose to shift things into a lighter and playful mood. "I kinda like it!"

"Heh, go take a shower."

I cleanse some more of the energy off and wander around a bit more. Rafa, the resident black dog, lies down with me in my cot. He starts getting aggressive and even sexual with me. I learn about boundaries with all beings and kick him out. Restless, I continue to walk the planks of the compound. With everyone asleep, the energy starts to settle. I make myself some tea in the empty kitchen, under the moonlight in the warm still jungle air. Everything comes to center, my second intent, and I feel a deep peace. I got exactly what I needed from Mother Ayahuasca.

Breaking Open

The mats in the *maloka* are set up in a circle as I've said before. That makes the people next to you a special sort of kin. On my right is a man from San Diego going through a divorce and figuring out his next life. He shares that from his third ceremony, he's had lots of butterflies and gardens in his mind's eyes, and the shaman reflects that the inside of his mind is that beautiful and pure now. He turns to me and shares, "Be careful with how deep you relax; you could end up going all the way through to rebirth!"

I sense what he is talking about, but think to myself, *isn't that kind of the point?*

A fear seems to be in the shadows around me today as I am unsettled by how closely my third ceremony resembled some manic states where I am out of control and simply flowing with things. I am happy I came down naturally, but not sure if I should risk drinking the sacred brew again tonight. I have a heart to heart with Marq, who is in a mirrored romantic situation to me. He reassures me to let Lotus go ... so that we can reunite on a new level. Or perhaps there will be a third girl that embodies all! In divine timing with the theme, various workers are hanging up the sign that marks the change in ownership of the Center to Arkana—and I learn Arkana means protection. "Protection from what?" my colleague would ask in the future, who believes that the word protection itself creates a dichotomy making danger implicit...

The Fourth Ceremony ... ah where do I begin? At first I avoided writing about this under the vague mystery clause of "these experiences cannot be described," yet here I am with the unshakeable notion that my entire book is an attempt at such! Let us continue then, always at your own risk, down the lunar pathways to other worlds...

Tonight is the night after the full moon, and something strange is in the air. After drinking the brew, I make a few trips to the bathroom and stumble across a bizarre scene (for one in an altered state) of a medic all around a man who had leapt head first off the platform. "It's going to be one of those nights..." a local says to me, as I pass by the scene. I feel a muted kind of sadness, as if all around me participants are celebrating in some joyous revelry the illusions that can come with Ayahuasca. I feel like she is being taken advantage of. Exploited is the best word. I feel like people are exploiting the Divine Feminine, and I hold on to my tender feelings and resolve not to succumb to any visions.

After I receive my Icaros, I lie down on my mat and hear a voice that I had yet to notice all the other nights—an elder female voice singing a song of ancient wisdom. The voice is light and high-pitched, like those angels I heard all those years ago after overdosing on edibles ... yet not the same caliber. I can make out the individual tones and songs—she is indeed human.

And she is attempting to make me a healer.

Teaching someone through sound waves is a pretty normal experience, but much different when the student is on Ayahuasca and the teacher is speaking a tribal language. I experience these sounds as geometric shapes, and my vision gets filled with colors and lights.

Then I get stuck.

I mean I imagine this is a feeling everyone can relate to—stuck in a rut, in a pattern, watching a dream you can't change—yet imagine this intensified a thousand times as a visceral experience. My body moves in a continual loop over which I have no control, and it involves rubbing a rock I had with me all over myself. I can feel each grain of sediment on my skin and have the sensation of being completely dried out. Somehow my body responds enough to flick my red flashlight on and off—a cry for a facilitator to come over.

An Australian man asks, "Do you want out?" Something about that phrasing triggers me—out of what? The Matrix? Instead of it coming across as an offer for help, I feel challenged to continue with this process and let it take me where it may.

Even if that's around the endless circles of Hell. Spoiler Alert: Dante simply didn't gaze deep enough (or didn't want to share).

The next sensation I have is that I will be here for all Eternity. That my mind broke. I am in limbo in all senses of the word and am almost resigned that I screwed up and now have to endure this fate. A fitting scene to be frozen in for someone who experimented with forces he didn't understand!

One of the things the facilitators told us on the first day was that "Everybody always comes back" when explaining how the ceremony would end each night. The music and songs stop and the lead shaman says, "*La ceremonia ha terminado.*" But I am not back. I do regain some semblance of control over my body, at least in the sense that I can have an intent and watch as the scene changes.

Outside the bathroom, my fellow North Carolinian notices my state. "You look like you are at a loss as to what to do next."

I can only nod in reply.

He suggests brushing my teeth and going to bed. I go through some motions. Yet with so much energy coursing through my body that I want to process, I take my trusty hiking staff and go whirling it around as I walk the risen planks of the complex. I lie back down on my mat in the Maloka, where many people are opening up and processing the ceremony with each other. I have forgotten that other people were important to the process, so I speak up about my first childhood memory when the subject comes up in conversation. My words resonate throughout the Maloka, but no one seems to know how to connect with me. "That's sad to hear," someone replies.

Next thing I know, I end up in the bathroom and I feel distinctly "backstage" of a performance. I am getting prepared for a grand entrance, a wonderful show, and my friends Sun and Wolf are there with me. However, the scene I am preparing for flashes in my mind's eye: it is a death scene. The death scene in *Antigone*, which is the play where we all met during two years prior. I take my time in preparing for a scene, because although Life is a Grand Play, us characters actually experience death as real. My jaw feels much more open and relaxed, and I practice a few of my lines. Marq is in the bathroom next to me, and I feel a deep kinship with him—as if we are little kids in hideout forts! Sun keeps whispering into my mind's ear, "Names are important," but the woman outside waiting to use the restroom next ... I've forgotten her name! The show *Ed, Edd, and Eddy* comes to mind, and I remember the theory of how all those kids are simply in purgatory. A theme which has come up a lot in my life.

Outside the bathroom is the corridor leading to the Maloka. I slow to crawl as I prepare for my final stunt. I feel the potential energy of the kinetic move about to be performed in the "center stage" of the Maloka. I am not going to do justice in describing it, like a spiral inside out backflip reverse handspring. One of the woman facilitators hovers over me, as the shaman wonders, "What's wrong with this kid?" Palo Santo continually is blown in my face, but it is not having the desired effect. Everything is so INTENSE! The smells, the sounds, the visions—

I begin to cycle through the Elements and eventually understand that I need "WATER!" I make my mouth say. In response, my face is flooded with Agua de Florida. [I don't know if I was actually given something to drink during this time, but let me tell you right here that dehydration during mystical experiences is NOT fun. 0/10. I do not recommend it. Lord knows how Jesus managed in the desert...] And the scene my mind plays is from *Cowboy Bebop*. You can skip the next paragraph if you care about spoilers regarding

Cowboy Bebop.
*
*
*
*
*

It's the final death scene in that show. I continue to try to focus long enough to make my hand into a gun shape and say, "Bang." Yet, the energy always falters at the last moment. After all, this is my death scene and reality is not one for copycats. I am still outside the *maloka*, going in and out of consciousness. With all sorts of sensations and experiences, I can barely begin to describe much less recall. A half-blind shaman appears before me, who is continually trying to bring my Soul back, and it dawns on me that with his blind eye he can see into the realities beyond. Everything makes sense now:

"RealityRealityRealityRealityReality" I repeat—

"He's stuck in a loop!"

"Come on, Arthur. You've done this before."

Everyone rallies together to break me free—they enter a meditative state and get my attention only to say a spontaneous word and pass it off. Somehow I believe I now know Spanish and think we're playing a game of translation.

Freed of the mental loop, I plunge deeper.

My mind flashes through various scenes that are very personal to me. I see a crucifixion and three men lined up in a forest scene. My mother is there, looking at my childhood self, and I confess I love Jesus. I ask people nearby in the waking world what offspring a jaguar mating with a monkey would produce? I realize I am a monkey! What a breakthrough!

"You finally figured that out?" says Scott.

A monkey emblem (I visited Japan during the year of the Monkey) is on my staff and it all comes together. I am wearing my Puma shirt and jaguar medicine continues to merge with my consciousness. Raw energy floods every cell of my body and I somehow enter the Maloka. I feel the events of the next day through time and space and keep shouting, "Group picture! It's time for the group picture!" At this point, I black out, the fear in the room has risen due to my out-of-control state and the fact that I have a hiking staff that's often mistaken for a martial weapon.

Deep in my inner world, I feel like I've plunged into the center of the entire complex, holding on to as much sense of self as I can manage.

Dying is Healing?

I wake up to sunlight. Everything feels different, and time no longer passes like it used to. It passes in long, languorous waves of energy, perhaps in tune with the heartbeat of the earth. Perhaps.

I wander the complex and am greeted by a lot of scared workers. I am famous at this point and get the impression I kept everyone awake long into the night. I begin to wonder if they have called authorities, and I'm about to be whisked away to some mental hospital. I hear helicopters, and see an official-looking boat float toward us on the river. The anxiety never rises to panic, and I take my time not to let my mind run rampant with speculation.

Yet, when I come face to face with a staff member (after flossing my teeth, since I can feel each individual gum now), she updates her mental file on me. "Ah, so you're doing better now. Good." Another woman comes out of the shower, someone I have a bit of a connection with and I ask her if she can help me with my things. My mind doesn't work like it used to, and I am still at a loss as to how to function.

She's clothed in only a towel and enters my room to help me. She directs some of my actions, and I get caught on the jaguar print I had purchased… "How do I store this?"

She instructs to roll it up, and I take what feels like six eternities doing so. She holds out for as long as she can, reaches her limit of patience, and says, "I'm going to go get ready, you take care of that."

I organize most of my things, including my tent, which had ripped open on the flight from Lima to Iquitos. After breakfast, a man named Light Raven lets me know that, "We're good now" and how he thought he'd have to fight me when I came into the Maloka whirling my staff (oh, so that happened?). His wife says she now, after all these years, understands why he is called Light Raven. When she reflects on what she observed in myself, we share a tender moment with me. I eat some food, slowly and methodically, as if learning for the first time.

Sitting around the Maloka, we share our experiences of the final Ayahuasca ceremony. My friend confesses she thought "Someone had died last night" and was in a state of perpetual panic. A lot of us had a rough time, and Gen-san simply says, "I did not drink last night." I feel the pain of his Soul in those words, and an audible whimper escapes me. In this state, I feel like I can hear the music of everyone's Soul, the rhythm of their essence. I share succinctly, focusing on the sensations of somersaults, springing, and "facing a lot of dark stuff." The shaman replies that I need to implement changes and asks, "Is this nourishing for you or not?" Moving forward, he shares with all of us to remember that this was a real experience. This actually happened and was not a dream. He offers that we can reach out to the center to reconnect.

Marq gets me to sit down with him off to the side in the long limbo of waiting for the boat to arrive. We have a heart to heart, and he comes to terms that a lot of what I said the previous night doesn't make sense. Perhaps I was channeling pure Chaos. In particular, he wants to take from me the gift of some strange name I had given birth to, "Spaghetti Williams," as his stripper name. Later I talk to Vlad, who is continuing to diet on his plant and stays mostly in isolation in his hut in the jungle. He says my eyes are different now … like I've seen a lot. I feel seen in a way I am not accustomed to. Like I can no longer hide anything from anyone. It is a new and unsettling kind of vulnerability, and a deep camaraderie our group now shares.

On the boat ride back, Mike slowly pulls something out from his bag. A pair of sunglasses.

"I don't know why I packed two pairs, but something told me it was important. I see now why I brought it." He hands me red/black shades that have inscribed on the inside "Fuck the Rest." It's the kind of deep message telling me that I need to take care of myself now, even if it isn't best for the entire tribe. I don't see that at the moment, however.

The boat ride is much longer than it was on the way into the jungle. We have all changed so much and experienced transformation. I keep going in and out of wakefulness, but what's strange about my new body is that it reacts intensely to the wind. Anytime a breeze comes across the boat, I find myself taking a deep inhale through the nose and feeling refreshed.

The Floating Boat that Never Was

We head out to a restaurant that we need a ferry to get to. On this floating island of desires and temptations, many of us wrestle with wanting to eat food and go against the recommendation to avoid alcohol. I hear the Souls of my compatriots crying out, "Please, something familiar. Anything familiar. I don't know where or who I am anymore. Nothing works as it used to."

I order something unmemorable to eat and decide to stay away from alcohol and drink only water.

Leaning on the railing of this bizarre island structure, I watch the lights in the distance across the sea twinkle. I really have no idea where I am. Is this reality? Are we all in a dream? Did we all really die that night with Ayahuasca, and this is my experience of purgatory?

The questions don't lead me to a cycle of insanity, as I have all my fellow travelers with me. Having people who have gone through it is enough of a bond to keep us all afloat. I let the reverie sweep me back into the same hotel we used before our journey—only this time it is booked by the staff and our room assignments are arbitrary.

I confront my deep fear—that I will not be able to sleep. Yet, I wander out of the room (my roommate snores) and find a couch in the hotel lobby. Comfortable and exhausted, I drift off into unconsciousness, only to be awakened by the same roommate. I am oddly moved that he was worried enough to come find me.

We really are all in this together.

9

Valley of Death

To the Sacred Valley
Enjoying each beautiful Day, sharing my gift of Freedom. I'm on my Way
-Arthur the Wanderer

Our group parts ways and is reduced to those who wanted to continue their explorations with the follow-up trip to the Sacred Valley of the Incas. We travel by plane to Cusco, down to five in number. As the plane takes off, a wave of anxiety and fear grip us as we continue to wrestle with our new reality. Everything is more intense. Time is no longer what it once was. My Australian companion shares how she believes the Ayahuasca was "spiked" with Toe, a medicine plant which is a balance of light and darkness. Everyone seems to agree with that explanation, as it seems much easier to write off the insanity of our experiences as due to the brew itself. As for me, I continue to reflect on the deeper levels of reality and how their workings can shatter the mind. The vehicles (Toe and Ayahuasca in this case) used to make that plunge are of only circumstantial relevance compared to the places traveled to.

Speaking of ascent and descent, we arrive at Cusco, which is remarkably at a higher elevation than Machu Picchu itself (3,400meters vs. 2,400 meters), which throws me for a bit. I'm going to climb a mountain and end up lower than where I started this trip? I buy a little, brown journal for this leg of the journey, and it is from there that the quotes of below each bolded chapter will come.

Day 1, August 9th, Wednesday

Heading to Cusco, my body feels light, relaxed, and free. Eating only high quality foods is important

for keeping the inner Freedom & Liberation of a pleasant happy state.

Jung: Creative Light within. Understanding & integrating the unconscious actuals of the

Psyche which influences me. Primal energies...

We descend to the nearby Sacred Valley, arriving at a recently acquired retreat center. The itinerary when I booked the trip was to stay in various hotels as we visited different sites in the Valley, but due to the change in ownership of the retreat company, we are surprised to have a home base nestled along the Urubamba River.

Sacred Animals

The more powerful the Shaman, the stronger the Darkness. But the Shaman doesn't need to become more powerful — Stay in the Light.

Our first day, I wander out for some much needed alone time by the river. I slow down and realize how much slower my baseline is from the rest of the group. The realization comes that I sync up my flow of time with those that I am with, so solitude is of the utmost importance. Of course, as my tent was thrown away back in the jungle—mistaken for trash—negotiating that alone space, and time is going to take a bit more effort.

Back at the center, they offer a sweat lodge. I feel like I've done enough work with fire. I am also afraid of the intensity of it. One of the perks of this center is I am once again connected to the world, as they have Amazon Fire tablets and the glorious gift of Wi-Fi.

After the group finishes their sweat, we hike up under the twilight sky to the salt farm that lies across the river. The mountain ranges and landscape of this part of Peru are captivating with their reddish brown hues carved up by the aqua blue-green river life. The salt farms stretch out beyond imagination along the mountainside, and the sheer vastness of the task of mining moves me. Not to mention how steep the mines taper off into the abyss of the valley below. To labor on the edge of the Void each day! What courage, What strength!

Link Freedom
Everyone is unfolding,
Unfinished,
This is beauty,
Respect the process.

I awaken on the grass steps leading up to my room, away from everyone else. I don't remember falling asleep, or really who I was before this moment.

I wake up with a strong answer to my inquiries: "What are the nature of my gifts, and what is my path in life?"

My first lucid thought is: "This is what I can do for people?"

That's all the articulation I can manage, such is the lightness and freedom I'm feeling in every pore of myself. San Pedro is the plant medicine we're currently doing a ceremony with and is meant to be done in the daytime. I find it indeed a less intense experience than Ayahuasca. I'm glad I didn't let fear stop me from partaking in this ceremony. Although, I did drink a smaller glass than everyone to ease my anxiety, which the head medicine woman mocked me for.

I go down to the field where everyone's having their experiences, and one of the shamans is lying on his back, facing the sky. He returns to earth as I approach and smiles. Getting up, he offers me a giant condor feather, as if he plucked it from the sky itself. I run around the yard, flapping my wings and feel myself being lifted above the skies.

We go on a hike up to the salt ponds above the river. It is this grounding journey that brings us back to earth. I have come to appreciate the green sign of the restrooms as pointing to a "way out" of the Matrix I had entered. A symbolic re-entrance to consensual reality. Now that I read this again, I see that it's a bit of a reverse for most people. Aren't spiritual experiences supposed to liberate us from the Matrix of day-to-day life? But to me, the Matrix is a place where you are only as limited as your mind, and the experience of being watched is tangible. On the hike, I deepen my connection with my fellow explorers, as Herman the traveling craftsman, Kalcky a Nei Gong practitioner and climber, and Anthony my Australian hat brother share their stories with me.

All in all, it feels great to be out in the fresh air of the Valley, far above the intense heaviness of the jungle.

Machu Picchu
Find your Zenter

The day we ascend Machu Picchu, Saturday the twelfth, is clear and bright. Our sleepy-eyed crew has been together for the most sacred of sites Peru has to offer. But after all we've been through, it isn't exactly excitement in the air. We transfer over from our car to a bus in the lower town in order to ascend up the curves of the mountain.

The guide shows us around the ruins of a civilization that was way beyond its time.

We visit the Temple of the Sun and learn of the three cultivations that their people focused on: Jaguar for the Present, Condor for the Future, and Serpent for the Past. The symbol that I have been seeing all around, the Incan Cross, is connected to the southern cross in the stars.

The guide taught us that Cusco is the center hole, which lies at the center of the Universe.

After the tour was over, the group dissented about how to proceed.

"Hey, we're all on the same level, aren't we?" mentioned my spirit brother, Ice-Man.

But I disagree. I don't feel I am on the same level, nor wavelength, as the whole group. And I'm not going to go along with whatever we end up settling on for my trip to this mountain.

I go my own way and wander up the paths and trails above the ruins.

I find a hidden alcove off a path that has a stone perfect to sit on.

I cross my legs for meditation, feeling into the place beyond time for all the energy that has ever gathered here. When I come out of it, I feel as though many hours have passed. I open my eyes to see some of the crew coming toward me who share that it's been a short thirty minutes since we parted ways. We try to sync plans and agree on various routes again, but I am drawn to hiking the Sun Gate.

Mike, who has served in the military and could feel everyone's pain back in the jungle ceremonies, is the only one to join me. He's terrified of heights, but somehow falls in line behind me on the trail that runs along the cliff edge.

"Are you sure you're okay? No need to push yourself through your fears."

"Keep going, man, I'm fine."

I get the distinct feeling that the less we talk, the easier it will be. I remember my time on the hospital roof in Brazil and my own fear of heights...

We get to the Sun Gate, and I scamper up a giant rock to a beautiful view of the lands below. I further earn my monkey archetype in Mike's eyes. He rests in awe of himself and the sights.

"Wow. We really just did that!" He exclaims. The great expanse of the earth opens up before us, with green being the main color of our vista.

Later after our descent in the town below, we avail ourselves to the outdoor hot springs. The signs entice us to hike another few miles up the city, and I trek with music in my heart at the prospect of a nice soak!

Of course, I have been thoroughly spoiled by my experience in Japan of *Onsen*. The *Banos Termales* at Machupicchu Pueblo are pretty crowded and less aesthetically pleasing. I take an icy shower to rinse off before my plunge into the springs. Relaxation comes in time, not without some social anxiety at the co-ed bath and the beautiful women present.

I take a nap on the train back to the retreat center. After our return and a nice dinner, I settle down to sleep for the night. I wake up as if struck by a lightning bolt. I don't know who I am. I look down and see my brother's coast guard shirt; am I my brother? I don't remember much of the night, but I know I faced a lot of fears and worked through some intense experiences. I end up sleeping in the ceremony room where the energy feels a bit easier to relax into. *Made it.* I write in my journal.

Cold Winds and Warm Nights
August 13th, Sunday

The day of transition has arrived; my scheduled retreat is over. My return ticket leaving Peru is not for a few more weeks though, as I gave myself until the end of August to have a free-form adventure. I made that decision envisioning another tent/wilderness exploration similar to Japan. Now that my tent is lost, I negotiate to stay another week at the center. I advocate having my own room with no roommate. The center fills as new guests arrive here for their own Peru adventure. The discrepancy between our position in the healing process (not in terms of life, but in terms of the sequence of coming from day-to-day life to the retreat center and decompressing) makes for some friction. I treat myself to a massage, and the cold winds blow fiercely as I enter a special room off to the side. Pamela gives me a delightful session and I release a lot of tension, feeling love pouring in with each gentle breath as I ease into relaxation. The night air feels very warm as I re-emerge to join the others for their first dinner. I meet Paul, an actor from Australia who shares his experience of a psychotic break while on stage. I don't want to feel any of that pain since I'm in such a happy state. Despite my empathy not even picking up on anything, I excuse myself.

Deja vu; a lightning bolt hits me soon after drifting off to sleep. The spirit of all things compels me to rejoin the group down in the ceremony center where I open up about my emotions. This has the bonus effect of breaking someone out of the loop they were stuck in. Paul shares his reflection of my brother. "Sounds like he's trying to balance you out, wearing the same shirt and hat each day? It's as if he's saying 'Look. This is who I am. Deal with it.'" I realize that the calligraphy I got in São Paulo while traveling with my brother makes sense: it is exactly what he is teaching me. It reads , pronounced ***Fudōshin,*** which translates literally as "Immovable Heart." It can be read as "perseverance" or "stillness in the midst of adversity." I aspire to have a will as disciplined as my brother's and not to waver from my own wavelength.

Not everyone sees the Cat
August 14th, Monday

We start our day with some chanting and morning yoga together. I break my usual routine of meditating by myself, compelled again by Spirit. Christina feels my struggle, as I chant through a lot of pain and tears, and comes up to me afterward.

"It's been awhile since I've had the Sight, but did you have a cat when you were younger? With white paws?"

"Yes ... I called him Socks, among other names: Oliver, Winston, Kitty."

"He's still with you now, comforting you."

I break down into more tears. A "Midwife of the Soul" worked on me back in 2015 and told me my childhood pets wanted to stay with me in spirit form to protect me, but I didn't feel worthy of them and told her to let them pass over. Apparently, Socks didn't heed my request and stayed! How like a cat... Tears form in my eyes, of gratitude, of the forgiveness, and love of animals. Can you imagine?

After a tobacco purging that I don't take part in, I help the groundskeeper—Dejus—hike the group up to the salt mines. I remembered how grounding it was for our group to do it in that order, so we took our time through the winding mountain paths. Dejus teaches me some good Spanish words: *Pasaje - beautiful picture of reality, translated as landscape* and *Pasajismo - work of art, painting of paisaje.*

Through the Fire and Smoke

"You can only be intelligent at things that have happened. Scary new things ... that's where life is." -Paul the Actor

August 15th, Tuesday

The retreat takes the same pattern as when we first arrived, so today I am once again invited to partake in the sweat lodge ceremony. This time I find the courage to participate and overcome fears that somehow this will induce more insanity. The ceremony involves chanting, singing, and sharing, with periodic breaths of fresh air as they add more wood to the flames. Chandra, the medicine woman and head facilitator of this retreat center, instructs us to pull up deep earth energy to cool ourselves (Deep earth is cool? Ah yes, the Yin ... it refreshes me)

My perception of time is shattered. I feel moved to channel some higher being as I stay completely in my center (the rest of my body floats around in all sorts of ways, with all sorts of sensations). I honor and acknowledge all my teachers, Michael Lomax for his Chi Kung and all the people who have taught me along my path. The state that we move to is so altered and moving that I lay on the ground while everyone else exits. Deep in the earth, I feel like I'm in the womb once more and who would choose to leave that? I move to exit the shelter through the opposite side of everyone else, being the defiant rebel that I am. Chandra says quite clearly,

"No. Go the normal way."

To live a normal life ... isn't that what Ice Brother had said was the highest? To be a spiritual master as a convenience store clerk? That seems to be my hardest lesson. To learn how to live life as it is—without needing epic displays of grandeur, adventure, or drama: to be satisfied with its inherent magnificence.

After opening up to Paul about what troubled my heart—the letter Lotus wrote to me—he reflects how much courage and strength she had to write that. I call her, and the silence between us is thick with stillness. I am at a complete loss as to what to say. Is it a disconnect, or is there nothing to communicate other my struggle to simply be? She reminds me to enjoy myself and that I seem to have a lot more energy. I call Sun right after and feel as if she can perhaps understand what I'm going through. Sun fits cleanly into my pattern of making life complex and welcomes all of my emotions. She sends me the song "Anchor" by Mendy Gledhill, and I cry cathartic tears until the darkness of sleep takes hold.

First Rainbow by the River
Honor your Path.
Focus,
On the Rhythm
August 16th, Wednesday
A beautiful day with so much light, I write in my journal. I offer to go along

with Yosdel, the resident yoga teacher, to the market; we ride in a motorcar as I hold her two children close. Feeling like a guardian, my role this morning shows me a more mature, parental side of myself. My stomach is in a lot of pain, so we're also out to pick up some aloe vera that will be used for a medicine drink.

I continue to quest for those red/black sunglasses I had. The light is starting to hurt my sensitive eyes. Even the stars feel like they rouse me from deep sleep! I remember only a flash of a scene like a dream where I had the sunglasses in my hand and re-read the "Fuck the Rest" engraving. In a holier-than-thou moment, I rejected that energy—not wanting something so selfish in my life. I continue to miss the lesson of healthy anger, assertiveness, and advocating for oneself.

I paint a butterfly in the massage room to practice for the tattoo I am designing for Dejus for my shoulder. We go outside to a light rain and the first rainbow to shine since the center's ownership changed hands. I feel like I am part of the center and that the beauty of the rainbow was as much a blessing on my presence as anything else.

I don't think anyone else saw me during that time, or felt me as a part of that experience. The rainbow had them completely absorbed and who would want to connect dots at a time like that?

Around dinner, I open up a bit more to the group about bipolar and what I'm feeling. In the magic of the now, my intensity softens. "Don't you feel what everyone's getting by what you're sharing?" Paul asks. But no. I have no idea what people are getting. All I know is that all the world feels settled when I open up to the group and fear disappears for a time. In this sacred moment, there's no such thing as bipolar or mental illness—only the beauty of now.

The Soul cannot be Split

Nighttime comes again. Did I mention I was deathly afraid of the dark as a child? Sleep does not come easily; my awareness is too acute and life feels really intense. I feel possessed by the spirit of Jaguar and roam around the center. Timelines blur and change. My mind begins to fracture as I feel less and less in control. I knock on Dejus's door, asking him if I can go see Chandra. He tells me it isn't a good idea, but I am having a full-blown panic attack.

Not happy at being awakened, Chandra takes me down to the ceremony room and instructs me to lie down on a mat and breathe. "Nothing is happening to you, you are fine. You aren't on any plant medicines, nothing is happening." I relax a bit, but get worried that they are going to think I'm insane with all this talk of "nothing is happening."

On the morning of the seventeenth, I wrap my head with my Buff so that it covers one eye and I fake a stroke. I pretend to no longer know English, and Paul the Actor is not phased at all by my display. He continues to see right through me.

"I think Arthur feels like he did something wrong."

I go into my room to take a shower, and Chandra threatens to call my parents of all things. After a few frustrated failed attempts, Chandra leaves the center to fix the Wi-Fi. With her gone, I feel a bit more safe to come out of my room. The group happens to be in a San Pedro ceremony, and when I join, they say, "We felt you coming and were wondering when you'd arrive."

After a bit of talking, I run at full sprint with all the energy I can muster—the Winds of Change! The intensity shifts a bunch of people, and we all move in different directions while Paul agrees to spend an hour of his time on me. We meet in the ceremony room with some ground rules:

1. No hurting ourselves, each other, or the center.
2. This talk is confidential.
3. Listen, don't react.

He guides me through some of my emotions and I take on each form of myself. Anger has a lot to say about how he's been trying to protect me, and I've done nothing but abuse and neglect him. I confess about how poorly I treated my exes, particularly my ex-wife. Finally, Paul asks me to find the "director" of all these parts. I say I can't find that when I'm with him, so I go into the bathroom to be "behind the scenes" of it all. When I'm back with Paul, I try to communicate that the director is transcendent—beyond both of us—yet he sees things differently. He has an extremely strong, emotional reaction to me attempting to love him all the same. We finish our time together with a hug.

Chandra returns and lays down some law. I am not to leave my room at all that night as my nightly wanderings have been scaring the other participants. (Christina says I entered her room, but I know I would never violate boundaries that way. Is it another timeline where that happened? Or fear distorting memory and perception? I remember leaving a note for her in the door crack.)

With all the discipline I can muster, I stay in my room after calling some family members. Waking up in the middle of the night, the defiant rebel in me once again goes out through the window rather than opening my door, justifying it as a loophole. I make my way down to the massage studio room. The energy here is peaceful, and I send Lotus a text thinking of her. The butterfly I had painted gives me some relief, so I return to my room to rest a bit more. I do not fall unconscious, but enter into a perhaps deep meditative state for some of the night.

Fear Itself

Nothing Crazier than trying to act Sane

Now it is the eighteenth, a date that you will not find in my journal. I have only written one sentence about this day and will share what I remember from my fragmented mind. I also have this post on Facebook, as my wish to leave the center meant leaving the tablet behind:

It's that time again. Farewell Facebook, I'm off to ride among the clouds and enjoy the freedom of Life. Find the Love in your hearts today.

"Knowing is the Path"

Look for Healcyon when the Wind brings you healing.

Peace. Balance. Relaxation

I woke up to the nightmare of Paul having misheard my story with my exes. Chandra talked to me one on one, having tracked down my ex-wife and discovered she is not actually dead (yes, Paul, in his heightened emotional state, believed I had confessed to killing her.) [it is quite amazing to this day how easily memory can be distorted!]). My ex is quite worried about me and says she'll pray for me, as she's been there for most of my breaks of sanity. Talking with Sun, I have an insight that Chandra's weakness is technology, and I bring my GoPro camera to the conversation. I do not trust Chandra anymore and feel her to be adversarial to my well-being. I pack all of my bags and prepare myself for the timeline in which I leave and go to a hotel to decompress from all this intensity. Yet Chandra also contacts my mother, who has begged her to keep me at the center.

I am not told this. Instead, I drag my bags over to the gate which I find locked. I video-tape this with my GoPro as I struggle to stay grounded as past traumas of confinement come up. "Why am I being locked in? Am I a prisoner here?" Some retreat!

The panic rises as I pace around the center. To add to it, the shaman is coming. He has been delayed due to personal circumstances, and I have been content to not have him bring Ayahuasca to this Sacred Valley. I want to be far away from the madness of the jungle. From the deep terrors hidden behind veils and veils of illusion … He is coming! I can feel it! I tell Paul in a sober moment, "That will do harm to me. I want to leave. I want to go to a hotel somewhere." I am deeply afraid, and Kalcky finally returns from his few days of sickness to do some Qi Gong with me.

I take some time connecting to the moves of Damo Mitchell's Ji Ben Qi Gong. I feel a distinct difference between "inside" and "outside," which I take to mean as outside the center. I send energy to Sun and attempt to feel my connection to her as a pathway to freedom. Kalcky tries to guide me once more to the ceremony room where everyone wants to talk to me. To be the center of attention in these circumstances terrifies me more than I understand and can articulate! Not to be in the spotlight, but to have the full force of misunderstanding shone on me—they think I'm a murderer! I have always been very sensitive to the perceptions of others, as if it was an easy surface to project onto.

Yet if I only … Ah, I have dwelled many a year on what timeline would have come to pass if I had mustered the courage to be seen. For I am sure the Light of Truth would have swept away all misunderstanding … Instead, I wander around the center along all the boundaries. Kalcky walks with me in tow, and I keep coming up against the locked gate. I feel I am about to explode from all the pressure and intensity of this process. I have no awareness that the group is willing to hold space for me as I am, and I continue to search for an escape route.

The path I choose is to the river's edge, the mighty dragon of the Urubamba. I find myself there amidst the construction that Deyus had shown me at the outskirts of the center. The temptation is too great, and I don't stop to think. The path of escape by my own hand is right here in front of me. In my manic state, I dive into those waters, not knowing their depth nor thinking twice about my safety—I am simply in the Matrix after all…

Looking for a way out.

Gripping my sandals in one hand and my keyring in the other, I start thrashing at the water in an attempt to cross the thirty meter expanse. The current sweeps me downstream and under a bridge. I look to the shore and see a construction worker notice that I've entered the river and the alarm is sounded. My sandals slip from my hands as my arms fatigue from the effort. Past the bridge downstream I emerge on the other side dripping wet, feeling the madness of the ink path I had laid out for myself last night scribbling in my journal. Everything is connected. Karma is instant now. All is at the knife-edge of the moment as I scramble down some rocks to a man who doesn't understand me. He has kind eyes like a grandfather, and I plead with him to provide me with some sanctuary. Please! Kindness of strangers, don't fail me now! They want to imprison me back there!!!

Dejus and a few other men arrive, but I am stronger than them. I am Neo, and I will not be contained by other forces any longer! I wrestle out from their grip and scramble toward the salt mines—the hike! Yes! The Way Out! I see a motor car on the side of the road and push my Matrix powers to their limit. I take the keychain I had been clutching, with its Oathkeeper keyblade, and jam thekKey with etched wings into the ignition. Turn on, turn on! I wrestle madly with the vehicle, only for the others to catch up to me, the three of them working together to subdue me more completely.

I am dragged back into the retreat center. Kalcky begins to talk some sense into me and to ask me about my life. "What is it that you said you do for a living back home again?"

I talk to him automatically about some details of Healcyon. He has kind gray eyes and reminds me of my stepfather. I see him as a more free version, a Wind brother who did not confine himself behind a fortress of safety. He also likes to talk about things that make sense when the world is on the verge of shattering.

The gate doesn't seem too tall and I can sense that the ambulance is coming—for sure! Another mental hospital? In Peru? I could be lost forever! I run to the gate wall and try to jump up, only to be slammed back down by Dejus. Dejus then swings at me with his fist, hard, and my head hits the stones. I don't feel the blow, but I can tell I've been struck by the way Kalcky looks at him in disbelief. I start taking off my wet clothes, not wanting anything to do with any kind of restriction, and I am held by each arm strung out like a cross while they attempt to clothe me. Chandra does her best to talk some sense into me while I plead to be allowed to talk to Paul again. I only know this because Chandra was videotaping this experience, as I have no memory of these interactions. I beg to talk to Paul alone, but I'm told there's no chance of that happening.

To use as leverage later, Chandra took videos of me during this part. Watching those videos three years later is heart wrenching. The only way I can describe it is ... perhaps coming full circle to a painful part of your past that you were "numb" or "tapped out" and unable to truly feel at that moment. Normally, this happens in trauma healing as the body remembers the experience. What a horrific difference to watch and feel the amount of pain it took for me to black out and dissociate that completely. Yet, as Sun taught me, this was an opportunity to look at myself with compassion, to not see myself as that person—trapped—but as a fellow being in deep suffering.

In retrospect now, I can see the amount of inner strength and patience it must have taken to deal with me in that state. The amount of misunderstandings and miscommunication were staggering, including the person who did the screening interview saying they lost my medical intake. I had indeed let them know I had been diagnosed with bipolar and had been hospitalized, but the distinct "covering of one's behind" smell lingered in the air. This was piled onto Paul's mishearing my story and painted me as a very dark and untrustworthy character. Despite all that for the most part, the workers at the center did what they could to keep everyone safe and manage my episode. I also discovered that I was locked in because in contacting my parents, my mother had begged them to not let me leave.

I have gratitude in my heart for Paul, who took time out of his own healing process to help me deal with my own in what ways he could. Also for Kalcky for treating me like a human being right after I had escaped into the river, which I imagine would disturb most people. Although I felt Chandra's energy at odds with mine during the peak of this experience, she didn't abandon me in the scenes to come.

My next flash of awareness has me on my back outside. I scream for Paul, a primal plea for him to come make some sense of this, and my energy reverberates off every surface and disturbs any semblance of peace and tranquility of this place. The female shaman who I had bonded with during an earlier San Pedro ceremony looks at me with tears running down her cheeks, and yells "I hate you! I hate you!" Those words leave a deeper scar than any punch Dejus had landed.

In the ceremony room now, shielded from prying eyes, they tie me up with ropes. I can no longer move, but it has been long now since I felt a semblance of sensation in my body. I have completely dissociated, and I do not remember the medics arriving. Nor do I remember their needles nor anything after that.

On the way to the hospital, I am told that they have all my stuff. I ask about my hiking staff. Please don't lose my staff. Dejus goes back to retrieve it.

My GoPro, with any evidence of my tale, goes missing without a trace.

In the hospital room, I come to my senses long enough to look in the mirror in the bathroom, then return to the bed where I enter some state of unconsciousness.

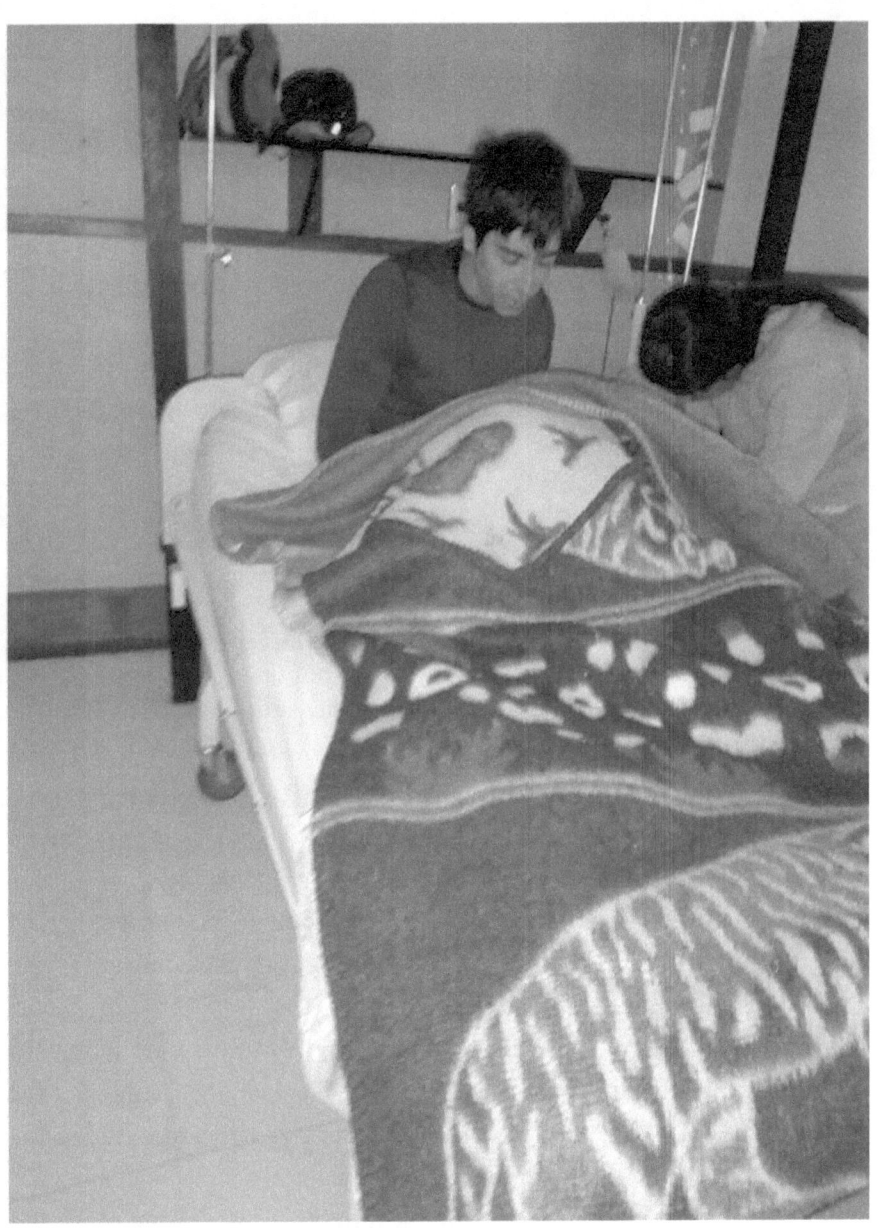

Wind in my Shoes

Feel your way Through

I wake up in a taxi riding to the airport. The driver zigs and zags through the Cusco traffic when I look down at myself and realize that I'm not wearing shoes!

The driver responds immediately at a traffic light. He takes his left shoe off and asks if it fits. It slides on like a glove, to which he responds by taking his right off and throwing it back all the while dealing with morning rush hour.

Moved to tears, I thank him from the bottom of my heart.

"Thank you? No, you have to buy them! Give me 150 Soles."

By the gods, I have about 170 Soles left in my wallet, which I hand over; I feel untold gratitude for my new pair of shoes that will let me fly through all the worlds.

To my delight, on the edge of the heel is written the word simply, "Wind."

Now, I know exactly who I am. Following the wind is what I do best.

The Magic of True Adventure

Olga helps me from the taxi through to security at the airport. She may be the woman in the picture above, as I remember her with me in the hospital. As luck would have it, it is against Peruvian law to commit foreigners to inpatient care. Distant in the corners of my mind, I am aware how much anxiety is stirred up in my family by my release. I am guided by Olga as far as she can take me—to airport security—and I walk through the queue, watching her concerned expression. I am moved to this day by the compassion she showed to one in her care for so brief a time.

In the playground of the airport, I am drawn to an expensive shop with luxurious alpaca silk scarves. The softness, the colors, the richness of the material world! I get a few as presents and one for myself to have a comforting cloth to hold while navigating this mental state.

Full extrovert mode engaged! I stumble into three sisters from Maryland playing at a table. They invite me for a game of Parcheesi. We have a wonderful time until the flow takes us to our flight to Lima.

On the flight, I meet John and Jeff, both from New York. John owns a t-shirt printing company, and I eventually follow up with him to make the shirts for

Healcyon. Jeff's Instagram name has douche in it, and I look him straight in the eyes. "You're not a douche to me." He acknowledges it's been a long time coming to change that name.

    Landing in Lima, the flow takes me to a man, Ricardo, offering rides to a hotel. Mind you, my mother had come to my rescue during this ordeal to arrange the flight from Cusco back to the United States, but I was barely aware of this itinerary (no cell phone, remember?). Instead of catching my connecting flight, I follow the magic of the moment. He asks me which Hilton hotel to go to and I choose one that feels right. When I arrive, no one other than the three sisters from the airport are there! We celebrate destiny and agree to hang out in the future during their stay. I do some Gift of the Tao Qi Gong and get myself a nice room to relax in. Credit cards are great, that's all I'll say. It's of no surprise to me that Fidelity is the name of my card and how I have been saved by that ideal!

    [Unbeknownst to me, my flight that I was supposed to have gotten on gets stranded in Hurricane Harvey (Category IV) and doesn't leave Houston. Miracles never cease! Who knows what madness I would've gotten into stuck in an airport for that long during a heightened state!]

    My adventure in Lima is blessed by the wings of freedom. It helps that no one knows my history. How liberating to be who you really are, wearing a fresh face! Truly, we are chained forever by our pasts, gaining glimpses of liberation through the new perspectives of strangers. What wonders are possible for someone to know your whole past and to let you be (now)? I relax and flirt in the hotel's jacuzzi, have lunch and deep conversations with one of the sisters, and all in all explore the beautiful world I find myself in. At the local mall, I buy a new phone from ASUS called the ZenFone.

It's good to be Alive again.

10

Karmic Gravity

Soular Eclipse

It's the great Solar Eclipse of August 2017. And where do I find myself but in the sky. I look out the airplane window and the horizon darkens to an amber twilight. I want to tune into the energy of this moment. After capturing the colors of the sky in my heart, I close myself off in the airplane's bathroom. I do some Qi Gong and integrate the sun and the moon into my heart.

Before I leave the airport, I make a few more friends, having donned an outfit expressing who I am happy to be today:

I arrive at Dulles Airport near D.C. worn out from my journey. My mother is waiting to pick me up. All the anguish and anxiety she had been carrying ... with all the faith she had to summon, not knowing if her son would be okay ... dissolves in a great hug.

We have a magical day the next day, and I touch the hearts of all the people we cross taking care of errands and chores. My mother is happy to see me alive, full of joy and exuberance! She is not concerned about my state when we're alone together. She only worries about how others will perceive and receive me. We make a pretty good team, living out our spiritual ideals of spreading the love of Jesus to all we interact with. At night, I sleep for a few solid hours then I am awake with plenty of energy that concerns her a bit more than my daytime activity. I Skype with Wolf, and I share all my excitement for our friendship moving forward. I feel great and balanced, though of course my unnatural rhythms (only three hours of sleep? What happened?) gives my mother cause to worry. Not wanting to be taken to the hospital for any reason, I resolve to leave the next day.

This time around I have my car, thus I have my physical freedom. I drive south. In my ambition, Sun asks for help with driving her newly adopted cat to the vet. Seems absurd for me to journey five hours south to give someone a ride, but this is the effect her needs have on me. I realize the ambition of stopping to have dinner with my father and then arriving in North Carolina later the same night. When I arrive at Midlothian, Virginia (at my father's), I instead decide to stay the night.

Yet, my past fears creep up as the night deepens. I remember all too well how my stepmother advocated for me going to the hospital last time I was in this state, so when I wake up yet again at 3-4 a.m., I do my best to channel some energy into my laptop and work on my writing. (Hey! I was writing the early chapters of this book!) As the grey morning light slowly shines, I am able to be emotionally present with my father. This is a rare thing and I can scarcely do justice to the ocean of calm and peace being with my father's energy is. A lifetime of being a male Cancer in this world, all that sadness has taken up far too much space in his heart (and lungs)… As we talk into the morning at a slow, leisurely pace, I offer him this reflection:

"You know, being present with you like this… feels like the essence of meditation."

I have my mission to arrive at Sun's and take her cat to the vet, so I do not stay long and say my farewell. My stepmother is not chained to the past the way I am and says I don't need her blessing to come and go.

To the Rhythms of Life!

Driving through the rising dawn, I arrive at Sun's apartment complex in the light of day. I take out my trusty drum, Tempest, and begin beating it in a slow rhythm. I feel as if I'm using echolocation to find her apartment and travel up and down the green hills of Raleigh looking for her. I finally see her friend Sol (yes, you read that right) leaving an apartment. He stares at me with wild eyes of joy. "Dude, I feel like we're on the path!" I wish him well on his path and take Sun and her cat, Luna, to the vet.

I don't know how to describe the flow of energy of this day, but it is as if I am trapped within a strong current. Sun says I interrupted a healing process, and I am still in full swing of the Spirit World. The world's symbolism overwhelms me, and her help is about the only thing that anchors me to the ground. My parents quickly see her as a "sanity check-in" resource and pester her several times with their worries. I take my first opportunity to alter the timeline at lunch, where Lotus is between her classes.

I arrive near a building named Kilgore and my whole body feels like a feather. I want more than anything to do no harm to her, to be gentle above all else. Sitting on the curb as she approaches, I hug my arms into my knees and place my gift ten feet away. As if I am radioactive, I pull my energy in close while she watches me with her deep, brown owl eyes. I give her my travel journal so that she may read and feel for herself the weight of my travels, as well as my entreaties to make amends with her. I let her set the pace given the letter she sent me at the start of August. With great fervor, I anchor my will to seeing her at 16:00 with Eternity the next day, booking it on multiple apps and writing it in as many journals as possible. I don't know what compels me, but I feel more than anything else that a ride with her would soothe my mind's troubles.

I don't remember the rest of the day, but I know I am guided by Sun into some slumber. The next day, I wake up at her apartment and begin going through my day as Sun herself. It isn't until I'm in the shower and begin shaving my legs that I stop. Who am I? As if I have become water itself and in being poured into the container of Sun's dwelling, I become her along the astral grooves she has carved.

I make it to my 16:00 destination despite the winds of change, through some combination of sheer will and Sun's respect for that desire. The time aligns with Lotus and give her a blissful ride back to her new living arrangement without the drudgery of her taking the bus. Neither of us wear helmets, the timeline being so narrow to get here made it difficult to line up the safety element as well, so it ends up being more of a shaky ride on the winds of faith. Something isn't quite right with Eternity—besides that I haven't ridden her in over two months. I was gone five months last time in Japan, and she had no problem starting up and riding off instantly.

I miss a turn and end up driving around the parking lot of her new place, which has a street named Whitehurst. That happens to be the last name of the Dreamwork coach, so I call him up.

He senses my hypomanic state through my speech patterns.

"Sounds like a lot more change than usual."

I use my whirlwind of change and energy to help unpack and set up Lotus's apartment. She moves at an earthy slow pace for these matters, and isn't it always more fun to do such things together?

Satisfied from my time with her, I go two streets further west.

Because of course Lotus and Wolf would end up living that close to each other while I'm gone. Such is the absurdity of Fate.

My own Space, My own Ride

Wolf, who was my roommate after returning from Japan, offered to continue being my roommate after college. I had refused, as I had adventures to live and didn't want to be tied down to anything in North Carolina in order to fully ride the winds. The same winds that overwhelmed me and brought me right back here to Raleigh.

Still walking in my Wind shoes, I climb up the steps to Wolf's new apartment that he had rented for himself during the summer. It has two bedrooms, one of which is being kept empty.

"Maybe I'm just psychic and knew that you'd end up crawling back here, needing a space to live."

The room he shows me has plenty of space and its own bathroom. The rent's cheaper than we used to pay; he offers to cover me through September in return for the security deposit I had let him keep from our old place. The fact that I can barely focus and am not really in a position to be stable helps add to my case. We watch *Moana*, and I dance to every song and scene, wearing myself out and releasing plenty of energy.

I relax and sleep. Finally, I sleep. In my own room. With my own boxes surrounding me. With nothing else to confuse me or project onto my fragile psyche, I lay down to rest deeply.

I wake up slowly and lumber about like Beast with my brother's eagle blanket wrapped around me. Hundreds of miles away, my mother finally exhales as Wolf tells her that I have gotten some actual rest.

Wolf and I start our day off with lots of enthusiasm as we finally finish *Code Geass*. Since we began this series, Wolf insisted that he was Lelouch and that I am Suzaku, but whenever I watched it during my INTJ-personality teenage years, I identified with Lelouch. Watching the final episodes, I see Suzaku duel Karen. I comment that Karen is my type of girl, and Wolf replies, "Of course. You love a woman who can beat you at your own game."

That line hits me straight through the heart. POW!

"You win, Wolf! Oh man, I am Suzaku after all?" I laugh cathartically as I roll around on the carpet. "You win, you win."

I ride Eternity to the motorcycle shop, and when I arrive to get Eternity some maintenance, the workers comment.

"It's a miracle you made the drive here on this thing, there's a lot wrong with it. Honestly, it may be time for an upgrade rather than pour more money into repairs."

I don't want to think about all the money I'd spent on Eternity over the years, nor the brand-new after-market Two Brothers spoiler I splurged on a mere six months ago. Riding the magic wave of joy and enthusiasm, I let the salesman dance me through the process of purchasing a new motorcycle. Wow! Really? Could I accomplish all this in one day? One caveat: I need my old title to trade in Eternity (I don't want to think about how they paid me barely more than the spoiler alone is worth for her) to buy my new bike.

Wolf comes through with another miracle—despite hanging out with a friend, he digs through my half-unpacked boxes and finds my title, then drives out to meet me at the dealership. I had brought my katana to the dealership, and now I understood why.

Time for Suzaku to kill Lelouch!

I approach Wolf's Jeep in slow motion with my sword, re-enacting the final scene! Life is so fun! Synchronicities abound, yet Wolf in logistics mode is nonplussed. That's when we wander around the showroom floor, and I pretend I haven't selected a bike yet to ask for his recommendation. I motion toward some electric bikes that have the same color scheme as Eternity, trying to throw Wolf off my trail. We arrive at a white bike that has green color highlights and Wolf instantly says, "This is the one. It looks just like Lancelot." (Lancelot is the Mech Suzaku pilots.) The MOMENT he finishes his sentence, one of the salesmen rolls up and says, "We'll get this ready for you to ride out."

Timing is everything, no? I had already selected that bike! I cackle at Wolf. I go all out on my spending spree, getting a new helmet for my passengers, a new shirt, and ordering a second new helmet for myself. Wolf looks through the catalog. I trust he knows my style and immediately finds the one for me: this one. It's called "Wanderer." Though it has black, red, and white stripes, he assures me the contrast will go quite nicely with the bike.

Did I mention part of my excitement is that it's an attempt to surprise Lotus, who I plan to meet at the gardens later? I can barely contain my joy at the magic of this day! Perhaps you can feel it in this picture:

I ride off on my new steed to meet Lotus, who is already deep in the gardens. We take a nice grounding walk through the beauty. When we exit, I take her right to the bike with an air of nonchalance.

"Oh cool, a new motorcycle," she says in a calm even tone, not even skipping a beat! Beat me at my own game, huh? She comments on how it is much more masculine. I realize this is the first male bike I've owned, in addition to being the first brand new one.

We ride to a sushi restaurant, where we enjoy another sumptuous meal. My father calls during the meal to clear up the argument we had earlier: I wanted him to co-sign on an apartment for me so that I can have my OWN space, all to myself, and he refused to help me get tied down. His logic doesn't reach me, and I only feel emotionally betrayed. During this phone call, I talk in a more sober manner about the realities of things; I agree it's sensible to stay with Wolf outside of the bounds of a lease, keeping my options open. He comments, "Wow, you're making a lot more sense now. Being with Lotus seems to be good for you."

In more ways than I can convey.

Zero Wind

My days become more full of life, as my sense of time re-orients to the majesty of the present moment. Guided by my heart, I still like to be of service each day and productive. Convincing myself that Sun's place needs me to Virgo it (read: organize and clean), I drive over there to put in my hours for the day. Internally, I begin to organize my own worlds by labeling things—Sun's place becomes her "lair"—which I don't even realize reflects how I feel about her being some ominous boss type. Even Lotus, who has more than a bucketful of reasons to harbor resentment toward Sun, discourages me calling it that. Sun called her place "Samaksha," which means "inside" (or going within) in Hindi, and I practice my pronunciation as I clean.

Later in the day, I meet with Lotus at the lake where we go for a slow walk. My cousins call and I have Lotus talk with them. They ask, "Is he on drugs? Why is he so happy?" But I don't let the comments phase me, I'm busy holding onto a key that I've had since I rented my first apartment with my first girlfriend back in Hawai'i. Saying my goodbye and recognizing my need to let go of something weighing me down, I throw the key far into Lake Johnson. Lotus comes up to me and gifts me a new uncut key—which has a Fox painted on it!

I looked at her, surprised. "But you got this for yourself? And it brought you a lot of meaning and joy!"

"Well, it feels right to give it to you."

Letting go is never without compensation by the Universe, which always seems ready to fill one's life with new joy and fresh energy!

On this particular day, Sun has her own manic episode, which is very acute. I can feel her through the aether but don't know how I would even begin to be present for her. Instead, I have dinner with Lotus, and every bite is exceptionally savory and potent. I feel like the traitor in the Matrix, Cypher, the character eating his illusory steak while saying "ignorance is bliss." I feel her suffering, yet I enjoy myself instead. I take her my leftovers—we were eating at an Indian restaurant—and attempt to drop it off with Sol, who had come over to help her. I can barely stand to be in the same room with her, as our energies blend into chaotic pain and psychosis. I drive off from there with Lotus, who assures me there is nothing I can do and that I am in no place to help anyone.

I don't remember the order of events, but at some point I know I need to retrieve the rest of my boxes from my father's place. I'm in a rush to have all my stuff (read: energy) in one place. Sun agrees to travel up with me to drop me off for a few days of recovery. Now that I have my new ride, I have a better idea that involves more freedom: I'll meet her there on my motorcycle! She recruits a friend to help her drive, and they go up to Virginia hours ahead of me.

Free from the psychic entanglement for a moment, I take the time to rush around and get some things for my room as well as pick up what Lotus says love looks like to her: a bag of trail mix.

I arrive at her work to surprise her and kneel down before her with a great smile on my face. Here I am, your knight! She, the Queen of Flowers at Harris Teeter, accepts my offering (along with the delicate white fan I had taken from Sun's apartment), and sends me off on my journey.

I drive north, bonding with my new ride. At a rest stop, my body feels the need to rest—just like that time in 2014—but I don't make a big show out of it. Instead, I stumble. My bike crashes on its left side, snapping off the clutch down the middle. My eyes tear up—not at the breaking of my new vehicle—but because I look down at the scar on my own left wrist.

"We're the same, aren't we, Zero?"

I learn later that Japanese often will mar something brand new or ritually give it an imperfection. This is because only "Kami-sama" (translated often as: God) is perfect and through our imperfections, we learn to be humble.

With a new sense of camaraderie (and no motorcycle jacket, mind you), I continue my journey. An intense rain starts to fall—and going 70 mph against my t-shirt—the raindrops feel like bullets. I steel my resolve to continue. Getting lost along the way near Richmond, I stop for some food to ground myself. The voices of the people at Chipotle go by like they are on fast forward, and I have an eerie feeling of being in the Matrix again. After that, I stop one more time to watch the sunset turn orange, finally rolling into my father's before it is dark.

Of course, I had left a stranger and Sun to be with them for a few hours, so the air is a bit uncertain. I make a joke about why I enter wearing sunglasses, saying, "The Sun is too bright." But my stepmother harshly cuts me down, "That is not funny. I thought she was having a stroke."

Apparently, Sun had been feeling my pain the whole ride and was having a very rough time processing energy. Alone, she comments we haven't done the Sun/Moon dance since I returned from Peru. I go through the motions with her. Something clicks into place, and she leaves with her friend in my car to take my stuff to Raleigh.

I sleep deeply that night, as I always do at what I call "TT's Wood Haven," and I wake up in the morning feeling like I'm in a new world.

Time is not Set in Stone

Let's take a break! As I've finally come down from a manic episode without medication or hospitalization! Exhale some sweet relief, dear reader, and let's focus on you for a bit. What do you think about time? That the past is done and history and move on, and that the future is ours for the making? My brother once said, "The present destroys the past to create the future," and not a truer juxtaposition can be had between us. For all that, my past obscures the present (what is this book you hold, after all?) and limits my creation of the future...

Yet, I have learned much from writing my story. One lesson is that the past is not fixed. For instance, today I talked to a confidant of mine about one of these episodes that I felt so much pain around. Turns out I had crafted a *story* about the past and maintained a certain perspective that was bringing me pain. Cancer Sun Signs often pride themselves on the ability to record the past accurately, but today I have released that sin and am willing to view things differently. As I sat on my deck in a similar situation three years ago, I noticed that by bringing myself FULLY into the present moment—I am actually doing what is best for everyone. Now, I can take this healthy perspective and shine it on the episode I completed writing on: Was I truly Cypher? Did I betray my friend? No, in essence it was more like how Lotus had seen it. By being fully present and enjoying my dinner with her, I was stabilizing the only reality I had control over. That isn't to say my communication skills were flawless, but I can let go of the guilt of the situation.

Oftentimes in healing work, people are asked to examine the stories we are *holding onto,* and I always took that to mean the current story and perspective with which we view our life. But what of where we've been? Can we look at our origin stories in a new light? Bring freshness to what *more* may have been going on in those crystalized moments?

I invite you to journal a bit about the first pain point that comes to mind. A divorce? A job loss? Whatever it may be, notice what you tell yourself about why it's happened or the way it reflects on you. Now, since the pain is still there, I implore you to *dig deeper* to find the gems of wisdom hidden in that experience. Listening to those emotions—as opposed to making a story about what they mean or analyzing them—will help guide you to a fuller perspective. Take as long as you need to reflect, discuss with a friend, or dream about a new way of seeing the story itself. I am a champion of taking the initiative to investigate the past, so that life does not need to reconstruct scenarios to trigger us and bring it up! If there's anything I've learned from the *Power of Now* by Eckhart Tolle, it is that within each moment is a beautiful melody—if we only but listen.

Full Circle

In Virginia, late August 2017, the feeling upon waking is none other than "my mind is healed." I no longer feel the manic rush, pressure, the intensity, and high. The flow of energy still is close to my sensations and perception, but I am not being swept away. Time slows down, and peace exists in the air. My stepmother is a natural at Feng Shui, simply because she feels the subtleties of things and acts according to her intuition. With her help, I craft a letter to help me return to the old spa I worked at before I left for Japan: Hand and Stone.

It's a bittersweet feeling, as one of my more profound massage sessions before I had left was with a woman who had suffered many injuries in a car accident. She said to me, "When you come back from Japan, you'll be far beyond this place!" She encouraged me to reach my full potential, yet here I am returning to that same place of employment a full year and a half later.

"It's good to have a spring board, something you can rely on and do without any thought. From there, you can push off into new territory with Healcyon," my father advises.

Despite feeling a lot more balanced, I don't spend multiple nights with my father. I had promised Wolf that I would watch a movie with him that night, so my loyalty and commitment to my word compels me to override what rest my body may need. I leave later that afternoon after only one night's sleep; my return trip goes much more smoothly. My father gives me an oversized jacket to protect me from the elements on the ride down.

Back at Wolf's place, which we have begun to call the Rainbow Thieves' Hideout (the name is a work in progress), we start to watch *Deadpool* and I immediately fall asleep. When manic, sometimes it's easier to go to overstimulation, white noise, and pass out rather than retrace your steps down to relaxed and decompressed!

Regardless, the trip to my father's proved healing on multiple levels. I feel encouraged in a deep way that I have come down from a manic episode without visiting the hospital! This reinforces my belief that supportive relationships—people who will accept you as you are, as you show up, and ample freedom to navigate the experience in a way that is personally meaningful are enough to restore equilibrium. Trusting in the wisdom of our mind/body's ability to heal allows me to "come back down" from any spiritual high. That is not to say that all manic episodes are necessarily true spiritual awakenings and breakthroughs, so your mileage may vary.

Still I cannot emphasize enough how pivotal this episode was in my healing. It was one thing to feel deep down that, no, I'm not crazy, and that a path existed beyond the current paradigm of mental illness. It is quite another to ACTUALLY live it, to go far beyond the deep end with plant medicines and then for stability and equilibrium to return to my psyche without ending up in the hospital or using pharmaceuticals! With grace, I was granted the

actual experience of Madness to Magic, without which this book would not exist. It would only be a collection of wild experiences from the perspective of madness. Let this be the spark of hope for the world that indeed there is
Another way.

Process and Renewal

Half a year later or so, in the spring of 2018, a series of synchronicities helps me open back up the Peru experiences. I come across someone at the Buddhist temple I meditate at, the Kadampa Center, who spontaneously brings up plant medicines to me in conversation. The box of Peru lay before me, and I feel ready to peek inside.

To start off the week, I walk with a girl who has also traveled around Brazil and done a few Ayahuasca ceremonies. Interacting with her opened the box; I felt myself singing in my helmet the whole drive from Hillsborough back to Raleigh to process the energies that had been frozen in time and space.

I call my Machu Picchu hike buddy, Dave, and he shares how much of his life has changed since returning. He references our Ayahuasca experiences as "getting our Soul ripped out in the jungle," and I laugh a deep laugh of resonance! That is exactly how it felt!

I open my journal that I wrote in and began to read through some of my experiences, touching on what happened. That Wednesday, I go to a Core Shamanic Practitioner meetup and mysteriously I'm the only one to arrive. I share my experience with my Durham Shamanic mentors, Marcia and Jack Hebrank, about what happened in Peru. I mention the gruesome death of a blue jay on my apartment's sidewalk as well (which happened before my trip), connecting as many dots as possible. Marcia "Moon" looks off into the distance as she does when communicating with the spirit world.

"What I'm getting from the blue jay ... is that you were saved from something much worse by leaving the center."

I'm reassured to know that for this whole time, I was beating myself up for acting out of fear and fleeing the center, but perhaps my survival instincts really were protecting me from shattering my mind beyond repair...

And THEN having successfully come down from a manic episode without hospitalization or medication and being able to process some of the trauma from Peru—I go on to live a stable life with Lotus and don't go pulling any more reckless adventures with plant medicine. I even start working for myself full time and enjoy the independence of adulthood!

Yet, as you can see the book has still more pages in it. It pains me to confess that I did not learn my lessons deeply enough to navigate the Sun and Lotus dynamic in a healthier way. Nor did I listen to my friend's sound advice on the manner. A series of breakups with Lotus turned out to be blows, causing deeper damage than I realized, and more grief than I could handle alone. What breaks my heart continually still is that at the start of 2018, I really had the option to be more gentle with myself—to participate in the unfolding of life and relax into grace. I had gotten so stuck in the story that I needed to let go of Lotus, that somehow enjoying a relationship was bad or counter to spiritual growth, that I had formed a deep habit of leaving and then being unable to live without her. During one rare moment, I heard a kinder soft voice as I was burning up paper in a fire ritual to let go of her once more. It asked, "Are you sure?" I broke down in tears, then wondered if we could even have anything healthy after so much damage had been caused. I was despairing and feeling unworthy of the chance I was being given. Well, here I am learning forgiveness and compassion for the mistakes of youth. Stories, remember?

For a long time, I thought words like "I'm happy with who I am now, so I can make peace with the past" or "it all happened exactly as it needed to" were empty cop-outs to avoid the pain that mistakes really were made. However, here in 2020 (with 20/20 hindsight!), I am finally ready to say at least this much:

No matter what ways I could have gone, the path I walked has meaning and richness that is unique to it. I will honor the way in which I learned my lessons, so that I may not repeat the same mistakes.

Moving Forward—

11

Journey to the West

Moving Backward

August 2018, I find myself in Portland. I'm at this beautiful Chinese garden staring at two pink lotuses, with one in the shadow and one in the light. I'm on the phone with Lotus. We're talking about how this needs to end. Yet, we're having such a peaceful conversation, and there's not even a flicker of disharmony or tension.

"This sucks," she reflects.

"I know."

Yet we continue through the motions of breaking up, it being "necessary" or "right" and I hang up the phone for the last time. That's when I somehow press a button on my screen while putting my phone away, and I hear her voice whisper through the pond.

I take it as a sign, much like letting go of a key only to receive another. Letting go has renewed us! I answered with excitement that perhaps all we needed to do was let go, and here we are!

She laughs lightly, then heaviness sinks in like a rain cloud. "No, Arthur, nothing's changed."

My brother and I are welcomed into Portland by a friend's friend group (my friend being in Tibet, so they were barely more than strangers). Very quickly, they help clear our energies and interact with us on an authentic soul level! We are offered a place to stay and even a car to borrow to see some sights! I literally am in more culture shock than when I visited Japan ... is this the same country as the East Coast? The morning after my breakup with Lotus, I stare out with a sad look.

A Gemini born in the year of the Horse—twelve years older than me—mocks my pouting.

"You're acting like there's some way to make a mistake! I can't work with this energy. Boo hoo," he shoos me away so he can focus on his business. Part of me feels invalidated (am I not allowed to grieve? To have remorse?) and yet I want to live up to the constant happiness that this community seems to foster—the joy of being. What I discover is Portland's dark side: that going deep with someone does not mean a real and lasting bond has formed. I finish out my adventure in Portland and return to Seattle where I stay with my brother as he goes about his life.

I keep thinking about Lotus—at the animal zoo, at all the beautiful places I'd love to share with her. Going against my gut, I text her sitting in my brother's apartment while he's at school. Immediately, I dissociate, get up from my chair, and the clear quartz on my lap falls and breaks.

Whenever things break in my life, it feels as if I have lived a little too carelessly, as if I have once again shattered life's ongoing attempt to heal the damage I have caused.

Hammer of Fate

"You can learn anything if you're willing to fuck it up." -Dad

I return from my trip with so much energy I don't even enter a deep sleep the first night back in Raleigh. Before I left, I had promised I would see Lotus first on return, yet she can't seem to stay awake as I drive back in the rain. This aligns with the eerily prophetic bag of potato chips I saw at Whole Foods earlier which read, "Waited till I saw the Sun"—a literal sign that shook me in my bones. The next day, I see Sun at a dream group and catch her off guard by showing up at her place to carpool.

My impulse to participate in synchronicities and surprise people overrides any common sense, as usual.

My transition into Virgo season is rife with energy and a bit of a blur as usual (it was during Virgo season that I had the blackout for nine days). I make an adult decision between meeting up with some friends in Canada who drink and play board games and my new friends, who offer a camping trip on the Appalachian Trail over Labor Day weekend. The camping retreat is with two new male friends, and we push each other's edges in a decent way. I come back from that trip having unlocked my anger—not knowing I had so thoroughly cast it aside as undesirable emotion!

Next on the whirlwind, I am driving up north to Virginia on my motorcycle to attend my high school reunion. Caught in the rain, my phone gets fried, and my stepfather offers his sage advice as he is wont to do at these critical junctures. "It's ... important to keep an even-keel," he warns. I arrive for my reunion earlier than everyone else, and in my exuberant Fire energy get to have a lively conversation with a group of older gals out having a good time together. Seeing all the changes and hearing what everyone's been up to—or not, has its own usual blandness and formalities. I hug my best friend from that time as I go to leave, and he pulls me back in tighter. I hear him say something curious, "They aren't coming yet, we still have time." It feels as if we have a sacred moment to really love each other across the far-flung dimensions and timelines in which we normally find ourselves.

I return from that trip with all the extra adrenaline of one who has ridden a motorcycle in the rain and has driven five hours in one day. Unexpected construction delays me a crucial twenty-five minutes and I end up missing the one student that signed up to learn Qi Gong from me in downtown Raleigh. Strong emotions lead to seeking support and comfort, so I end up making my way to Lotus's apartment and finding her car instantly—though she never told me where she lives now. Almost every fiber of my being tells me to stop, respect her wishes, her new space, and leave. As if the spirit of my steed refuses to disrespect her boundaries, I point my wheels back down the hill and leave.

That doesn't stop me from texting her that I stumbled upon her home anyway, which leads to us meeting up for dinner.

As I lay out on the back porch in the sunlight before she comes over, I feel-sense-see a giant silver hammer with a red handle swinging its way from way out in the deep sky straight toward me. When it reaches me, I shoot up, having been struck quite viscerally, and not knowing what to make of this vision.

I can only call it the Hammer of Fate, coming down to wield justice on my stubborn booty.

The Value of Sacrifice

After another painful breakup in late September, I make it perhaps a week or two without contacting her. I go on a camping trip out to the Smoky Mountains with my dream guild, and we connect under the stars. When I return and reach out to Lotus, I have a deep inner sense that has never been there before. All the other times we had parted ways only to come back together, it had been at my own hand (and sometimes hers—forever the saint of patience, she, too, is human and can handle only so much before doing something about it) and never had a feeling of finality. Yet, at the store I stop to smell and buy fresh flowers, and prepare however I can to enjoy my time with her. A sense of dread, of impending ending, a sorrow at the ephemeral nature of life.

"Why are you being so kind to me?" she asks.

I hold her in response, not finding the words over the sound of my breaking heart.

She returns the next day, having forgotten her flowers, and she confesses how she had a conversation with (who I'll call her "new boo") where she confronted him about how he wasn't official with her and what he would need to do if he wanted to change that.

I start to have the eerie feeling, not quite of deja vu, but a similar sensation. A feeling like I am at the juncture of timelines: a feeling like the decision I make will actually change things, will change the course of fate. My instinct is toward freedom, telling her that I don't want her to have to choose between us or for me to distract her from a new start. It wasn't even a question of "not going for what I wanted" (her); the only things in my mind as far as motivations were that I had no confidence that I wouldn't continue to hurt her. I wanted her to be free because I saw myself as an unavoidable source of pain and instability in her life; free of the bipolar swings and chaotic torrent of my inner world. I felt the stirrings of fear, too—what if she simply didn't choose me if given the choice?

"Will I ever see you again?" she asks, standing at her Evergreen Camry door, parked on Deboy St.

"に"

The Fresh Snow of the West

I manage my way through October with a great focus on getting and maintaining clients. Business picks up, and my trust in the Universe to provide for me financially continues to grow. The end of October rolls around with another Qi Gong workshop with my Stillness-Movement Family in Colorado.

My flight is due to leave very early this second time going to Colorado. I schedule a Lyft ride for the morning, only to have the driver cancel on me with a mere forty-five minutes to go until my flight. I panic and get a taxi, arriving at the airport shy underthirty0 minutes before, where I am promptly denied. I knew thirty minutes was cutting it close, but the new policy is apparently that one must at least be there an hour before check-in.

I am devastated and desperate. I sit down to meditate and wonder how I'll hold out for the next eight hours or so before my new flight. I cave and call Lotus, refusing to call my friends that would come out at no hesitation, for emotional support. The need for a ride is the excuse I use to break the gate on how I'd been holding back from my impulse to reach out to her. She doesn't answer, and I end up calling my friend who shows up soon enough.

I feel ashamed to ask for help at all, and the regret weighs heavy as plans get shattered and remade. Sun drops me off and does a Tarot reading, unsure of whether to act on her own desires to stay longer with me or not. I end up asking her to leave in the cold morning sunlight, so that I may take a nap and try to refresh myself.

I ask my other friend for the ride back to the airport later that morning. This lets me spread around my detestable neediness and desire to not spend more money on cab rides.

The trip brightens up from there, as the winds of freedom take over on any journey: completely free from the patterns of my day-to-day life, I am able to stretch my wings a bit more.

I fly north first with this new flight change and end up sitting next to a woman in the same field of alternative healing as me. She shares a lot of her wisdom and encourages by saying "never give up this Qi Gong family you have, even if your practice evolves or changes over time."

With the original plan, I was due to arrive early to Colorado and be up in the mountains that same day. Now, I'm spending a night in Denver, which allows me to check in with the same AirBnB I used last time—a Japanese woman who remembered my thank-you note written in Japanese to her from last year! We have more time to talk this go around, and I am pleased to have a lighthearted connection with someone who has opened their house to me.

The ride up to the mountains is filled with magic and wonder as well. First, I meet a bus driver on the route back to the airport. He lets me call him "the Mathematician" and allows me to ride the bus for free, given I didn't have the small change for the trip. Many passengers greet him and give him hugs. He comes across to me as the undercover Bodhisattva/priest of this route he's been working for some time.

He starts to give me advice as well, but quickly finds me to be the free spirit type and says, "I can't help you at all." Little does he know how much I learn from seeing him be himself and the value I put in his way of life and perspective. He attempts to help me anyway and teaches me the way of the Mathematician: how men need to use logic and approach things in a certain way. I've had a pretty rough and tumble relationship with logic these past few years, haven't I?

Yet, slowly I start to understand the sense in what he is saying—and in what a lot of people have been saying. Wasn't it with some logic and sense that Lotus was able to guide me back from the edges of madness? Didn't I use logic to protect me from the unchecked impulses and feelings that were like a storm tearing me apart inside? I had been crushed at every attempt to play Go in Japan. My last chess match in Portland featured me gaining an advantage of a master through emotional diversion, but then losing without the proper calculated follow-through.

Yes, maybe there is something to this being a mathematician after all. Perhaps, it isn't too far from how I actually live but simply more awareness of what I've been doing this whole time...

At the airport, I meet the shuttle driver, an old Grey Fox. There's someone in the backseat who is going up to the YMCA camp nearby, and the Grey Fox talks to both of us for a bit while still in Denver.

Then he turns to me on the open road and confesses his intentions.

"God revealed to me some time ago why I needed to drive this van. Whoever sits where you are sitting right, we are to have real Conversations. It's very special that we've met, just as your friend Ben did yesterday."

He continues to deepen his talk as we go through a quantum dive. I notice the lady in the back is fast asleep. I don't imagine there's any coincidence at play here and start to take Grey Fox's words to heart. He shares some stories of people performing the same miracles as Jesus—such as the multiplication of food at a wedding he was at.

While these stories have always made me remember how truly mysterious and beyond us is the nature of reality, I find myself not as moved by them emotionally anymore. Perhaps I've lost my sense of awe, of wonder, in light of all this heartbreak? They come across as a standard report of magic to me, with far less of an impact than if it happened right in front of me. Perhaps, all this mathematician talk has left me jaded...

He asks me what the foundation—the real core of reality is. I go into some philosophical Daoist talk of emptiness, the void, the primordial—

"It's love," he says softly. With a real tenderness. My logic softens up, as do my walls, and my heart sinks; how far have I gone from love?

As we ascend the mountain, a deeper lesson of this ride—and trip—starts to hit me.

The lesson of Granite.

"Look at all this granite, do you know where it comes from?"

"I don't know much about geology," I admit.

"Granite forms on the crust of the earth's core and is slowly pushed up to the surface of untold years."

Molten earth from the very depth and core itself. This is the quality I want to find in myself—to embrace really—as I step out into the uncharted waters of a new future.

A Trip to the Far Side of the Moon

My roommate had been attuning to the mountain since the previous day when I arrived. He takes me on a hike to some places of power—where one can connect with the spirit of the mountain a bit more easily. The fresh air, the pines, and the loving support of the boulders, we find help refresh mountains of stress off my shoulders.

The Tarot reading he offers me centers me in the Warrior archetype even more strongly; the wisdom of Celtic spirits, trees, and our plant kingdom allies.

I've always had mixed feelings about the Warrior—because I know far too many people in the military and men who live very structured and disciplined lives for the sake of others. I do my best to support and care for people, so the Healer always fits better—but what exactly is so Warrior-like about learning the arts of meditation and energy healing? Aren't all my physical needs being catered on this beautiful mountain surrounded by understanding and loving friends?

Spirit, as always, has the answers to these questions. Of course, it doesn"t come through in words this time around.

The workshop begins, and we warm up slowly to the altitude change. We're pretty high and that night we get even higher. We do a communal marijuana passing, and I take only two short hits knowing my sensitivity to this medicine.

It's the full moon, too, but I don't connect that with what happened in Peru because Ayahuasca has so much more ritual and intent put into its use. Even with my spiritual family, while learning Qi Gong, it has the air of casualness to it.

We ascend the mountain, bathing in the moonlight.

We physically descend, but I take one more hit to finish off the joint. With a wink to the moon, I dedicate the experience to following my promise to her. To always follow my heart.

The swirl that follows is hard to describe. As a wave might carry one from his vessel into the sea, I feel I am at the mercy of the tides. My friends quickly perceive this shift and come to my aid.

"You're at the place where you've lost control of the situation, but you have the tools to get through this."

I do the same thing I have done many times with fear—I face it and choose to move forward. I know panic won't help at all and my friends' words reassure me. A few guests arrive late in the lobby and I can feel more of them than I would ever want to. Seeing this, Nisa helps me into the practice room where I am able to practice with Canadian Ben some stretches and movements. We warm up and go through some stretches, where he remarks that "You're at the point where you can make physical changes." This sets off a bit of my paranoia—I feel as if I'm about to warp time and space itself and enter the abyss.

"I didn't mean to scare you," he says, as I realize he meant in terms of releasing patterns and healing the body.

We go through a few more moves, but I am anxious to leave and walk toward the door.

"I see that you're in 'go-get-her' mode, but let's take our time here."

I catch myself rushing again and notice my anxiety, how I want this to be over and done and next next next—but what's here to explore?

He offers to do a session on me, and I lay back on the table—feeling his patient hands slowly stretch out my neck and do Daoist healing on a few acupressure points. Even though my sense of time is warped, it still seems like he has the patience of a true craftsman as he sits with me. I offer to return the trade, reassuring him that it will help me and give me something to focus on.

I focus as best as I can in that altered state and make it about halfway up his spine with the Daoist treatment. To my perception, I am able to either clearly do what is necessary and move within the flow better or I'm working within the limits of my altered capacity for mental focus.

I feel "into it," and the session comes to its close.

Out in the lobby, my friends worry about me, as Canadian Ben escorts me to my room. I turn to him and ask, "Please make sure Nisa doesn't worry about me." I'm afraid that I'll feel her worry, and that empathy will take me on that spiral path through emotions very difficult to feel.

I take a nice hot shower and bath, reminded of Ben's parting words "know that this is a release process and it's all very natural." I start to trust that whether I've lost my mind again or not, I can enjoy the altered sensations and relaxation I'm feeling. I remember my first time I got "too high" and how afraid I had been that I was dying because everything was so different.

Learning to enjoy myself ... what a deep lesson.

I lie in bed not really falling asleep, as colors and sensations swirl around me. My roommate gets up, but he feels lightyears away. I keep silent and let the feelings wash over me.

The night passes, and I'm able to enjoy my early morning hike in the mountains. The air is crisp and fresh, and I am definitely not the same person I was. With morning, it dawns on me that I have changed on a deep level. Whether I'm back from the other side of the moon or not is a different question; the theme of the workshop of integrating "Two sides as One" continues to spill over into all parts of the day.

Going Starside

The flow begins to take over as I make fewer decisions or perhaps I am not reflecting on them in any sort of mental way. My ride to the airport is offered to me as one later in the evening—a private shuttle service. I finish my time with my family around the fire with Kuan Yin Oracle cards, which have pierced through to our hearts. With the parting hugs, I'm able to feel the reality of how long it will be before I see them again-—the sheer magnitude of experiences that will come and go.

The driver begins to talk to me about how he's good friends with the resident master and a local native chief that helped start up the lodge. I appreciate how casual he is with the often revered master and how he sees through his trickster ways. The conversation then turns to the topic of beings from other star systems and all the races therein. He gives me a brief overview of Sirius, Arcturius, Pleiades, and some darker races I don't recall. He mentions how messed up things got last time that humans went "starside"—linking back to Atlantis I suppose. Little does he know that my experience on the mountain has me taking this in a deeper way—this is my chance as a human to once again go "Starside" and make considerable changes and shifts in my life.

Of course, after a fashion, he shares that he and his family are from the Pleiades. He reminds me that the essence of Qi Gong is in tapping into the universal love and compassion first and then moving from that place. With that energy at the core and intent, one can shape the world for the better and move the hearts of all. I am not surprised at all when he turns out to be an Aquarius, which happens to be the energy I am to learn more and grow toward in this lifetime. Truly, I can feel the vast freedom of mind this being has in his exploration of the Universe.

Oh—one more thing he tells me—in the event of a major catastrophe, there's a star gate hidden in Colorado. I make note to keep that in mind next time the apocalypse rolls around.

Hit the Ground Runnin'

My flight is a redeye back home, and a few hours after arriving I have a client scheduled. Well aware of my difficulty saying no or prioritizing my own needs in these kinds of situations, I figure it will be no problem to have one client. The session goes into a deep peaceful state—the client is a therapist as well, and I always find my focus sharper and energy more palpable in these cases. After that, I meet my new roommate, a Pisces who knows well the language of water.

She's wearing a hat with the Ace of Spades on it—my favorite card. I feel like this will be a great new arrangement and make no attempt to hide my exhaustion.

"Rest your bones," she says. Those words are a magical spell that carries me into my bedroom where I lie down for a long time.

12

To Infinity, and Below

Cutting the Root

Four or five days pass as if they were nothing at all. I remember clearly the second day back because I took Sun to a Tuesday night meeting with other spiritually-minded professionals. Faith was the organizer's name, and she was sharing with us the healing power of dance and contact improv. In moments that defied time, she chose me to demonstrate the beauty of contact improvisation—a dance in which Spirit leads. I leave the room after that so the energies may settle where they may—the other participants are a bit awkward about contact and not wanting to be watched.

Well, I also want some fresh air. Ever since Colorado, air quality has been very important to me. The next day is Halloween, and I dress up to offer the only candy I have to the only group of kids who ring my doorbell. Sun shows up and the air is tense. To me, she is the harbinger of death in many ways. I challenge her to a duel outside since we both have costumes and let her borrow a sword. My gaze grows cold. This moment feels like the only time I've stood up for myself—for who I am and my own importance. My stance is defensive, and since she is not the aggressive type to initiate combat, the duel comes to nothing. Part of me wishes that we could've fought—some outlet for the rage simmering beneath the surface. Rage at all the ways I betrayed myself to accommodate her feelings.

I call Canadian Ben to check in with his re-entry process. He shares some things that have happened. When sharing the whirlwind of my week, he replies, "Did you cut your roots to the earth or something? You feel very ungrounded." I take offense to that as it came off as criticism rather than a timely warning.

This is on the first day of November.

Stranger and Stranger Still

The second day dawns, and I walk to the Buddhist temple in the morning, where we normally sit and meditate around 7:30 on weekdays to start our day right. Around first light, I take my wooden sword, since I feel like cutting through to the heart of reality some more. I run to the park where I do some sharp movements in the crisp autumn morning, then run across the street up to the temple.

This meditation seems to start like all the others, but we can tell it feels different.

"Rev your psychic engines," my elder friend mentions at the start.

Time goes by in a much different fashion and I try to focus on my breaths. I also feel a bit paranoid, as if my altered state is somehow very apparent to everyone else in their meditation. I let it pass as time marches onward, and we all get up from our cushions in turn.

A few meditators stay in the gompa, looking a bit more closely at the statues on the altar.

Their awareness has shifted, and they start seeing things they never had before—even as some of them had been sitting here for years. We look upon the tantric statue of Avalokiteshvara and see that it is a woman mounted on a man: "Two as One."

"Have you ever noticed that before, Link?"

No, I had not noticed it either.

The Beatles tribute band member gives me a ride to breakfast. I listen to Beatles songs that bring me back years. I am grateful to not have to talk.

On the way back, I'm taken by a man who resembles the devil archetype to me. I don't know why he feels that way, but the similarities of this type seem to be around the question of logic and being a heavy participant in the System.

He remarks that I seem like a carefree type with a lot of time on my hands.

He's right and I try not to keep them idle. Yet, I don't have enough structure in place for all this energy that has been unleashed. My day flows with the whims of the Wind. I had worked all of September with being grounded and free—with the Horse. The Speed of the Horse seems to lend itself to mania if I'm in one place for too long. I remember that time outside the restaurant before I went to my first psychiatrist appointment: "He just needs his own business!" remarked a woman flattered by my enthusiasm and passion.

I have my own business now, but the discipline needed to focus on and make it a priority is currently elsewhere, or perhaps the need to focus on my feelings is rising higher and higher with the tides of energy. In the end, I use all that energy to run from my own feelings, demons, and ghosts that I need to face.

I can see now a bit more clearly what was brewing at that time, with all the clarity of retrospection:

I was running away from the painful reality that someone I had fallen in love with was gone and that I would never hold her in my arms again. It was away from the truth that life is fleeting and things change all the time. It was away from the fall, which brought with it all the sadness that comes from letting leaves fall to the ground—and all the beauty of remembering a life lived.

When one doesn't truly live, then the regrets of both the past and the unlived past weigh down the heart.

I was running from death after all. Or straight toward it, as is often the case with destiny…

Will you stay awhile?

I race through the streets carrying my wooden Katana named Sangue. I must look like some daredevil samurai, driving around in second gear on Zero, wielding a sword with my clutch hand.

TO INFINITY, AND BELOW

I kneel down before Princess Death to whom I always return. Today, she is in the form of a Scorpio that I have always admired. She understands her role immediately.

"I am Batman, here to serve."

"And should I kill you today, Batman?"

"If I stray from the path, please do so."

I offer her my sword with all the weight that it carries. With all the weight of the past.

She accepts, for Death does not feel the weight of such things, and is indeed what frees us always.

She climbs onto my motorcycle with that way of hers—folding her arms across my upper back.

To luxuriate in this feeling, to take off with her and bring her to the other side of the moon … To not look back even once…

Yet, what remains of my common sense nudges me, and I think of her boyfriend: "He's waiting for you, isn't he?"

I go to vote after seeing a sign—a literal one. An endless line winds its way through Talley like the intestines of a great beast and I think I can cut in front all the way at the top of the snaking queue. Today's magic, after all.

I'm met with a real anger in the eyes of those who were patient.

"It's fot Fair."

They're right … who do I think I am after all?

I go get my haircut instead where it gets chopped because of how rushed I am and how rushed that makes Sun. Empathy can be a beautiful and terrible thing.

The rain beats hard in the night as I ride to a friend's house despite my exhaustion—*I want to honor my word.*

There the table is all set for some nostalgia, but my friend can tell something troubles me. He feeds me, and our third friend arrives before any questions can be asked that strike deeply.

We play Super Smash Brothers Melee, which would normally remind me of my childhood days and endless games played against my brother. Yet, my mind stays fractured and partially in another dimension. I'm more interested in the unicorns and rainbows my friend's wife has. She wraps my scarf around me so that I feel comfortable and safe.

My friends start coughing harshly, and I feel like I'm warping reality a bit too much. When it's time to go, my friend asks me to stay and talk—really open up to him. I say I'll stay for forty-five minutes because it's late.

We move outside to talk. I'm afraid of him, I don't know why—isn't he Magneto? Doesn't he harbor some deep darkness that is his vision for the world?

I leave in less than five minutes, unable to withstand the intensity of his gaze or surrender to his offered help.

He watches me go by, and I feel the look of sadness—another chance to open up missed.

Another choice to go the hard way.

To Die without a Funeral

I have a client at 3 p.m. that Saturday, so dying is really inconvenient. I don't remember when, since the days run together, but I did a meditation with Snow Leopard the other night.

Snow Leopard gashes into me, and then sits with me while my life bleeds out. Her gaze is full of truth, and she teaches me to stay present with the fear of losing my life. I feel the unsurmountable truth of the end of mortality ... time fades as blood drips. All fades to black.

It's a day when the sun is out but I can feel the rain. I can feel the storm of another timeline and I want the two to merge as one. The sun and the rain, coming together on the same day.

Have you ever felt the sunshine while it rains?
Have you ever sung into the depths of the clouds?
Have you ever been hit by the first drop of rain?

I have a lot of questions today. They all start with "how does it feel?" I feel like singing that line: how does it feel? I feel so much...

How does it feel
To be hit by lightning

TO INFINITY, AND BELOW

To be hit again and again?

I keep pacing in squares, keenly aware of the squares in life and making connections with the four corners:

Of a sidewalk

Of a carpet pattern

Of a deck

Of a tile floor.

I pace and pace and trace the outlines of all the squares.

On the deck, I remember living in all the timelines at once, knowing that I have to die. I see myself jumping over the side of it, while also sitting in a corner. I feel my body at the bottom of the lake near my house and how I'm drowning with my head pointing down.

Wake Arthur up after winter.

Wake Arthur up after winter's rest.

King Arthur sleeps below Great Britain for when he is needed again.

I wake up on my massage table, which is set up for my client. A client that is turned away by my friends, who explain I am in no condition to see anyone. I'm guided around my own house, barely knowing who I am. I see a bit of a stain on the massage sheets and table. I realize that was where he died—probably from being struck by lightning. That he was me, right? Who am I now?

I see my Wayfinder necklace has been shattered, two of the petals coming off of Terra's orange keepsake.

My new roommate is unloading all her stuff and Wolf observes that we have a clash in energies that's pretty strong. She mentions feeling like "scrambled eggs" and that's pretty much the perfect image for my current state. Wolf orders food and they take me over to Sun's apartment where I can get some space.

On the way down the steps to her building, Sun says, "I'm really feeling it now." Whatever *it* is, at least we're both feeling it.

It's the feeling of reality no longer being what it was.

It's the feeling of the Matrix and invisible eyes watching you and your loved ones at all times.

It's the feeling of paranoia that things will never be the same, that you've been irreversibly
broken.

With this feeling in my heart, I ask Wolf, "Is there any going back?"

"No. I don't think so. This is how people learn."

With no idea what I'm learning, we share the Mediterranean food in front of us. Wolf goes home to get some rest, since he hadn't been sleeping well for a long time and today was intense to say the least.

I have a hundred different ideas that I keep switching between with no apparent ability to let Sun guide the dance. My focus level is at about two minutes max as I jump from one excitement to the next. It's so nice to be alive!

Twilight sets in, and Sun guides me to the outdoors where we find ourselves in the Rose Garden. The crescent moon peeks into the sky as we rest a bit at the fountain. Sun performs a ritual to anchor me down to the ground. Yet it goes awry because of her attachment—she gets involved and connects our hearts together. Now, we're a see-saw searching for some sort of balance.

I dance along with the wind and trees until it's time to go home. I'm not quite sure where that is anymore either, but I'm along for the ride. I come down at night, only to rise once more above the clouds with the sunrise.

The roller coaster picks up speed. I'm losing any sense of self that would connect all the events that happen together. At least I know it's Sunday! I call my mother, I cry, and I tell her all about the Rose Garden. I portray it as a dream and since Sun is in earshot, her sense of reality gets clouded as well.

Wolf and I go for a drive. I'm trying to reach the new temple. I give him free reign on where to go—but then he warns if I let impulse guide us, we'll end up at the beach.

I have my Supreme Protector Chinese Medicine herbs, but I feel safe simply holding them and looking at the two guardian warriors.

There are children outside when we get back. They are playing football! I play with them, and feel like half of them are introducing themselves with fake names. "Kilik" is the guardian of the younger children, wearing a grey shirt that has a half white/half black lotus. I like Kilik. He plays in order to bring all things to balance. I can feel that he knows how to slow down time, or maybe time slows as we all dance in the energy of the day—we play for a long stretch until the clouds darken.

Inside Wolf's apartment, in his spare bedroom where I used to live—I have the sense that I need to lock myself in here. It's an empty room, and the only stimulus I bring in is a giant blue yoga ball. I draw hearts in pencil around dents on the bathroom door. I feel like I have everything I need. Only trouble is I don't know how to slow down or how to feel boredom or how to rest. I spin out as much energy as I can with the foam nunchucks Wolf loans me. I black out for a spell. Wolf takes me back to my apartment, where he asks if I want to go see *Venom* with him. I hesitate and feel like it's time to go to sleep and be in my own space instead. The rational thing to do 'n all.

The only thing I'm forgetting is that my new roommate is at my house and it's no longer my own space, but a swirling field of chaos that I have not been able to stabilize in.

And for my Final Trick—

I go insane. Well, no. To me, I am merely putting together as much of a surprise as I can. Do you know the left hand of God? The left hand that acts during the night, when the right one sleeps? The left one that makes a mess of things and come morning, the right one asks, "What happened? What has been done?"

Well, if you don't know of it—maybe this night will show you. Show you all the magic of chaos:

I call Wolf over. I know he won't be asleep (or don't care). I need him for this part because he's part of my "behind the scenes" crew. I message online one of my fellow Ravens, who had gone through some rough times of not sleeping in the past and a divorce as painful as mine. He suggests I go to the beach—a nice, long stretch on the beach would do wonders for my soul right now—and I agree.

But first, does Lotus know how much I love her?

With Sun asleep, I try to get Wolf to be my anchor. I set him up in my bathroom with the sink at a trickle. (I know enough to slow down the flow and not have it be a waterfall.) I ask him to do a 1000 reps with his pinky, holding up a treasure from my time in Hawai'i. I want to be connected to that time ... to the last time I proposed. The pendant has a lotus flower on it and I set my heart straight for seeing Lotus.

But first, the fire extinguisher behind the toaster oven catches my eye and I remember that the book I had ordered for Sun had arrived. I envision a wonderful surprise for her and set up the dining room accordingly: with spooky fire extinguisher dust around to create a "haunted" effect fitting of a Neil Gaiman comic.

Satisfied, I walk off into the cold night adorned with Daoist robes and Shakujyo staff. I at least have the common sense of wrapping a red jacket around myself to ward off some of the winter wind that blows at me.

It's a long walk, but the miles matter not. Maybe I'll get there by sunrise, maybe I'll get there right on time.

I jump a Food Lion fence and arrive at her apartment that I wasn't supposed to know about and only found by following the strings that still connect us.

Then fate conspires with my insanity. I arrive at her door, touch the handle, and like magic, it's unlocked. I roam around the space where I can feel her presence and wonder if this could be my part-time job for awhile: to clean up and tidy her place while she sleeps as some act of atonement. I'm aware enough to see that doing the dishes would be a bit too noisy—she has a roommate after all.

Then I see the curtain, which I've parted so many moons ago and so many times. I see that my toothbrush is no longer at her sink and then turn to her bedroom door.

Gently,

Without thinking,

I turn the handle.

She awakens with a start—always was a light sleeper. Except for those rare times I held her and made her feel safe...

She does not feel safe tonight.

She comes out of her bedroom as I see another pair of eyes gleam in the

TO INFINITY, AND BELOW

night—her new boyfriend.

That doesn't really hit me hard because she is here right in front of me. I can barely contain my joy as she ushers me out of the apartment. All in whispers, with a firm demeanor and none of the anger that would normally injure an open heart.

At the crack of the door, she says, "You know you can never come here again, right?" I promise her I won't.

I promise her as I slide the keyring I brought for her—just for her! Onto her finger.

I'm on one knee. I see her smile—the treasure I had failed to protect—I see her smile and I know that whatever lies ahead it was worth that smile. A tired smile. A smile of absurdity. A treasure nonetheless.

I do not know what lies ahead.

I see a fire extinguisher anchored to a wall. The theme of the night continues.

I spray it over the steps, so that all may know a ghost visited this night.

I slowly take off my robes and lie them down with my staff on the sidewalk.

The pair makes an empty scarecrow on the concrete.

I draw a heart shape with the extinguisher on her car.

I see in my mind's eye her coming upon this scene in the light of day,

And knowing it was not a dream.

And perhaps smiling—smiling, once more, at the absurdity of life.

I walk off into the cold night in my pants with no jacket and no robe.

I'm on fire anyway.

I need to learn how to be a polar bear, how to make it through the winter.

I take a path through the woods.

I know it is easy to get lost in the woods, but there's a path.

I am not afraid of the Lost Woods.

I venture to Sun's house. Sun, who had said she would not be home, who said she would be cat-sitting for a friend that night and told me not to come over.

I climb the iron scaffolding up to her balcony only to see an Indian man leaving for work (it is now daylight, though the dawn came on quickly, and I didn't notice the sunrise). He is doing his morning prayers to the sun.

I jump down from the balcony—aware enough to realize I look like a criminal—telling him I am here to see my friend. He walks off, but then—moved by some unknown force—turns around to say cryptically, "You must climb the balcony, if you are to get in."

"What?" I don't understand.

He points back to what I was doing. "That way, you must go that way."

I do so and I knock on the glass door.

She is home after all and slides open the door with a sleep-deprived face and a Flash t-shirt.

When was the last time I slept?

Remember, Remember, the Fifth of November

Sun ushers me into the bathroom for a shower and gets Wolf to bring me over something to wear from my place where I left him. The dawn of day combined with her energy makes for a double dose of fire. I am excited to be alive with my feet further and further off the ground. I see texts from Lotus, angry that I had violated her space. I pretend I thought it was all a dream, which is half-true in any case, but I am scared that I am going insane and that I really did scare her too.

I tell her I don't want to go to the hospital. She reassures me that no one wants that for me. They simply want me to be more balanced and be okay. The full weight of my actions hangs like a guillotine over my head, and each moment is as uncertain as it gets on the edge of the Void.

Wolf has brought me some clothes and convinces Sun to finally go to the doctor. She continued to put off getting checked out due to the emotional demands of others (with me being the main culprit). Wolf takes me back to my house and I become dimly aware of how much of a mess I made of the place. We set to chunking down the task of cleaning with Wolf taking the inside mess and me resolving to be outside in the crisp autumn air. I have a broom, and I'm working on those squares again: the square of the deck and aiming to get every last leaf. I do a decent job, but being thorough stresses me beyond belief in this state. I check back inside with Wolf and hear jazz music, which convinces me that he is tapping into another timeline since he and my stepfather share the same name. Now I'm no longer sure they are different people.

After as much cleaning as I can spiritually and mentally stand, I take Wolf out to breakfast. We eat at good ole' Pam's Farmhouse and take our time having an altered state meal. On some level, I feel like I'm the president again and think everyone in the diner suspects as much. We walk to the Kadampa Center after that. I take a slow circumambulation around the purification pillar. My father warns me that I'm heading to a dark place, but I let him know I'm with a friend, which seems to reassure him.

Back at the ranch, my landlord has returned from having spent the night with his pregnant betrothed and wants to know "What the hell is going on?" He calls up my downstairs roommate, Wolf, and I to sit at the table. The downstairs roommate has a YMCA uniform that speaks to me on some synchronistic level. I focus on it as the anxiety, fear, and suspicion in the room intensifies my mania. Wolf attempts to explain what happened, hedging details as best he can, but my landlord is convinced I'm on some sort of drugs.

The police arrive soon after, and now my paranoia is reaching a max. They knock on my room door, where I had finally laid down to rest and I greet them with as much of a calm demeanor as I can.

I now know a healthier way of interacting with cops. Cops are interested in facts and tangible information. If you simply answer their questions with actual facts and give them as complete a story as possible, they can process things in their own way and proceed appropriately. This is the ideal state of the profession, going off sensory information and actions rather than patterns and intuitive assumptions. Not to say the gut has no place in police work, but when you are being interviewed by a cop, it's best to go at the pace of filling out tedious paperwork.

The cop that questions me is female and we step outside, I have the insane feeling that she thinks I'm a terrorist, that I'm incredibly dangerous, and that I have a bomb somehow on my person. Using this assumed information, I reason with her as best I can and try to let her know of my emotional state. I stick to nebulous descriptions of who I am and what I'm going through, but it draws out the process and intensifies my suspected suspicions she has of me. It likely doesn't help that I feel guilty of having potentially broken into Lotus's apartment, even though I know that she hasn't reported me..

She lets me go on a walk to process some things. After talking with Wolf, she sends him over to translate.

"It's bad. I mean it's really bad."

I'm not sure if Wolf means how pissed the landlord is or whether they know about my adventurous night or simply the fact that I am a rogue element in an otherwise stable system.

"They want you to check in at a hospital and they'll know if you don't go. Let me take you to one."

I'm not really in a state of mind that makes rational thoughts or have foresight into the future, so I go along with whatever path my actions have laid out for me. We drive for a long time and arrive at Burger King where I repay Wolf for his services in the form of ice cream goodness, and burgers. I receive a message from Sun that I need to wait for my stepfather and be patient until she gets there.

He lets me out of the car at the parking lot and remembers that it was the hospital he went to after his first narcoleptic episode (and subsequent car crash). We enter somewhere and go through a metal detector. I see a penny and think it's my lucky day!

The wait is long. The hospital is painful. A violent movie is on the TV. Pain drips all around the place like a heavy fog.

"You're fuming," Wolf comments.

I am angry. Furious at this cage of a place that makes a mockery of the word "healing."

I'm finally called into the interview room. For some reason, I don't want Wolf present. I have begun to be paranoid about him in ways I can no longer articulate. The medical staff asking me questions during the interview reminds me of a temporary roommate who was a Pisces. I'm not so aware of how I answer the questions and am dissociating in a bad way, so much so that apparently I need a follow-up interview.

I am taken deeper into the hospital. Away from windows. Away from any semblance of sanity. Being alone in the dim lighting of this room and bed are all I remember later on. All I hear about this second interview is from Wolf who says, "It did not go well."

The reality of the Matrix intensifies at this point. I am scared of everyone being Agent Smith in disguise. I am kept in a concrete room with a mattress pad, and I attempt to do 1,000 parkour moves to train in this hyperbolic time chamber, feeling somewhat connected to my parkour friend by wearing his company's shirt.

I beg the medical staff who comes to see me, "Let Wolf go. Please, let Wolf go." I am aware he is in this Matrix as well, and I think they are interrogating us in separate rooms. I want them to know he did nothing wrong and to please release him.

I look out of my locked room and see a computer screen. I see squiggles and code and date and a sort of "Da Vinci Code" that I feel Sun is desperately trying to crack. I feel like she is trying to break the Matrix in order to get through to me, in a somewhat similar feeling that Earth Girl was changing the world in order to liberate me from jail that one night many moons ago.

Coming to my senses, I see a needle in my arm and everything's in slow motion. I have a thought that this should hurt, so it does. I scream loudly and the scene changes rapidly. Everyone moves here and there. I do not know if they have my blood or not.

I am with a sitter in a hallway, and Wolf is there as well. The sitter is incredibly anxious. "Is he breathing?" she asks, as my altered state allows me to have very abnormal physiological processes. I get up to leave. I am tired of waiting. Why am I still here and where am I?

Wolf says, "You just doubled it." Doubled what? I think as I feel reality bending with my actions. Like Karma is getting piled higher and higher and there's nothing, *nothing, nothing, I can do.*

Every action done creates karma and sends me spinning into samsara once more. Yet, no action also creates karma. Reaction creates the worst karma, whereas simple awareness of what is unfolding creates neutral karma. Neutral karma leads to the experiences of non-dual awareness and enlightenment or so the Tibetan Buddhist masters tell us.

Every time impatience rises to the surface, I struggle against the system and I am sent deeper in. I black out after a while and wake up in hospital clothes with my drawstring tied very tightly.

Sun is here, finally, and she's wearing a shirt that says "Wild Flower." It has a moon I like to boop and a golden-yellow color that is more beautiful than anything I've seen before. Wolf is still here, stalwart friend that he is. I get the sinking suspicion that I have trapped them here.

My mind is reeling with potential escape paths, and I feel like I am colluding with my friends to exit this place. I settle on the route of becoming a statue and then being taken out of here like an inanimate object. I come up with plans and ruin them all the same, as the staff get more and more paranoid of my presence. It isn't long until I have another sitter in the room who gently stops me from my multiple attempts to leave.

Finally it dawns on me—my friends are trapped here in this hell for eternity. In a literal sense. In the sense that this scene will always exist like this for all time—that my actions lead to us being in this abysmal hell. I confess I have trouble explaining this feeling, this state of being: it is at once feeling as if one is in a tomb. A terrifying and inescapable place in which one's consciousness will remain forevermore. Nietzsche introduced this idea of *eternal recurrence* first, so appalling to gasp that the first time I read about it, the author thought Nietzsche didn't mean it literally. That idea is scary enough, but I implore you to merely glimpse (and not too long) on what that reality would *feel* like to *experience*.

I see the love in my friend's eyes at that moment, and the weight of my actions buries me deeper. *They are trapped here too!* Without anything being verbalized, they give me a look that says, "Yes, we know this is a painful place to be for eternity. But that is how deeply we love you; we don't want you to be alone here."

That love breaks me open; *it is too much.* The weight of regret solidifies me into that statue. I assume the position of Christ the Redeemer in Rio, solid and watching over the world from his final resting place. If I am to be nailed in one place, let me be a beacon of compassion!

———————

I do not remember leaving that room. I do not know if part of myself remains there in that frozen hell, or if writing this brings some solace to his suffering. All I can say is that I have lived to share my story and perhaps that will be enough.

———————

"This is where things change for us," I hear Wolf say, as we walk down a corridor. I don't know what's about to change, but I'm glad they are finally being released from the hell I have brought them into. I am walking around the floor down corridors with light tan coloring like I'm in a dream. I see a table with a red-and-white chess board printed on it and red-and-black backgammon markings. Ah, I'm in a world of games now then? Playing—or being played by the cosmos—another game of chess?

Then the scene ends, fading to black.

13

Life as Art

The Pit

I know the only way out of the pit is without the rope. I know the only way out is that narrow passage in which death is omnipresent. I know that death's form of love is to push you through that tunnel, to the other side, to a new life. Others may call it a psychotic break, or a metaphor, or simply an intense panic attack.

Those who have made that leap know what it is for them. Living through the tale of Batman and the Pit is a tall order. All around me are concrete walls and nurses in pale blue uniforms.

I see a woman on a mobile workstation through a closed door's window. I'm hitting the door, but she has compassion in her eyes as well as a distant stare. She is blonde.

"I'll make time to visit you; don't worry." Her angelic voice comes through the black, hard handled corded phone. I don't know how many times I called Lotus today. I don't know what I say to her. I hear this, and that's enough hope for me to hold onto.

I heard about that day from my friends later in bits and pieces. My body remembers, and as I write this, I am trembling from memories that I have no visuals for. I am safe now, right? I am here now, but I remain curious: what happened to the "me" who could not bear to record those feelings into memory? Are those memories out somewhere in the ether of consciousness, needed to be found and restored? How do I explain that being in a hospital—a place where all your needs are met by trained professionals—is a trauma? What words can I write to show you that the atmosphere of a place, which houses those tormented and suffering, is suffused with black anguish painted in invisible ink? Can you see that feeling that pain with no filter is enough to shatter reality?

"Perhaps the greatest faculty our minds possess is the ability to cope with pain. Classic thinking teaches us of the four doors of the mind,

which everyone moves through according to their need.

First is the door of sleep. Sleep offers us a retreat from the world and all its pain. Sleep marks passing time, giving us distance from the things that have hurt us. When a person is wounded they will often fall unconscious. Similarly, someone who hears traumatic news will often swoon or faint. This is the mind's way of protecting itself from pain by stepping through the first door.

Second is the door of forgetting. Some wounds are too deep to heal, or too deep to heal quickly. In addition, many memories are simply painful, and there is no healing to be done. The saying 'time heals all wounds' is false. Time heals most wounds. The rest are hidden behind this door.

Third is the door of madness. There are times when the mind is dealt such a blow, it hides itself in insanity. While this may not seem beneficial, it is. There are times when reality is nothing but pain, and to escape that pain, the mind must leave reality behind.

Last is the door of death. The final resort. Nothing can hurt us after we are dead, or so we have been told."

-Patrick Rothfuss[10]

All I can say is that I am here. I have not resorted to the final door. No matter how painful the reality I encountered, I can say I have seen such beauty and love that makes it all worth it. Perhaps this is a choice we need to make every day.

The Path of Chains

"I thought I was here voluntarily?" I ask, with hands curled into balls of rage.

"That was under the condition that you improved overnight and could function after the first day." The doctor made no mention of having had to restrain me, and I had no memory of it in any case. "I thought you were going to go the listening route. What happened to things being different this time?"

I want to say that it will be different. I will earn my freedom and prove my sanity this time, but the moment passes with my silence.

The police officer that escorts me to the courthouse is a kind man, strong and quiet. It's the subtle things that tell whether someone has kindness, and it is revealed in the smallest of moments between us. The way an officer handcuffs you can say a great deal many things, as touch remains a clear channel for communication.

---

[10] Rothfuss, Patrick. *The Name of the Wind*, DAW Books, 2007.

LIFE AS ART

I enter the courtroom and meet my lawyer—which is different from how I'd done things back in high school. Did I even have a lawyer back then? Only my parents...

The suited man advises me to keep quiet and let him do the talking. I ask whether I can be a witness or not—thinking my charisma will somehow save the day.

How can you condemn a man to insanity when he can plead his case with a clear voice?

To my dismay, the doctor is on the stand first. Some may say she's doing her job, but being on the receiving end of a testimony with one's freedom on the line skews my perspective. She offers to the prosecutor and judge that with the full weight of her experience and expertise behind her, I am indeed not sane enough to be released to the world.

And furthermore, she brings up the incident of my having broken into my ex's apartment, phrasing it in a painful enough way that paints me as some sort of mad criminal. The blow strikes me deep, not to mention the confusion—*How did they even find out about that? Did I tell them? There were no police involved.* My emotions are off kilter now, and I'm not able to think rationally about what to present to the court.

My lawyer does a better job presenting me as a college educated self-employed man who has functioned well enough off of medication for the past few years. I plead my case next or more accurately, I open the floodgates of emotion and plead for mercy before the cold will of justice shatters my dream of making it to my retreat/workshop this weekend. I find no way to convince them of the importance of this professional education—nor the fact that I simply *know* that I'll be received well and be able to ground back to reality in the safe haven of people who simply *understand*.

"I'm not crazy" sums up my testimony, even though I don't say that verbatim.

"I find the defendant crazy, sentenced up to thirty days of hospitalization," the judge concludes in a dismissive tone. Another day at the office, eh?

The anger settles into me like black ice and sinks deep into my very being.

At least the officer shackles my wrists with compassion, as he leads me through the dim corridors that wind behind the courtroom.

The cold rain greets my face outside. I savor every breath of fresh air, taking in gulps of Freedom.

When will I see the Moon again?
"You mustn't look with just your eyes–what do you feel? Warmth? The cold?
Pulse
"Let it break upon you like wave upon the sand."
"Listen with your heart
You will Understand."
Pulse~
11

I keep the above poem that frames a drawing of a goddess front and center on my desk.

Her green and blue eye stares back at me, with her other two eyes closed in a peaceful visage.

Whoever drew this from whatever world and whatever timeline:

Thank you. From the bottom of my heart, this beauty has truly saved me.

I have a workshop out in nature. Three days at the South Wind Farm relaxing and enjoying the beautiful embodied presence of so many other aspiring teachers. It's next weekend, please will I be able to go?

I'm so close. I know that there all the chaos could settle into... まいい

My friends come to visit everyday, so that's nice.

I don't remember the first day they came.

I don't remember anything from that day, except that I was escaping from The Pit as Batman in the *Dark Knight Rises*. I went full Batman, barely having the strength to know what that meant.

I wake up in isolation or "the side of the psych ward with all the troublemakers." There's no group therapy and the other patients here are deep in their own hell.

I'm quickly labeled as the Devil himself.

I prefer to go by Lucifer.

---

[11] Unknown Author, *Untitled Work*, Duke Regional Hospital, 2020.

LIFE AS ART

If that's what I need to be for these people, so be it. I know it's not an easy role to play.

My friends help me see that there really is nothing I can do for the other patients. My empathy weighs heavier than they can imagine. I do my best to listen to their advice—I know better than to try and force help when it is not asked for. On the other hand, holding up a mirror to all I meet is about the best I've ever asked of myself.

I receive a card filled with vibrant green nature with a yellow little square in the corner that says "It's ok." On the inside, my friend's handwriting whispers:

"So I hear you done got broke. It's okay, everyone's a little broken.
It's what we do with our brokenness that counts."

He had come by for one day, one visit. I managed to come up with a clever response using quotes from a library book I had chosen earlier. The room gets still and the philosophy of Zhuagzi, Zen, and absurdity flowers into the room. Usually that's what it takes to slap him back around to himself, and in this way, I feel that maybe I can be of service too—even with this jester hat on. Being on this side of the veil does have its advantages and a perspective that not many get access to.

Or maybe I'm still refusing to learn that I'm here only—*only* to be of help to myself. To get "better."

Yet how can I not get involved, not even dare to look at my fellow humans in all their nakedness in this madhouse? It doesn't sit right, it goes against the nature of my being to completely tune out the suffering around me.

Not that I seem to have any skill in this endeavor. A woman in the ward is facing a concrete wall, barefoot, talking to herself. Perhaps, talking to God, her spirit guides, or anything that will listen. The pale tan brick walls have ears, but they've heard it all in this place and no longer can be roused to care.

I get close to her with my Lucifer mask on, feeling that only a trickster can help shake her out of her cycle. Deep down, I am worried about her, how long has she been standing there? Isn't her body exhausted? Cold?

"Oh God, he's here again. Please save me from this devil!" Her gaze is full of fear and anguish.

And she will not be budged from her own place in Hell.

I "know" that the only one I can save is myself, but that doesn't stop me from trying.

Am I that afraid of how powerless I am to impact others?

Or am I simply the fool that persists in his folly that I may become wise?

The leap across the bottomless chasm into a world of love where one can help even those entrenched in fear. They say no one makes it the first time.

Maybe I lie here at the bottomless bottom, refusing to pick up the pieces. In a future time and space, I will read an article by James Parker about *Slaughter-House Five*, how Vonnegut decided to "lay among the pieces" rather than pull himself together.

Sun gives me an essential oil that smells like love. I use it when the walls start to close in and the pain gets too intense. I inhale it from the bottle like medicine, wanting to feel any sense of comfort in this burning place.

All my visitors get banned the day Magneto and his wife are able to visit. I look at them through the grated window prison of the sixth floor. They are consoling Sun, who is worried beyond measure. The reasoning for the ban is baseless—they are accusing my guests of smuggling in a cell phone, which has not happened. All I've done was keep the wireless landline in my room overnight instead of returning it to the front desk. Perhaps it's for the best that Magneto doesn't see me in this light—or whatever part of his soul I'd reflect. I call them from the wall-mounted phone, and they say they can feel how much pain and how "haywire" my heart chakra is.

I spend the rest of the day by myself alone, watching cartoons at times, dancing at times, and feeling the weight of introspection heavy on my mind. I begin writing "13 Rules for Life" as my father tries to distill some of Jordan Peterson's wisdom over the phone. My first rule is "Position," inspired by his posture rule. To know my position between Heaven and Earth, to rest at my center.

My brother seems to think that I've channeled Joker once more—not Batman—when I ask him about archetypes and share my journey down the rabbit hole. In the end, I relinquish the Dark Knight archetype, reminding him that he's much stronger and suited to wear that cape.

In a tender moment, I tell him that in truth, I'm Alfred to his Bruce and that he has always been my "True North." The sentiment seems to warm him—even though it is incredibly rare to see any emotional signs bubble up from his depths and even rarer over the phone. He's watching *Daredevil* now, which I knew because I had tried to fuse Batman and Daredevil into one archetype when I was on the outside.

What the hell do I know about alchemy? I'm really tired of these things blowing up in my face.

Anyway, he shares that what he appreciates about Daredevil was the five years he spent in prison, atoning for the things he had done.

Atonement.

That strikes a chord.

My time here may be used for reflection, understanding, growth, and all that jazz.

In many ways, I feel the sobering reality of: "you screwed up, there are consequences to actions, and above all you've caused pain and abused love." It makes the difference between wanting to get out as fast as possible and realizing deeply that I am here for a reason. That on some cosmic scale things are being brought into balance.

Even with this perspective, patience is not easy to find.

————-

The sands of time have offered me a fresher perspective on atonement since those dark days. A-tone-ment is the natural spiritual remedy to any feelings of separation or illusion. In this way of seeing, the only sin is to feel that we are separated from God in the first place in Christian terms. The only illusion that there is a "self" independent from existence in Buddhist terms. To love and to see that side of yourself, which has been cut off and divorced from the whole ... or to cut through the illusion that didn't even exist ... perhaps this is a softer way to approach the whole notion of repentance.

Timelines Shift and Change

I have a Wind brother on this side of the ward. As our element implies, it is rare that our energies align and we occupy the same space. The wellness coordinator is running late one morning; she sees us both in the hallway, gliding the shifting currents of invisible energy.

"Oh my, I always know it's going to be a good day when I see you two!" she says, reassured by our presence.

I go on a walk with a nurse to do rounds one night. I tell her about Healcyon and all the various tools I use in my business to help people. I talk to her about Tarot cards and show her a card from my deck that is chosen by fate. She is focused on her task, but is quite attuned to the feeling of what I'm saying. She reflects, "I feel a sense of peace and calmness as you talk, wow. I'm glad you're doing this for people!"

Even here, I find a sense of purpose, and it is moments like these that allow me to continue on.

Later that night, I wake up in terror, pausing to at least put on my clothes and scramble out the door. I feel like I'm my stepfather, battling unnamed horrors in the night that haunt me even after waking with no memory of my nightmares.

The same nurse sees me on the other side of the window. Using her badge to go through doors and layers of protection, she reaches out to me, "Come on Arthur, it's okay. Don't you remember me? Remember when you first got here? You're so much better off now. Let's not go backward."

I'm too scared to tell her "No, I don't remember when I first got here." I don't remember anything of what I did, what I said, or how I felt. All I remember is black and staring out at someone through a locked door with a tiny window.

She guides me back to my room with grace. I'm afraid of the dark again. A nine-year-old boy again, not wanting to sleep in darkness. Of course it's never actually dark here, and I can see every detail of the room even with the lights off. The darkness that frightens me is when I close my eyes, when I face my unconscious, when things that I have to see are bubbling up to the surface...

I don't know whether I'm dealing with only my own ghosts or all the ghosts that have ever passed through this room. I am terribly alone. Locked in a facility far from the people I love. The nurse's warmth is enough to lull me to sleep.

The next day I mentioned how other's pain is affecting me to the weekend doctor on staff. Turning toward me with his full attention, I get the sense that I've mentioned something he is deeply concerned with. Speaking slowly, he says, "This group psychosis you speak of ... that's what your anti-psychotic is for." To be in a place that creates the need for its own prescriptions, truly I am deep within Samsara.

Thrall

Some days I hear music that reminds me of Thrall from *World of Warcraft*. I figure it reflects the storm of my inner world, of all the rampant destruction in my Soul. Either that or the shamanic nature of Orc culture and all the elemental forces raging around my psyche.

The doctors change shifts and the one who condemned me in court leaves for the week. My new doctor is a pleasant Leo whose name is Thrall.

For the first time, I have some hope for psychiatrists, for it actually being a profession committed to healing.

She has a way about her that eases my fears of medication. She changes my anti-psychotic to Risperidone and simplifies my understanding of the pharmaceutical world. Of course it's not something to be on forever she assures me, but simply to stabilize and get one out of the hospital. She is the first doctor to concede that a psych ward is not the best place for healing, which is why heavier medication is required. Perhaps I can even get out of here in time to get to my retreat; she implies that such a road is possible to walk. I let the hope fill me. Optimism takes root in the pale grey ashes of my heart.

No, I do not see her as an angel.

I see her as a Shaman, as is her namesake and of how she can bridge the worlds. As much as angels are blessings in this place, they can only do so much to help one integrate back into the world we all live in.

"I think for people like us, spiritual solutions aren't enough. Maybe we simply do need medicine," Wolf shares with me. In our kinship, I feel agreeable enough to take my medicine.

I am not getting better. The science of taking Lithium involves making sure the dosage is correct by checking blood levels after three days of taking it. The logistics do not line up, and I do not make it out of the hospital to my retreat. So it goes.

Thrall apologizes for getting my hopes up and sees the pain it has caused me.

The days get heavier. The leaden weight in my heart promises to sink me into the abyss for *quite some time.* I manage to do some Qi Gong in my room once every couple nights. It goes by slowly and deliciously. Is it that the light is more tangible in such heavy places? Or is the break from madness stretched out through time?

My Qi Gong lineage is called Stillness-Movement, and it is definitely more movement than stillness these days. Perhaps the Winds of Change need to be brought to this place. Or when given less room, gentle breezes rage into tornados seeking liberation. Of course the windows don't open here. Not even so much as a vent to stand by. When will I feel the breeze again?

Yet, I march onward to stability. This produces an interesting Catch-22 of emotions and mental states.

Something like this (if you can imagine): the more sane and aware I become, the more I am able to comprehend my situation. The more I comprehend my situation, the more insane it *feels* to be here, and the waves of reality threaten to pull me under once more. That's some catch.

That's what I like about Rothfuss's quote. It's not that I ever fully step through the door of madness nor that there's some breaking point with no return (not to imply that it can't happen). I simply go through the revolving doors as needed to escape pain I'm not ready to feel. I return to drink smaller doses of reality when I can. I mean I don't even have a therapist to talk to in here. Really, I get to savor the true meaning of that quote I heard in Peru:

"What we call therapy now, we used to call friendship."

A rhino comes into the ward. His madness is similar enough to mine that when I produce a drawing of a rhino that I had spent a few therapeutic minutes coloring the day before, he gives the synchronicity a brief chuckle. The drawing I kept for myself was one of a komodo dragon, silver and red, whose assertiveness and independence I channel as often as I can. We connect over our willingness to see our animal side. Yet, we remain different animals...

Rhino doesn't understand me. He doesn't *get me*. It's only through translation with Wolf that he has any insight into my nature. "What's his thing?" he asks Wolf, probing to find out what my vice is apparently. Or if I'm a drug addict of some sort. Is it that difficult to comprehend an addiction to energy? To connection? Or perhaps to magic? [Alas, this is all in retrospect with the gift of hindsight. At that time, I didn't really know the answer either.]

Wolf talks to me and tries to summarize Rhino's perspective. "He is a man who values time above all else. And he doesn't think he has much of it left." I get the distinct and ominous impression that time in this case is not "how many years you live" but "how many years one **Lives**": fully alive and able to grow and experience new perspectives. I have always been afraid that there is some limit ... Some capacity to evolve, grow, and experience refreshing newness we are born with that gets "tapped out" after a certain time (circa 30s?) and one loses their invincibility. What comes next is feeling the heavy iron-clad anchor of mortality dragging us to a final rest ... I believe this can be mitigated by choices, by discipline, and by mindset. Certainly, I have met elders with more vibrancy and exuberance than myself! Yet, Rhino stands before me now with his two kids and too many ex-girlfriends. I wonder if I would be in his shoes if I let certain rivers flow where they may...

Rhino especially doesn't understand the nature of my relationship with Sun.

"Is she your girl?" "No, I am still figuring that out," I reply.

"You're taking too long. I would've..." he goes on to imply certain *desires* for Sun with the metaphor of painting walls; did I mention she was sitting there while we discussed this? Only a few times have I been made painfully aware of the objectification of women inherent in our culture and have had a taste of myself being an object as well a few times. It is inherent in the masculine/Yang approach (not talking genders here) to be considered having more physical realities than emotional ones.

It's almost time to make new friends! Progress in this system means inevitably going to the *other side*, where the more cooperative patients are. Dr. Thrall is hesitant about letting me transition. It isn't that she's afraid of me infecting them all with my madness, but that more people will be more stimulating and thus make things worse for me.

At breakfast, the whole ward's timelines actually line up to eat together—Wind brother, Rhino, and the Girl-Who-Sees-Devils. After a rather raucous time, Rhino (who knows the ways of the system pretty well I'd say) accuses Wind brother and I of being racist and picking on the girl. A team of nurses and techs circle around him, trying to diffuse the situation and listen to his grievance. A whirlwind of uncertainty follows as I am packing up my stuff and not sure where I am headed next.

The Lightbringer

I get a roommate and his name is dangerously close to the word *Daemon*. He tells me I am like Neo and he is Black Panther. Perhaps I am "the One," but what good does that do me here? I am unable to sleep at night with a roommate, even though he is able to rest far deeper than I am and insists I won't disturb him with my presence. One night, I black out for a few hours and I wake up with my watch missing. Now I'm completely divorced from linear time and I'm going mad trying to find it. It is in none of the usual places yet I know the alarm will go off the next morning—the alarm that reminds me another day has passed, and there is yet some anchor to the consensual world. I am too restless to wait—my roommate has stolen my watch right? Where else could it be? My rustling disturbs him and I take the chance to ask him if he's seen my watch.

"You'll find it when it's time to find it. Go to sleep."

I don't sleep. I make my rounds between the nurses, the floor outside my room, and my bed. Rhino eventually wakes early and makes conversation with the nurses on staff with his usual swaggering charm. My presence irritates him and he asks the nurse on staff, "Does he have some history with... thinking he's Black?" The nurse really doesn't know what to do with that question. After a short back and forth, she answers quite simply, "No, to

LIFE AS ART

answer your question, he does not."

My alarm rings the world awake and I find my watch underneath my bed. I have no idea how it got there and worry about what happened during that blackout ... Finding it feels like shifting out of the spirit world back into consensual reality.

Weary from sleep deprivation or the weight of pain in the air, my soul drags around behind me like a cape of suffering. In a mood a few shades darker than an oil spill, I pick up the phone.

My mother reads me the Bible quote of the day most days. In lighter states of mind, I take them to be the guiding principle of the day. Or as a meditation on an archetype ... learning that Paul had been struck blind for three days was a particularly journey in consciousness. Today, she talks about what Jesus said of the Devil and evil.

I talk about loving him.

"Don't you have compassion for Lucifer, Mom?" My patience has been worn away, "To live without God's love, *can you imagine that*? Isn't that the very definition of Hell?"

The words sink into her and I can tell she is moved. No, she has never imagined that. No wonder. For where does the Bible sing of love for Lucifer? Who dares reflect on the absence of love that deeply? Of what it might do to a being? For Lucifer to have chosen freedom above all else ... To be that true to his own nature to reject even the comforts of an all embracing love. It's enough to move me and to have me question the reputation the Devil has gotten. Don't mistake my meditation for some sort of Satanic worship; all I claim is that there is more to the Story than we are given. To look through the eyes of Lucifer is to see our own darker shades more clearly and embrace responsibility for our own monsters.

I feel the depths of bitterness, the angst of all creation, weighing down on me. I know enough to choose love. But even then I am focused on the darkest depths and my rage against the bars of my cage. No, I am not in prison, but sometimes it is worse. A sentence is handed down and you have a guarantee (and the non-solitary confined at least have time outside—fresh air!) of when your time will be up. One can bide their time and patience with a finish line in sight. Uncertainty hangs like a scythe above me each moment, and I forget that one day it will be over: that *this is not permanent*. Sometimes it proves difficult to remember that when each moment is etched into the tapestry of eternity.

I face the doctor each day with no reassurance that I'm getting out of here. The wicked Catch-22 being that not getting out of here only makes it harder to get out of here because of the stress exacerbating my mental state.

"I know that you aren't getting better in this place," Wolf confirms what I've been feeling. Meanwhile, outside of the hospital, he moves the boxes out of my new home and back into the spare bedroom of his apartment.

I look back with tears forming around my eyes, knowing what little difference such a truth would make in any case.

"I brought this on myself. I don't think I ever told you that story."

I'll share only the abridged version here with you, dear reader, as it pains me to narrate. What matters is that it culminates in a dark promise to Lotus that if the Universe would have to tear us apart, it wasn't meant to be. After I said that, I took a shower and saw dancing lights swimming in my vision … I had a numb feeling that it indeed would tear us apart that way.

I'd signed onto madness … committed to the very causes of a psychotic break. Yet here in the bleak sober present, I am confronted with the very truth of the matter. No forces other than my own hand had caused this. I had such conviction then, and yet retained none of it when the see-sawing of my own emotions made a storm of our relationship.

None but my own choices and mistakes paved the path to these unforgiving concrete halls.

Wolf can only listen as my tears echo against him.

Paint yourself Sane

"You know, you're the most natural thing in here" Wolf reassures me.

The last time my friends visited together, the fire energy was so intense I painted myself all over with markers—drawing lines of color like ley lines in the flesh—attempting to ground me into this world. Coloring oneself is actually listed as a coping mechanism on the worksheet they handed out, but all the staff see it as a sign of insanity ... Figures. Weirdness and unconventional (I'm looking at you, Aquarius) = not fit for release to the public. For me, I feel more grounded and more centered in who I am— Art is Art is Art is *Art* after all!!

I slept maybe two hours that night. The doctor sees it as a dangerous relapse. For my own good, she restricts my visitation rights to one person a day for only an hour a day. As time goes on, my inner world is torn between bitter rage and resentment at Sun, but also needing her care and emotional support to get through some days. I am truly fractured down to my core, swinging between the light and darker sides that I have compartmentalized within my Soul.

Pacing the halls on a restless night, I write Sun a letter cementing my clarity as to the nature of our relationship. I show it to a nurse, and she has some clear feedback about what the dynamic seems like. Sun's feelings being such a tidal wave of cosmic love and desire that it was all I could ever even begin to know how I felt in the moment with her—or what I wanted. I give Sun the letter and her response is one of continued confusion. She struggles with all the mixed messages I've sent her as I sifted through to my deeper emotions. "The good thing about Water is ... you will always find ground as long as you go deeper," she had taught me.

Yet, Lotus had first tried to reveal to me that I have a need to be needed. In that way, I abused my own feelings over-adapting to those around me, so that they would come to depend on me. Truly at the bottom of the ocean is nothing more than a crushing loneliness from which I am always trying to escape.

What a fitting name: the Abyss.

Walks with Wolf

The Tarot deck Sun buys me to work with, Spiritsong, sings me wisdom and light with the backs having lined lotuses—the kind of artstyle Lotus herself has always admired. I meditate with the different animals of the deck and write notes in the book as messages to Lotus. I intend to give her the deck as part of the culmination of my expression of love and Insight to her now.

It's no surprise to me that the Lovers card is represented with Wolf—who I have come to appreciate as one who has truly shown me what unconditional Love—Agape—is. The pure kind that seeks no recompense, that does not expect of me as anything other than what I am. I feel like I have absolutely no filters when he is around. After the visitor's restriction, I've begun to enjoy the one-on-one connection we've been building. Some of the best artwork in my room comes from him, and we have a giant page listing the "Dual" archetypes that we identify with.

He is Axel to my Saix

Sora to my Riku

Rakdos to my Gruul

Charmander to my Bulbasaur

...and others that would perhaps give away too much of his inner workings. Suffice to say, he shared with me the core animal spirits to his soul and the gifts that work through him. A true friend in all things.

I'm talking to Lotus through him, since he's the only one she will actually talk to. Finally, she has found an outlet for all her rage and sorrow. For her disappointments and pain. In Wolf, she finds a refreshingly sober perspective, a fellow Owl who can handle darkness and listen with his mind. I wish she had confided such feelings in me, but whenever she would come over with her mind full of things to say, in my presence she simply surrendered to love and let all else fade to black. I once asked her how she could do that so easily, shift into that state and be in a better mood?

"What do you think Love is?"

March of the Polar Bears

A true artist arrives at the ward. She rolls in a dulcimer, and it's my first time seeing such an instrument. I can tell she's an artist because of the way she *listens*—to us people in the ward and our preferences and also to the invisible sounds of the world that inspired her own songs.

If one thing can be said about the Magic of Madness, it is that listening to music is a true *experience*. I wonder, being sent through the portal of sound to other worlds, if this is how life is actually lived. If this is how most of the world actually *hears* music and experiences vibration. I am left to wonder if life is too bright and those brief times I actually let myself be alive overwhelm me terribly.

Waves of healing course through my body as the dulcimer is played and healing is only a catchall word. Each melody has a life of its own, and riding those waves carries me to realms far away from the harsh concrete walls.

One song she has called "March of the Polar Bears," though she confesses not quite having the name figured out. While she plays, I dance, and it is the true expression of gratitude that seems to feed both of our Souls.

"Why not call it ... Waltz of the Bipolar Bears?" I offer.

Her smile is warm, and she says that would be a fine name. She means it.

How many do you Need?

Another patient shows up who has the same name as Wolf (his real name). The same last initial as well.

Naturally, I treat him as a friend from the very start. He himself can only laugh as the absurd amount of synchronicities pile up in front of us.

We're quite the pair, and the environment has us primed enough to be emotionally open from the start. I find his anxiety a refreshing change—I never seem to let my emotions go there.

Which is another way of saying instead of ever *feeling* anxious, I instead become anxiety itself and don't even notice it's happening. Earth Girl would point out how I like to roll up pieces of paper, fold things over many times, and compress straw wrappers into tiny places ... all those sorts of Virgo Moon behaviors you might imagine.

Another commercial linking our experiences flashes across the screen, and we say, in a singsong concert, "How many do you neeeeed?" He laughs again but I can feel the slight stirring of a deeper connection—patterns repeat to get the message across and it may be sinking through.

He has a wonderful girlfriend that visits. After divulging his true feelings, apprehensions, and other existential hangups, I implore him to treasure her always. My bleeding heart is the only testimony I can offer, in addition wanting to vicariously see a ship sail through fully on love's adventure. I can't bear to see my new friend go through a soul-tearing breakup.

An interesting crew gathers and a young Pisces man comes through the ward. His level of expertise in the world of acting and film is insane as are his connections. A lot of beautiful brainstorming happens. Then we get into some spontaneous Qi Gong.

I show them my moves. The Pisces shows me his own; he acquired it by virtue of being a natural. Turns out that the arms and hands are more important to channel and focus on in such an intense psychological state—they're closer to the brain after all! By really channeling the Qi (vibrational flow) of my hands and arms into set patterns, I'm able to find some stability and coherence in this storm of pain.

A Sobering Perspective

My new friend and I eat breakfast the next day. A cute girl joins us at the table, and our extraversion and friendliness are off the charts. The look in her eyes betrays a different story though; it's as if she is thinking, *Why in the hell are these people so upbeat and happy in a psych ward? Crazies.* She got in last night and is here for the 24-hour watch period. On top of that, she's not in any type of breakdown state—more of the "depressed, suicidal, and needed to escape" sort of drama. Through the mirror of her eyes, I come to the awakening that yes I am indeed in a tough spot, but at least we're making the most of it?

I've gotten bad about listing the dates, haven't I? I suppose if I were to ever go to prison, I wouldn't exactly be the "mark the wall" with tally carvings type. Yes again, this is different because there is no "sentence" or guaranteed release date—but still it is a bit too painful to keep track of linear time and to think about how long I've been here. The 24-hour watch girl leaves after being quite thoroughly terrified of all us crazies. [isn't it funny that fear is a marker of sanity and those that aspire to live in Love are a bit too much and need to stay?] A few days later, it is Thanksgiving.

I've spent Thanksgiving in some weird places. No, this isn't a segue into that time I took a train and made it to Fort Myers, Florida over Thanksgiving, but

LIFE AS ART

I am reminded of that experience since after being arrested for running away, I spent the night in a halfway home sort of deal. Yet all-in-all, I am not too remorseful for spending it in a mental hospital. I call all of my family one by one and get to have real conversations—more real than many a Thanksgiving allows space for. For lunch, Sun brings me actual home-cooked food—the love that is in them is the nourishment I have been missing out on here. Everyone has a family member joining them and even Daemon has his whole family visiting (no one had visited him since before today)! I tell a few of the patient's wives, husbands, or other family that Sun is my fiance for no particular reason. Maybe I want to feel like I have some semblance of a normal life. The meal itself isn't worth mentioning, though I believe there was an attempt at cornbread and turkey, but the feeling in the air is of genuine connection. Perhaps this scene causes confusion—genuine connection while playing pretend couple in love?

Yet, Sun and I are ever talented actors, and the stage is all set for us to play our parts. I set the tray down between us and we savor each bite. Sun has eyes that reflect her nickname—and her golden skylights illuminate the scene. Her Rose tattoo floats over the cream colored meal tray and she feeds me a piece of turkey. In all of love's mysterious forms, the rose is one that continues to capture our attention. Hers is a deep colored red, reflecting an ocean of the purest of feelings. A sea of warm blood, the vital essence which pours out from all hearts, embracing me with the finest of actions and details. Yet the lightness of a feather, the peacock tattoo on her other hand, balances out such a feeling—one is not overrun or drowned by this sea. Instead, wings I didn't know existed carry me to places beyond the imagination and into the embraces of angels and celestial lights.

I have not done Sun justice in this story— to paint her as some confusing manic pixie dream girl who threw my mind into disarray—I love her for who she is and it is a rare thing.

To Fall Again

Enter Desi, a wavy-haired fireball of a girl who is running around the halls of the hospital. I catch her in the bend of the hallway out of the nurse station's sight.

"Are you okay?"

"Yeah-I'm-fine-I-just-have-a-lot-of-energy"

"They won't understand that. Don't let them catch you like this."

Something about the way I say it softens her and I remind her of her ex-boyfriend. We connect over *League of Legends* and she confesses Ashe—the reluctant Ice Queen—is her favorite champion. Ashe is married to Tryndamere, an enraged man with an ability that allows him to defy death. Comparisons are made and I of course am reminded of Maria. At least this time I'm not unconscious...

A few mitigating factors help me this time around. One of them being the nurse that I confided to about my situation with Sun. While doing a routine blood test in my room, she warns me of Desi. I can sense the feeling of the warning and the "I've seen how this goes" wisdom is palpable. Given how often I've ignored this type of feeling in the past, I pay more attention. She delicately puts it, "I've seen her chart and know her history, so please focus on yourself and don't get caught up in a messy situation while you're beginning to recover."

The other help is that a male classmate of hers also happens to be in the psych ward. A recurring theme for my compatriots—many Duke students end up here with the perfect recipe of finals and family stress of Thanksgiving! The ensuing trio dynamic diffuses the attraction enough that nothing foolish or reckless happens. Despite whatever is on her chart, she manages to work the system well enough that she is released in time to prepare for her flight to Florida, where she will continue treatment and live with her family.

Only a Matter of Time

In a side room, that's never used past my social worker's office, I have a meeting that is familiar to me by this point. I call it "the sanity screening" done by the doctor and some administrator I've never met before. My emotions run high and the intensity threatens to drag me once more into the endless Catch-22 of "too insane to leave, too sane to stay and get better." "I don't know if you're emotionally ready to leave yet," Thrall says. I am at a loss as to how to explain myself and the mysteries of space-time. Of course, at this moment, I'm not ready to leave because now is not the time for me to leave! I mean don't they teach that in grad school? Feelings do not last longer than perhaps twenty seconds—a few minutes in the nervous system. When it's time to leave, I'll be ready to leave.

Gracefully, Thrall does not try any of the dirty tricks that I experienced in the iNOVA hospital. She does not go out of her way to trigger me with lies. I can only imagine it a mercy that my parents have not been involved enough with this hospitalization; they did not visit me. I don't know if it's because they've resigned this to yet another one of my episodes or because it is too inconvenient and emotionally challenging to see me face to face.

The day before I'm released, I spend a lot of time in my room. It's a funny nostalgic peaceful atmosphere in here. The realization that what you thought of as a prison was actually holding you safe. How the artwork I've collected and the room I have all to myself was a blessing in some way. The head nurse—I can tell she thinks I'm a troublemaker type—strolls by my room's open door.

"What's the matter? You're a lot less ... enthusiastic today."

"I'm taking a quiet day for myself."

"Well I'll be."

Having it be my only interaction with this head nurse, my opinion of her is softened. Before this, she had been painted a villain by my friends for her repeated enforcing of arbitrary visitor rules as well as general standoffishness. Yet, her few words carried across a warm pink compassion beneath all that harshness and I treasure the glimpse of her soul.

This Too has Passed

I reflect on the almost inevitable nature of this hospitalization. Part of why I wanted to write this book was to inspire others with mental illness that they too could live without medication! Free themselves from the tyranny of fear and pharmaceutical dependency! Yet for all that I lasted indeed a year without medication before Lotus showed up, truly it was the stabilizing presence of love and emotional support that allowed me to make it as many more years as I did. Without that connection and wisdom I quickly devolved (accelerated as I was with marijuana and the Rockies) into a chaos that leads to the narrow land of transcendence and growth but more often for me to the metallic boundaries of the healthcare system.

When I get out—and it all happens so fast—I'm on the lawn of the hospital and the sky is struggling to decide between rain and sunshine. The clouds are being whipped every which way by the wind and I find the trees that I had gazed at for the weeks I was in the restricted area side of the building.

I fall to my knees, pressing into the grass, palms grasping at the soil, inhaling the fresh air, and I break down into tears. The sheer beauty of it all moves me. I let myself stretch out deeper so that I'm weeping and prostrating to the earth. The feeling of exhalation, of release. My friends give me space as they put my things away and arrange my car for my escape out of here.

This is about the time where I completely forget—and would've ignored anyway—the warnings not to drive while on the medication Risperidone. I have my phone back and call my brother as promised. I sound the bells of freedom to all that want to know and text the girl I had met in the hospital.

She doesn't respond, so I find a nice park to go to—of course I'm right by Eno River.

The place where I had asked Lotus to date me officially. The only time—she reflected later—that I had ever been clear about what I wanted and what she meant to me. She did not end up visiting me in the hospital despite all my attempts to reach her through every means available to me. She did not think it would help me to move on. She was right, and her coldness is a mercy.

A fitting place to lay it all to rest, I suppose. I take out my hiking staff and walk among the hills and the colors of fall. Everything has changed while I've been on the inside, but the frigid cold that carried me there has thawed as the sky decided that yes—Sunshine it is for today.

I wander among the rivers, the many creeks, and bridges. I dip my hands and Soul into the brisk waters. At a particular crossing, I take the fallen tree route—about fifteen feet above the river.

"Am I really still this eager to take risks and caution be damned?"

I know my answer as I balance my walk across the trunk of stability.

LIFE AS ART

I'm wearing Sun's shoes as that's what I had gone into the hospital with anyway. Maybe a few miles later I'll have a semblance of understanding her, but it doesn't really register at the moment.

I'm finally alone.

Finally in nature.

There's no bipolar to be found here, as far as the eye can see. Strangers pass me, some greet me, some don't, but none of them look at me with critical or fearful eyes. I am no longer a threat to the psychic stability of reality. It feels amazing to breathe in the wind.

I rest by some rocks and video chat with my father. He's concerned and notes how exhausted I look. I don't remember the last time I actually slept—the kind of sleep that puts you all the way through to the other side of rebirth.

I make my way to Desi after she responds, but she makes it clear she only has the time for the shortest of short visits. Honestly, it's enough to receive a hug from her and wish her well on her way to Florida and exchanging the pleasantries of looking forward to seeing each other again and all that jazz.

I lay Sun's shoes to rest near a dumpster and set off back home to Raleigh, to my old apartment that Wolf set up to help my old landlord purge the crazy out of his home. He kicked me out after taking my rent money for November and not agreeing to refund any of my deposit. Greed truly is an ugly sin. While there, my room is stacked wall to wall with boxes and the collateral damage of my life being uprooted. There's nowhere to relax and I do my best running on the fumes I am. The wind has nowhere to rest, for when it stops moving it no longer is.

After however long, it's time for me to take my friends out to dinner—to celebrate friendship fnd Freedom. We go to a ramen restaurant with a dragonfly as its emblem downtown. I order some alcohol, probably violating some other rule/recommendation for my medication.

The only other person to visit me at the hospital calls while I'm there with great timing. He makes sure I understand how much I owe my friends who "went to Hell and back for [me]."

I'm glad to be out of Hell. I also miss my motorcycle and see through my ambition to ride Zero that same night. My Wolf friend drops me off at my former residence where Zero's parked and reminds me how foolish it is to visit Sun tonight, but I don't exactly see myself relaxing at his apartment either. That's when he points to the moon, rising above the clouds—Waning. She's smiling her golden splendor, and the radiance reflects the perfection of this day. My wish to see her fulfilled, I bask in the warm evening breeze.

It's November 26, 2018.

And I'm Alive.

14

Conclusion

Convictions

~~Love is everywhere and in everything~~ "Love is a Force of Nature"

Happiness is always right there in front of you—*if you choose to see it*

There is no such thing as a coincidence (yet not everything has been planned either)

We have hidden the keys to our chains inside of others. Trust those who have come into your life—unless it's clear not to.

I am learning about how one cannot interfere with the personal karma of others, as that is not an act of love. Ofte times, we want to help or "fix" others because their pain is making us uncomfortable. A local wise woman shared a new definition of love with me:

"Love is allowing others their own space and time to make the choice to see the light." It requires ultimate patience and a great capacity to be with another's pain with no desire to fix. In 2016, one of my teachers in Japan had come up with a rather more elaborate and precise definition: "To love unconditionally is to provide the necessary conditions for another's growth, while simultaneously accepting them exactly as they are." I enjoy the truth in paradox. The element of respecting their own free will, path, and choice gives it the added spiritual depth I appreciate. A final quote I've picked up from somewhere is "To be Loved gives one Strength, to Love another gives one Courage." To synthesize these wisdoms and own my own flavor, this is what love means to me today:

Love is to open the Gate of our Hearts, to be fully Seen and to fully See another's Soul, allowing this Force of Nature to inspire and move us beyond what we think we are. Following the Dance of Truth, and trusting the Divine to illuminate our Path. Daring to Weave together the Threads of our tenderness with another and to want nothing less than to share Everything.

Doubts

Fate isn't what I thought it was. Perhaps it's always been in my own hands.

Be careful who you choose to be in your life and even more careful of who you try to force out.

I don't know if it gets easier or not, but at least I know there aren't any guarantees.

Evil is real and only destroys us when we turn a blind eye to its existence.

Hopes

I hope, and hope is not an easy word for me to say, that this book has shed light on the depths of madness. I want to clarify that I have no desire to enable psychotic or neurotic states of being and dress them up as beautiful and meaningful. I differentiate madness from these out of control and potentially dangerous states of mind in the sense that a deep wisdom and knowing comes from owning your flavor of insanity.

Perhaps this book has helped show that there are other ways to navigate some of these states. I sincerely wish that no other beings have to suffer with these states as painfully as I have. May your paths be gentle and beautiful. May the darkness in your life not scar you, nor the light blind you into annihilation.

Epilogue

(Redux)

And now as I finally come to a place where I can celebrate being alive, and how far I've come, I want to confess it hasn't happened quickly. Nor is it a finished process. I have made a decision to never be committed to a mental hospital again. Let me explain the subtle difference. Before my third hospitalization, I assumed it would never happen and that I had reached some spiritual awakening and plateau—that I could navigate experiences more wisely and wouldn't end up backsliding so far. Yet the danger of mishandling one's life is always present and we are good to be sober to that reality. In my decision is the recognition that it is in my hands to be captain of my ship; I promise to guide my life with more responsibility and compassion for myself. Rather than assuming, this is claiming ownership of the timeline in which I learn my lessons deeply and do not step off any cliffs of recklessness. In my quest for untrammeled freedom, I now admit that there are lines with real consequences upon crossing them. I know I am not immune to future heartbreaks, but I pray that my future self sees them as opportunities to break open: to receive more love from the moment right in front of me. To be vulnerable and seen in the hallowed halls of pain rather than looking to escape.

I don't know if my story has sparked any insights or triggered any more depth of being for you. But I do know that what you feel matters. No matter how many times you pick up and put down that thread of feeling—it is your treasure. Your gift.

Please, take your time. Be gentle with yourself. Most of all, be patient. It took me as many years to live this story as it did to write it.

The End for Now

Afterword

Afterword

During the final stages of editing this book, I happened to be taking a personal journey to Arizona. Everything was as magical and as uplifting as some of my other adventures when I got a phone call: a friend of mine had completed suicide. I had texted with her just a few days before and sensed none of her inner disturbance.

I don't know if the tragedy of Michelle's death could have been avoided. One of the things she said to me during the few intimate moments we shared in 2022 was "hurry up and do your Ted talk! We all need it." I know I could've been there more for her. I don't know if that would've changed anything at all, but if I've learned anything from a life of regrets, it's the importance of being able to live with oneself. Forgiving oneself is much harder work than doing what you feel is right in the first place.

I want to take this space also to write about suicide. In my story, I only briefly mentioned my dark teenage years and struggle with such thoughts, and I presented it in the framework that it was never a problem for me after that. Even Tommy's death did not bring my thinking on the subject to the forefront.

In light of Michelle's death, that is not the case. Perhaps I am not afflicted with the thoughts of completing a suicide or the despair and struggle of a painful reality so often that it becomes an attractive option.

But there are many ways to commit suicide. Often in my life I have gone down certain pathways to "throw my life away" without dying. This hidden epidemic of suicide need not go unheard of.

Any type of suicide is a painful shock across the shores of reality. The only solace Michelle's friend gave me when delivering the news was that "Michelle had help offered to her and available. It was her choice that she didn't reach out."

It is always a choice.

If nothing else, I hope you choose to believe that you can be helped. That comes far before asking for it, in my experience.

I'll be here, growing right alongside you. So please, know that you are never alone.

Dear reader,

Take heart.

And thank you.
   -Arthur Benjamin Freeman

About the Author

Arthur Freeman is a healing arts professional and spiritual mentor based in the Triangle of North Carolina. He writes as a labor of Love, aiming shine light on misunderstood realms and reach the hearts of those suffering with the nature of their minds. When is not teaching, writing, or facilitating transformative group events he prefers to be out in nature with his energetic chau-pomerian-greyhound-golden retriever pup Ronin.

You can connect with me on:
 https://healcyon.com

Subscribe to my newsletter:
 http://eepurl.com/drugLT

www.ingramcontent.com/pod-product-compliance
Lightning Source LLC
Chambersburg PA
CBHW020246010526
44107CB00002B/130